P9-CLV-075

B Wyn $ 19.95
Wynn, Ned.
We will always live in
    Beverly Hills : growing
    up crazy in Hollyw 808707

SEP 0 3 1992

JAN 8 1991

SM

HARRIS COUNTY PUBLIC LIBRARY

HOUSTON, TEXAS

WE WILL
ALWAYS LIVE IN
BEVERLY HILLS

WE WILL ALWAYS LIVE IN
BEVERLY HILLS

Growing Up Crazy
in Hollywood

NED WYNN

William Morrow and Company, Inc.
New York

This book is dedicated to the memory of Ed Wynn and Keenan Wynn and to my loving mother, Evie

Acknowledgments and thanks to Lisa Bankoff, Ben Benjamin, Casey Coleman, Donna Cook, Michael Georgiades, Phil Goldberg, Jath Hathaway, Lisa Henricksson, Bob Horrigan, Evie Johnson, Schuyler Johnson, Doug Tibbles, Steven Ujlaki, Jann Wenner, Tracy Wynn, and Adrian Zackheim.

Copyright © 1990 by Ned Wynn

All rights reserved. No part of this book may be reproduced or utilized in any form or by any means, electronic or mechanical, including photocopying, recording or by any information storage and retrieval system, without permission in writing from the Publisher. Inquiries should be addressed to Permissions Department, William Morrow and Company, Inc., 105 Madison Avenue, New York, N.Y. 10016.

Recognizing the importance of preserving what has been written, it is the policy of William Morrow and Company, Inc., and its imprints and affiliates to have the books it publishes printed on acid-free paper, and we exert our best efforts to that end.

Library of Congress Cataloging-in-Publication Data

Wynn, Ned.
   We will always live in Beverly Hills : growing up crazy in Hollywood / Ned Wynn.
      p.   cm.
   ISBN 0-688-08509-1
   1. Wynn, Keenan, 1916–1986. 2. Wynn, Ned. 3. Motion picture actors and actresses—United States—Biography. 4. Fathers and sons—United States—Biography. I. Title.
PN2287.W9W96   1990
791.43′028′092—dc20
[B]   90-37030
                                                              CIP

Printed in the United States of America

First Edition

1 2 3 4 5 6 7 8 9 10

BOOK DESIGN BY MARSHA COHEN

If all my words were stars on silver strings
Or oceanic jewels, or from the well
Of my heart's blood, there are some things
Of which I could not tell, could never tell.

I could not tell how autumn sadness stirs
Sere memories and balked desires half knowing,
Or how the summer moon, behind old firs
Smiles secretly, triumphant and alone.

Or, how far mountains move majestically
In evening shadows when the embers die,
Or why night is still, or of the fire,
High tumult of the wild geese in the sky.

Or where dead leaves go, or the leaves that blow
Down drifting winds to other lands than these,
Of summer isles and silent snow
And dim disasters under sullen seas.

Least could I tell you what is in my mind,
Seeing your face on mist I half forget,
Half hope, remembering the wind
Stirring your hair of old regret.

—SHERRY ABBOTT
"Autumn"

It was 5:55 in the morning. I was standing in front of Westward Ho market on San Vicente Boulevard. I had dragged myself to the market because I needed a drink. Just a couple of nice cold beers to put out the fire in my stomach, and a little half-pint of tequila to still the rockslide in my head. That is all I needed. The market opened at six, and I was there five minutes early, just in case my watch was slow.

At six sharp a white-haired man got out of his car in the parking lot and joined me at the door to the market. He was wearing a bathrobe, was unshaven and bleary-eyed and needed a drink as much as I did. He looked me up and down. Even a smile hurt. I squinted at him. It was a real effort to speak. So I didn't.

The manager opened the door and we went inside. We both padded softly to the liquor shelves, pulled down our favorite medicines, paid, and left. On the way out the older man turned to me. "Give us a call, huh, son? We'd love to see you."

"Sure, Pop," I said. I watched my father return to his car. He waved. I waved. He drove off. I slipped back to my apartment as swiftly and smoothly as possible, holding the bottles gingerly, as if they were condor eggs. We both knew I wouldn't call.

CHAPTER

1

---

*I remember warmth and light. A ramp of sunlight, orange;
and late in the day it slid through the window and bumped
against me like water, urging me gently down on the rug. I
remember that if I held my hands in this light, it seemed
that tiny planets swirled through my fingers. If I closed my
eyes and pressed my knuckles hard against them, the planets
streamed down my fingers and through my eyelids bursting
inside my head in a lash of colors.*

*Nurse took my wrists and pulled my hands away from
my eyes. "What's he doing? Here, look at Mommy . . . look,
Neddy. . . ."*

There are days in Los Angeles, in the spring or late winter, when
the sky is bright with clouds and the air smells like warm stone.
Then the same birds, safe in the hedges, mouth-off to the same cats,
who drowse on the brittle lawns and listen. It's 1944 again. I'm three-
and-a-half years old and people are taking pictures. For *Photoplay*
magazine.

I sit on a stool in the kitchen. My mother wears an apron. I
have never seen her wear this gay little apron before. I don't know
why not. It has little people on it dancing and picking flowers, and
a house with a curl of smoke from the chimney, and a woman at
the front door of the house holding a pie which children and little
dogs, standing on their hind legs, want a piece of. Yum. I love this
little apron. And I love my mother. And to have my mother wearing
the apron makes me feel like wet clay. I waggle my head from side
to side and let my tongue hang out. I groan with pleasure. I wish
she'd wear it all the time.

"Neddy, look over here—that's it, don't get slap-happy—look at
your mommy." She stands at the sink washing dishes. I have never
seen this before either. It's very funny. And my father, he stands
next to her drying dishes. Oh, it's so impossible, so wonderful. Awash
in miracles, I laugh.

I love these people, the man with the camera and the lights,

9

and the lady with the pencils and the paper, because they make all kinds of things happen that never happened before. My father gives me a dish, a very big dish, and tells me to dry it. But it isn't really wet. I don't know how I'm supposed to dry the dish if it isn't wet. "He's so literal," my mother says. She sounds very proud of that. She turns to the people with the camera. "I just don't know how he got to be so literal." Then she smiles at me, and I know: It's good to be literal.

"Well," huffs my father, "he certainly didn't get it from *my* side of the family." Then he hoots like Woody Woodpecker. Everyone laughs. So many good things to be. I think I'll be them all.

I look for June, the cook. It was June who really did the dishes. She plucked the chickens and rolled the pie crusts and shelled the peas at night while Joe Louis fought on the radio. "Your grandfather knows Joe Louis," June would tell me. "Your grandfather knows President Roosevelt, too. He's a great big radio star, Ed Wynn, you oughta be proud." I would try and think of Grandpa Ed and Joe Louis, together in the radio. I'd squinch my forehead, proudly, and nod. Later, I thought, later I will look inside the radio and maybe I'll see them there among the glowing tubes.

Now June is hiding behind the people with the camera and giggling. She thinks it's funny, too. I bet she likes the people with the camera. Her white uniform sings as she moves her huge body and claps her hands. This is so much fun. I love it when June claps her hands; dark brown and still covered in flour, white dust billows from her fingertips. Flying desserts, I think. Chocolate éclairs in wedges like geese fly past my head, I turn to look. I call and they wheel in the sky, cream puffs with wings. Soon I'll eat them.

"Neddy, look—say cheese." *Éclair*, I think. I won't say cheese. Ever.

June stood every day at the kitchen counter rolling and trimming dough for pie crust or in front of the stove worrying eggs with a spatula, her hands and arms switched with tiny scars left by the popping fat. Once, when she showed me the scars, I kissed them to make them better. When I looked up, she was crying.

She saved the fat in a coffee can under the sink to use again, because, as she told me, we were at war. "Your family's lucky," she told me. "Your daddy's a movie star and you got butter. Thanks to Mr. Louis B. Mayer." She wrapped up most of the butter and put it in the new Frigidaire that hummed in a corner of the kitchen. She glanced quickly around and patted me on the head. Then she put the rest of the butter in a little bag in the small icebox in the butler's pantry.

It was a real icebox, one that used ice. Not like the modern

Frigidaire. Once a week a man came to fill it. He was tall and wore a leather pad on his shoulder and balanced a big block of ice there with huge iron tongs. I needed some of those iron tongs. Sometimes I confused the iceman with the rat catcher who came with traps for the basement. We had rats.

At night I could hear them scuttering behind the walls. On errands, I supposed, very busy, I hoped, too busy to take time to stop and listen at the molding by the closet door, to hear me breathing, to see if I was awake. I held my breath and shivered as they dashed along the wall-hidden highways that cobwebbed the house, the block, the neighborhood, secret roads that netted the world. And late, in the deepest part of night down at the very bottom of the house, in the concrete tomb where the water heater hissed and bubbled and the fire in the furnace made puppet shadows on the wall, in great basement meetings, they spoke. In my bed on the second floor I shivered because they spoke, I believed, of me.

He showed me a dead rat once. Huge, it grinned at me and stank, its lips skinned back from its yellow teeth, eyes like tiny pollywogs. Terrified, I thought, oh, please, I didn't do it. It wasn't me.

"Old bastard. Must be six, seven years old. Older'n you, kid." He grinned and threw Old Bastard in a sack. His trap was streaked with blood and entrails. As he left he wiped it casually along the hedge to clean it. I stared at the bits of hair and flesh that remained, dangling from the twigs. They bobbed and wiggled as he passed, the flecks of purple blood dark against the dusty green leaves.

"It's just extra," she said. "Your family's got plenty, so this here is just extra." June put the butter in a larger shopping bag. It was heavy. She gave the bag to a Negro man who smiled down at me, took my whole hand in his and pumped it up and down. He had a rag in his back pocket and smelled of onions and gasoline.

"You gonna be an actor when you grow up, like Keenan Wynn?" he said. "Like your daddy?" I nodded solemnly. I desperately needed a rag in my back pocket.

"Do you like butter?" I asked. He nodded his head.

"And chicken, and beef . . ." he grinned and patted the bag. June shushed him. "Well, are you Joe Louis then?" I asked. He laughed and danced away, ducking his head. The bag swung heavily against his leg. He brought his free hand up in a boxing pose. I breathed in the gasoline. It smelled good.

"I'm better," he laughed. June snorted.

"You get outa here now," she told the man. He moved off into the hall, and she followed him and whispered something in his ear. He turned and they both walked to the front door and opened it. The man kissed June on the cheek and squeezed her. He flicked his dark eyes at me and then walked quickly away down the driveway and out onto the street where another man waited for him. As I stepped to the door to look, June moved to block me. But she was too late. I saw the other man, and I saw my dog Cocoa with him. They were walking away together, Cocoa and the strange other man. Down the street away from the house. I called, but they just kept walking, and the first man followed them, his bag—filled with butter and chickens and children and puppies—bumped against his leg as he went.

"Keenan," the man with the camera is talking to my father. "How about outside. Anything you want to do outside?"

"Bikes," my father answers. My mother glances sharply at him. "Bicycles, Evie, not the motorcycles." My mother smiles thinly. "Don't worry, I'm not about to take him on the motorcycle." He shakes his head.

"You don't like the motorcycles, Mrs. Wynn?" the lady with the pencils asks, a little too interested. "Are they a sore spot between you and Keenan?"

"Oh, no, we can sit on the motorcycle. Let's take one on the motorcycle." My mother is starchy, pert. Like June's white uniform. "And then we can do Cocoa. What about Cocoa, Keenan?" Mother turns to the lady and smiles brightly, her cheeks as hard as coconuts. "What about our dog, Cocoa? We can put a ribbon on him. Neddy, darling, we can put a ribbon on Cocoa. Won't that be fun?"

Fun? Oh, at least. Isn't this the day I ride the moon and speak to the King of the Sea? It must be this day, a day of cameras and pencils and miracles. I sit on the motorcycle with my mother and father. We don't go anywhere. It's like the dishes. And then we put a ribbon on Cocoa. Cocoa looks so funny. Maybe there's a pie for Cocoa.

Cocoa stands on his hind legs wearing a coat and maybe some gloves. He asks politely for pie. I give him a slice. We dance together, Cocoa and I, and Mommy, and Daddy, too. We hold hands and dance in a circle and stick out our tongues and sing about pollywogs and pencils and chimney pie. . . .

"Say, who ya gotta know around here?" It's Uncle Van. He has appeared out of nowhere and is now sitting in his convertible in the driveway, his red-blond hair trimmed short, his freckled face as open as a stack of pancakes.

"Van Johnson . . ." the lady with the pencils says and moves her fingers urgently at the man with the cameras.

"Uncle Van! C'mon! Uncle Van!" I shout. The joy is piling up and I might not make it. I might lose consciousness. He cracks his gum.

"Can I get in on this? Who ya gotta know?" he jumps out of his car. In three steps Van crosses half the Earth to lift me up and kiss me. One of his strides is ten for the iceman.

The man with the cameras is tossing tripods in the air, tripping over cords, dropping cameras. "How you wanna do this, Keenan? . . . Van, you wanna sit there with Neddy—help with the ribbon bit? Keenan, Evie? . . ." If he keeps talking maybe Van won't disappear in a puff of smoke.

"Hey, V.J.," says my dad. His grin widens as Van gets into the shot with us. Mom stands back watching as the men put the ribbon on Cocoa. It's like the dishes and the motorcycle. We pretend. Cocoa grins. He's pretending, too.

"How's the Merc?" my father asks Uncle Van. "It's a goer, isn't it? A real bomb."

"I like it, I like it," he answers. The lady with the pencils is writing furiously.

"Do you come over often, Van? I mean, you seem almost like one of the family," she says.

"Oh, I am." He grins amiably. The woman purrs.

"The Man Who Came to Dinner," my father says.

"The Man Who Couldn't Say No," my mother says.

"The Man Who Couldn't Say *Oy Gevalt*," says Van.

"And still can't," says my father. The woman is charmed. She laughs.

"How do you spell *Oy—Ge—veld*?" Immediately everybody starts spelling: O-Y-G. They don't know that they are doing a bad thing. They are ignoring me.

"Uncle Van," I shout, grabbing his lower lip and giving it a good twist, "Cocoa can talk. We were singing. He asked for pie!" With my free hand I smack him in the face.

"I always knew there was something about that dog. Pie, huh?" Van pries his lip free and tousles my hair. Primly, I pat it back down.

"Don't, Mommy brushed it."

"Oh, she did, did she? What kinda pie?" he asks.

"Maybe you should ask the dog," my dad says. They all laugh.

"From Mommy's apron."

"Some apron."

"Some dog."

"Some Mommy." Uncle Van whistles. Mom blushes and puts her hand behind her head and draws one leg against the other, pinup-style.

"Gable!" I shriek. Everybody laughs. I'm back on track.

"Who's Gable, Evie? Is that Clark?" the lady asks, her pencil hovering above her pad.

"He means Betty Grable," my mom tells her. Her pencil ploughs into the paper. "She just adores Neddy."

"Oh, Betty. . . ." she yawns. "We did a layout with Betty just last week. The same day we did Lana. Such a nice girl." When I act like that my mother says I'm being *blasé*.

"Pretty, too," my father offers. Everyone nods.

"Oh, yes, pretty," says the lady.

"Very pretty," Uncle Van agrees.

"Attractive," my dad says.

"Terribly attractive," says Uncle Van.

"Gosh, yes. Nobody more attractive." The lady and the man nod their heads together.

"Gorgeous, even," says Dad. Now he's got them.

"Oh, yes. Gorgeous. No argument there."

"Absolutely stunningly beautiful!" he yells now, making his face red and angry like Hitler in the cartoons. There is silence. Then Uncle Van rubs his chin.

"Wellll . . ." he says doubtfully. Dad suddenly jumps on him and wrestles him to the ground. He rubs his knuckles on Uncle Van's head.

"Ab-so-lute-ly-god-damn-stun-ning-ly . . ." Dad says and grinds on Uncle Van's head.

"Ab-so-lute-ly . . ." cries Uncle Van.

The lady is uncertain. She looks nervously at my mom.

"All right, Keenan," Mom shouts, "Van, that's enough, now. Stop it!" They stop and look up at her like little boys. Mom looks down at them severely. She thinks a moment then says, "She's—*cute*, OK?"

Uncle Van and Dad scratch their heads.

"I don't understand, Evie," says Dad. "Who's cute?"

"Betty Grable!" says my mom.

In unison, Dad and Van shout, "Betty Grable!" Then they begin hopping on the ground thumping the grass and beating their chests like gorillas. Van jumps on a chair and starts clapping his hands like a seal. Mom howls with laughter. Dad yells like Tarzan. Cocoa barks. I'm in heaven. My feet begin to leave the ground. Soon I'll fly.

The cameraman tosses fourteen tripods in the air, drops eleven cameras and nearly strangles himself with a cord. They'll make him an editor for this.

There's no stopping me now. I tell the lady about all the other people I know. I tell her about Cesar Romero who's handsome and lives up the street and Mickey Rooney who's funny and short and Gene Kelly who teaches me to sword fight at Metro and Peter Lawford who's English and wears loafers with tassels and Laird Cregar who's very fat and plays with me in my sandbox. And Marlene who brings me meatballs with colored toothpicks and kisses my neck. The woman stares at me with her mouth open. Her pencil writes in the air above the paper. It might be a magic wand. Or a dagger. Or maybe she's just new.

"Dietrich?" she says politely. My mother nods.

"He just won't eat unless Marlene brings him her special meatballs. He loves them, don't you darling? She's coming by later. . . ."

The woman turns to the man with the cameras. "Fred, I think I'll call the office," she says. He nods vaguely. He has stopped doing anything now. He gazes at the trees. Does he see the fairies there?

"Evie, dear," she continues, not blasé anymore, "would you mind if we just sort of stuck around this afternoon, you know, in the background quiet as mice? I think the fans would just eat this up, and the studio would love it. A typical afternoon with the Wynns. . . ."

"Of course, Audrey. But I don't know who else is coming today. I spoke to Ty this morning, and he . . ."

The woman holds up her hand, "Please, you won't even see us." Then, softly, "Ty? . . ."

"Power," my mother says. The woman tries to close her mouth but she can't because her teeth are dry and her upper lip catches on them and stops about halfway. Then she turns and heads briskly toward the house, first trotting then stopping to turn around every few feet to wave, then trotting off again.

The cameraman stares into space. Managing Editor, nothing less. The fairies giggle and wave at me. Maybe they're just some baby pomegranates bobbing behind the leaves. I wave back, in case they're not. Too bad he can't see them.

"Nap time." My world implodes like a dark star. Nap time. I look up. It's Nurse. She smiles. She is kind and I love her, but nap time is not nice, not kind. Why pretend?

Why not just say: Time to be boiled alive? Time to get eaten by wild animals? Time to get the flesh ripped off you by tiny gnomes? Nap time. No one else is napping. Betty Grable is coming over. Marlene Dietrich is bringing meatballs with pretty colored toothpicks. Ty will bring his Deusenberg. I am not napping.

I open my mouth in a silent O. Nurse, bending to pick me up, senses what's coming and turns her head to avoid the worst of it. But it will do her no good. With sufficient air gathered in my diaphragm like the pressure in a steam engine, I release the piston, open the valve, and begin to scream. No negotiation, no pleading, just a primordial swamp scream, the sound a pterodactyl might have made.

It prunes trees and sets concrete. Shingles peel off roofs and fly up into the sky like playing cards. Insects pupate, fruit ripens, babies speak, and Cocoa, quaking in terror, walks over to the brick path, squats, and craps.

The scream stops abruptly. Fascinated, solemn in the presence of this new geology, I watch it coil neatly on the walk, a mustard-yellow snake. It looks delicious. Suddenly everyone is leaping up as if the pile of turds might suddenly run amuck. I see the people running down the streets, yellow turds behind them, smelling horribly. I am transported. I spin in circles on the grass like a lunatic dervish.

"Ohhh," my mother says and covers her mouth.

"Goddamnit, Cocoa! Shit! Get the hose. Where's the goddamn hose," my father is bellowing.

"Don't swear, Keenan," my mother says from behind her hand. "Cocoa couldn't help it."

Uncle Van is the best. He is wrinkling his face and saying something like, *Eeeuh eeeuh eeeuh eeeuh eeeuh* over and over again and holding his nose like he did when I was a baby in an earlier house and did what Cocoa did, only in my crib. That time he threw up.

Dad, meanwhile, turns on the hose, which starts thrashing around and spitting making everyone dance to keep out of its way. "The hose," he shouts, "get the goddamn hose, Jesus Christ!" I swoon into a bush.

Helpless and hysterical I lie in the bush and watch a sow bug crawling on a leaf. This is better than I thought. Maybe today I won't get to meet the King of the Sea. Or ride the moon. But I have solved a great mystery: I can control the world with my scream.

As I stepped to the door to look, I saw another man out in the street. And I saw my dog Cocoa with him. They were walking away together, Cocoa and the man. I called, but they just kept walking. "June," I said, "where are they taking Cocoa?"

"Nowhere, get inside now." She tried to push me in the house, but I slipped around her and out onto the porch. I yelled to Cocoa. But Cocoa didn't turn, he just kept trotting away. I sent him words from inside me, but inside I heard no answer. He just kept walking toward Sunset Boulevard with the two men. Sunset, where I could never go, where the earth curved, where even the rat roads didn't reach. I started to cry. June took me inside.

"Stop crying, now. How do you know that was Cocoa? Your daddy's a movie star, ain't that enough? You can't just have everything, you know." She went to the closet and got out the Johnson's Floor Wax and some rags. "You wanna help me wax the floor?" she said. She opened the jar of wax and handed it to me. I smelled the wonderful smell in the jar. Is Cocoa gone because he went to the bathroom on the path? I must be careful not to do that. They might send men to steal me too. I sat on the stair and held the jar of wax to my face and breathed deeply.

*   *   *

Although my eyes began to hurt, the colors were too beautiful to stop. And so I kept pushing until my eyeballs throbbed and a white-and-black pattern appeared. The white background rippled and flamed behind jagged black cracks that opened in it, tearing at my eyes and at my hands to stop me from pushing. This was the very color of pain. But I knew this secret about pressing on my eyes: that if I kept pressing long enough, a moment came when the pain would simply stop, when all visions, all sensations, all feelings would cease, and I would float free.

Cocoa never came back. My mother said he was stolen. I kept very still about the men. She said don't worry we'll get another dog, but instead of getting another dog, which I needed, we got a duck and another little boy. The duck was OK, but the little boy was unnecessary. I already had plenty of friends.

There was Maria Cooper who lived across the street, and Tommy Capra down on Barrington who had a huge spider that lived in a rusted toy truck by the kitchen. There was Peter Fonda whose mom was sick a lot so we had to be quiet. And his sister Jane, who was older and tried to boss us, which was OK because she also showed us her underpants. There were the Wellman kids, seven of them, and Jackie Hathaway and Bobby Walker and Wes Parker. They were my friends and I could play with them whenever I wanted. I didn't need another little boy, especially one who lived across the hall.

But my mother was insistent. Which made no sense, really, because she told me how hard it had been, getting this little boy in the first place. She said the doctor had to cut her open to get him out of her stomach. What was she doing with something like that inside her anyway? Had she eaten him? I had to sit down on the tub for a couple of minutes after she told me that one.

I realized after what happened to Cocoa that I had to be careful. So when she suggested that I try and be friends with what's-his-name, I said I would. I knew his name was Tracy, but I didn't feel I had to memorize it, as he'd probably do something bad before long anyway and then, bye-bye, little boy, regards to Cocoa.

I crept into his room and stood by the door. He was lying in a cradle, and hovering around him were what seemed like a hundred women. He was crying, which was basically my job, and they were making little noises at him and shaking rattles and showing him toys to make him laugh, toys that I needed myself. I thought, I will make him laugh and they will give me the toys.

He was naked and his little weenie was sticking straight up in the air, which wasn't all that remarkable except that he was peeing.

It was arcing through the air like a fountain and splashing on the carpet. They had been rocking the cradle, so it came and went in wavy lines back and forth like a lawn bird. Everyone cooed and chuckled and ran around spreading diapers and dabbing cotton balls and swallowing safety pins.

During a lull I sidled over and looked into the cradle. It was all white and blue and Tracy a pink lump in the middle. The light was coming in the window and settling on him, warm and pleasant. He smiled and stuck his fingers up into the light. He smelled of Vaseline and rubber, and I wondered if he could see the planets. I bent over closer to see if he was watching his fingers. My plan was to teach him about the colors in his eyes. This turned out to be a mistake. Without warning, staring up at me and gurgling, bubbles at the corners of his mouth, his tiny fingers hypnotizing me with the joy of his infancy, he peed on me.

"Well, why can't you take him back?" I wanted to know. My mother was in her dressing room sitting at her makeup table. I loved her makeup table with its big lighted mirror, and the crystal bottles and satin-covered boxes of perfume and powder that sat on its mirrored top. Red lipsticks and rouge for her cheeks, red polish for her fingernails, and dark soft pencils for her eyebrows were buried in the drawers with shiny compacts made of ransom gold and Spanish silver, treasure for little pirates.

Other parts of her hung from racks along the walls. There were shoes of every color tucked in the pockets of special bags that hung in the closets along with dozens of dresses and blouses and sweaters in rows behind sliding wooden doors. Sometimes I would go inside the closets, close the doors and stand there in the dark smelling the wool and the leather and feeling the silk and angora, feeling my mother against my skin.

But today I just turned and looked out the window at the backyard and the fish pond. There were fairies there and elves waiting in the dell where the long moss grew in the shade of the big rocks. They were waiting for me to come out and look for them, lying on my stomach with my cheek on the cool stones.

"You can't take babies back, darling. You have to keep them when they come. He's a very sweet baby and I know you'll love being a big brother to him and teaching him things."

"Like what?" I would teach him nothing. Or maybe I would teach him to jump off the roof. Good. Or I would push him very high in the swings at the park. Very very high. Very good. Yes, I could teach him things.

"Well, you can teach him to talk." I was already bored with the conversation. Anyway I wanted to see the fairies. I didn't really mind about the peeing anymore. Just the idea of all that teaching gave me a happy glow. I hugged myself.

"OK," I said. "Can Maria read to me today, after my nap?"

"After your nap."

"Just for your information," I said, using my latest expression, "Maria doesn't have any brothers or sisters."

"I know," Mom said. "Aren't you lucky?"

Sometimes in my naps I slept, other times I laid awake or crept around in my room or looked at books. There was a wonderful painting on the wall, a painting of the Land of Make-Believe. I would study it for hours. That was where the King of the Sea stood on a shell and blew a trumpet and where the moon rode under a flying cow and where trolls hid under a bridge near a Cave Where Nobody Lived.

After my nap my parents sometimes took me across the street to Gary and Rocky Cooper's house to play with Maria. She was older and she could read, so I tolerated her. And I had the comic books, so she tolerated me. Sometimes she'd come over to my house instead and sit on my bed and read to me, Porky Pig or Bugs Bunny. Once we heard Tracy singing this funny little song he called "dere dere" in his room and we laughed helplessly into the pillows. Maria was my friend, not his.

I remember going to swim at Ty's house, which was just down Saltair, or up to our friend Watson Webb's, who had a cigar-store Indian in his yard on Crescenda. There would be afternoons by those pools, afternoons of such color and intensity that I would shut my eyes and lie on the wet hot cement making machine-gun noises and air raid sirens into my cupped hands. The women were so beautiful and animated, their hair pulled up under bright bandanas and floppy hats, their wise legs and downy tummies slick with oil, that I would have to press my face against the sun-baked odor of their bodies and breathe them in like oxygen.

The men were loud and foolish and strong, their long arms and chests swathed in hair and gemmed with drops of sweat and chlorine; they gleamed like gods and tossed me in the air as if I were a penny. I thought of them when I saw *Fantasia* and called out "Ty" to one of the golden satyrs after the rain storm. My father's eyes glistened in the dark and he held my hand and squeezed it again and again while Beethoven roared in my chest.

It's 1945. We have a movie camera with color film, and now Tracy is in the pictures. My father picks him up and sweeps the sky with him, erasing thoughts of me. Tracy screams and studies the clouds and the bellies of birds before diving to the lawn to sit like a curly-haired Buddha, his face fat with the knowledge of buggies and bottles, of cribs and strained pears. Peter Lawford is there in his tasseled shoes, and my mother's brother, Uncle Irv, who was a soldier in the war, and the nurse, Mrs. MacGlendon. They sit with Tracy and hold his wrist and shake it, making him wave at the camera while I swagger around in my green corduroys with suspenders and my striped shirt, kicking the wheels of his baby buggy to make sure they won't fall off should he ever be in it going fifty-miles-an-hour down any hills or steep driveways or anything.

All day long my acres rose and fell around me like a friendly sea: There was a dandelion walk lined with pink amaryllis in full bloom. Behind it were orchards of avocado, persimmon, pomegranate, and lime. There were peas, string beans, rhubarb, and cantaloupe. There was a garage, a gardener's shed, a greenhouse where Slinky the duck lived, a playground with a swing, a slide, and a four-seat merry-go-round, a fish pond with minnows and pollywogs and elves, a flagstone patio, a barbecue house, and a flower garden. They held me, imprisoned in a paradise that I would never leave.

In the home movie again I am running along the amaryllis path, smelling the flowers and laughing. Infatuated with their scent I run in a kind of trance. But what makes the feeling complete doesn't show on the silent film: the sound of Tracy crying from inside the house. He has done something bad and is being punished, and the sound of his loud wailing across the lawn affects me like a tonic. It increases my giddiness until my knees won't hold me and I fall on the ground laughing hysterically. His misery intoxicates me. *He* did it, I cry, him, not me. Not me.

But at night the tumbling lands and glimmering ponds all disappeared with the light, leaving me alone with the bone-forming darkness that lived in my room. I would lie on my Procrustean bed afraid that something or someone would chop off my fingers or toes should they hang even one millimeter over the side. Huddled in a tiny ball, I saw lurking animals and dripping heads, nightmare shapes and drooling shadows, and a grinning wolf-faced tree at the window. But scariest of all was Old Bastard. Back from Hell he roamed Earth again, or at least that portion of it which contained my room.

He had gotten out of the rat catcher's sack somehow and had grown. He stood five feet tall, though his broken back bent him nearly in half. His lips still curled back from his luteous teeth like old cabbage leaves, his pointed snout tested the air like a trunk. He was sniffing for me. In a particularly throat-freezing twist he now wore trousers and a vest, and carried a cane. He would be at the foot of my bed when I awoke from sleep in the dead, toadstool hours, and he would stand there in the dark watching me.

My arms and legs were useless. Fear had collapsed my ribs and shriveled my spine like a burnt match. I shrank to the size of a prune pit. I couldn't move. But worse than that was the fact that I couldn't make a sound. Where was my terrible scream now? Oh, please, I thought, go away, Old Bastard, please. Don't be you. Be someone else. Be Porky Pig.

This went on night after night; I knew he would be there waiting for me, and he always was. Sometimes, frightened beyond shame, I wet myself. Then I would lie in the clammy damp of my own piss until the early light of dawn brought back the chair, the toy box, the bureau, the pine-tree bough. Only then would I get up and creep away to tell the nurse of my crime and watch as she stripped the bed, her angry lips clamped and white, while I lay naked and shivering on the toy box waiting for the men to put me in their bag and take me away.

But one night something different happened.

He was there as usual, leering at me while the wolf face gazed through the window. I screamed silently for my mother or father to come, but of course they couldn't hear me. Then a sound came through the door, a kind of toneless sing-song: *dere dere de-dere dere.* . . . And suddenly Old Bastard quivered and started to come apart. He wavered a moment then simply drained out of the air like sand in an hourglass. The wolf-faced tree looked surprised and then the face dropped away so that only the moon shone through the familiar branches.

My voice came back and I started to cry. Mrs. MacGlendon came in to see what was wrong. She picked me up and took me into her room for a while, and I stood and watched Tracy in his crib. His arms were raised over his head as he rocked back and forth singing tunelessly to himself, *dere dere dere dere de-dere dere.* I came to a swift decision.

"Can Tracy go *dere-dere* in my room?" I asked.

"No," she said. "But I'll leave the door open, so you can hear him."

I went back to my room. No wolf watched through the window, no Old Bastard lurked in the corner. Satisfied, I lay there and thought of mothers and fathers and swimming pools and little brothers who sang valiant songs while their big brothers led them through the dark falling forests past the troll-watched bridges to the wildly cheering shore where the King of the Sea rode on his golden shell.

It may not have been that night, but some night, maybe more than once, it seemed to me that just before I slept I heard a loud noise downstairs. A thump, then breaking glass. I listened. Was that my father shouting? Did I hear my mother sobbing? Or was it just Old Bastard, stomping angrily away, furious at his banishment? As I strained to hear, all that came to me was *dere dere dere de-dere dere*. Yes. Old Bastard. That must be who it was, breaking things and shouting. Never mothers and fathers. Never them. Then I took my fists and pressed them against my eyes as hard as I could.

CHAPTER

2

The sun was high, and the horses were lathered. Billy and I were hot and dusty. We needed water. We'd been pinned down in an arroyo near the border now for twelve days. I'd taken a bullet in the shoulder somewhere outside Laredo—maybe it was Abilene—or San Antone—and it was starting to hurt something fierce. All our vittles were gone and we hadn't eaten in weeks, and if I didn't get a drink soon, I'd die. And if the Indians, who were stalking the rim of the canyon waiting for dark didn't get us, the buzzards, circling now above our heads, would come in and eat the flesh from our bones. We'd never see our mothers again.

"I'm thirsty," said Billy.

"I'm powerful thirsty," I allowed.

"Me, too," said Billy.

"We're gonna have to shoot our way through those Indians to get over to the river," I said.

"What river?" asked Billy. I looked at him sadly. "Oh," he said. "Yeah."

"I'll give you the high sign," I said. "We'll circle around. Cover me." Billy nodded.

"OK," he said. I was his hero. "What's a high sign?"

I pulled my two-fingered gun from my belt, cocked the hammer, which looked just like my thumb, and gave the high sign. "Oh," said Billy. Neither of us knew what cover me meant.

Then, slapping our corduroy-flanked ponies, we charged up the steep bank of the arroyo and out onto the blacktop prairie where the Indians, some of whom were playing four-square and tetherball, scattered before our buffalo rush like startled quail. I made sure that some girl Indians squealed as we rough-shouldered our way through their game. That's what happens when a couple of tough hombres, pinned down for days without food or water, decide to get a drink.

After a brief and violent battle in which several skirts might have been lifted, we bent over the drinking fountain at the edge of the playground and sucked at the warm, precious water, to which we owned the rights as far as the crow flies, laying our lips on the stained porcelain fonts and taking turns holding the faucet for each other like cowboy buddies do out in the West.

"What's your name?" asked Billy. He was an overweight little kid with high brown shoes on, heavy steel-braced shoes; he couldn't run very well because something was wrong with his feet. And he didn't have a gang to be in so I told him he could be in mine. There were only two of us. The others were all dead.

"Frank," I said wiping my mouth with my sleeve, another cowboy trick not unlike a high sign. "Frank McGillicuddy." Billy stared at me in admiration.

"OK, Frank," he said. "Can I be in your gang forever?"

"Yeah," I said. A shadow . . .

"Ned Wynn!" My stomach wadded instantly. The principal of the Brentwood School was an angry, jowly woman dressed in sepulchral bombazine, her swollen feet erupting over the tops of her tight shoes like soft, gray magma. I wanted to put my finger in the billowy crease where the shoe bit into the foot just beneath the ankle. What was in there? An ancient, mossy incrustation? A squamous rind of skin that I could strip away like bark off a eucalyptus tree? I yearned to poke a finger there, to rub the pale flakes and watch them settle to the floor like old plaster. "You will come to my office promptly after school."

She turned and walked past my teacher, who was standing nearby, her arms crossed. The principal stopped and turned to me. "He is to come to my office directly after your last class. He's been bumping into little girls." Both women looked at me as if I were news of a failing market.

"That's Frank McGillicuddy." Billy was still standing there. You can't hang *him*. "Can I still be in your gang?" You can't hang *Frank McGillicuddy*, for God's sake. The teacher grabbed my hand and jerked me away toward the classroom where I would probably have my appendix removed with sharp tin can lids. "Bye, Frank!" Billy waved. Bye, Billy. I'm for the noose this time, Old Pard.

I had been sent to the principal's office every single day now for a month. This was because I had become somehow, suddenly, inexplicably, bad. The fact that I had been bad was a new experience for me. I had never, to my knowledge, been truly bad before. I had done things that displeased my parents, but I had never had strangers in charge of me telling me I was bad. And then punishing me. It was both bewildering and humiliating. Ashamed, I had tried to stop being bad. But it was impossible.

There were three of us who were especially bad in our homeroom: me, Debbie Daves, and a kid named Larry who always had snot running out one nostril. Periodically, Larry would scoop some of this snot onto his finger, play with it for a while, give it a little airing out, and then he'd pop it into his mouth. Then he would look me square in the face and chew it vigorously. Finally he would swallow it. Once, when I watched this performance too closely, he grew nervous and punched me in the forehead.

The teacher, in a burst of modernism, tried child psychology on us. At the end of each day, she handed each of us a slip of scratch paper and three crayons: one yellow, one green, one black. The yellow crayon was good, the green was OK, the black was bad. "Now, I want you to evaluate your deportment." I nodded. This was the same as *cover me.* "If you think you've been an angel all day," she said, making it sound like pure folly, "then put down three gold checks. If you think you've been good for a while and just so-so for the rest of the time, put down a gold check and two green checks. If you've been bad, put down a black check and any other combination you think you deserve. If you've been very bad, put down three black checks. We want you to evaluate you own deportment." Cover me, Billy, I'm evaluating my deportment. "You are on your own honor to grade yourselves honestly."

The first day of this new regime I had tried to pants Betty Lynn Dupy, put my finger on the water fountain and made it squirt through the open window of the bungalow wrecking a papier-mâché mask left over from Halloween, thrown away my report card, and put dirt in Stephen Loesser's sandwich. I gave myself three gold checks. From then on my self-evaluation was heavily edited.

After we three bad apples had crayoned our inventories to the teacher's satisfaction, we were sent to the principal's office for review. She would look over these pitiful scraps of paper with three little squiggly checks on them, little Tibetan prayers in the wind. If there was so much as a single black check we would be terrorized for a half hour and then I, at least, would be spanked by my father when I got home. Like clockwork. One black check meant a spanking.

I tried desperately to be good, to avoid having to put a black check on my paper. One day, through some higher grace, I actually managed to be absolutely good. I knew I had been good. I could feel the goodness in me, radiating from me. I had put down three gold checks. Their pale grace shone back at me like tiny angel hairs. The teacher had beamed her approval. The principal had even smiled, an alarming expression that made her look like a week-old jack-o'-lantern. I had gone home. Flourishes and coronets. Dad had not spanked me. I had gotten milk and cookies. I had done it. I had licked the being-bad problem. The next day at school I was full of the power to be good.

I am sitting in class. My desk is across from Debbie Daves whose scuffed, bony knees put wings in my stomach. She doesn't know it, but she is my girlfriend. Someday I will hug her knees and then we'll get married. Right now she is paying attention to a boy on the other side of her. His name is Teddy, and I hate him with a black intensity that borders on dementia. Agitated, I begin jumping around in my seat, alternately grinning and scowling like a primate, a chittering gibbon whose lips and eyebrows fly up and down like window shades in a vain effort to attract Debbie's attention away from my enemy and back to me. It's not working. They giggle and make faces at each other.

Now I'm desperate. What if he hugs her knees? I open and close my book with a loud snap. What if she lets him hug her knees? I drop my book with a bang. What if she asks him to hug her knees? I drop out of my seat to the floor flapping like a fruit bat. Debbie turns to me. Seeing me down on all fours, she starts laughing. It has worked. She swings her knees around and for one glorious moment I see her legs all the way up to her underwear. She loves me after all.

"All right, young man, to the principal's office. Right now. March!" The teacher has somehow appeared right in front of me, grabbed my arm, hauled me off my feet, planted me in the aisle and shoved me toward the door. "March!" I turn to her. For a moment she looks very sad. She shakes her head. Then she places her hand on my shoulder, a little more gently than before and guides me out of the classroom across the schoolyard toward the principal's office.

I know that hidden faces are turned toward the notorious Frank McGillicuddy as he walks across the silent plain where only moments before wild Indians and rock-eyed cowboys had warred over water rights with nesters and cattlemen. Now only the sounds of the cars on San Vicente Boulevard and the wind in the high eucalyptus trees are left. And a thousand disapproving eyes, hidden inside the shuttered classroom bungalows, stare out at the shamefaced criminal trudging through the heat waves that rise from the softening blacktop. A great dirt hole in the middle of the playground, that desperate arroyo, is now full of tiny finches and blackbirds pecking in the sparse weeds searching for crumbs from our squashed chocolate chip vittles. Can I be a blackbird? Can I fly away, my midnight wings shiny and quick in the sunlight?

"I've called your father, and you know what that means." The principal stands before me. I sit in a straight-backed chair and look at the tiny watch that is pinned to the front of her jacket. It is not time to go home, but I am being sent home anyway. A very bad sign. "You know what he'll do to you, don't you?" Even her marvelous humped feet don't interest me anymore. "Bumping into little girls and now crawling around on the floor in your classroom and dis-

turbing the whole class. What have you got to say for yourself?" She
stands so close now that it's like looking at the side of an elephant.
There is no view around her. I look for an edge, a corner, but all
there is is the black crepe expanse of her middle. She is a mass that
extends in every direction without borders or limitations. "Hmmm?"
She grabs my arms and lifts me out of the chair.

"I . . ."

"Do you know what he'll do to you when you get home?
Do you?"

"Spank me . . ."

"Eh? What? Speak up!"

"Spank me."

"Yes. And what did he do to you yesterday?"

"Nothing . . . I got milk and cookies, I . . ."

"I mean the day before yesterday, what did he do to you the
day before yesterday?"

"Spanked me." But what about yesterday? Yesterday I was good.

"And the day before?" She looked at me. Spanked me. He
spanked me. She knows that. But what about yesterday? Let's talk
about that. She shakes me till my head wobbles.

"Spa-a-an-anked me-eee-eee. . . ."

She grimaces and pushes me back down in the chair. Then she
walks over to her desk and sits down, her movements ponderous
and tired. She breathes heavily and grunts as she sits. I think it must
be hard to be her. Maybe she needs special shoes like Billy has. I
look out the window. We are on the second floor. Looking out, all
I can see are telephone wires, treetops, and sky. I sit there and wait
for my father to come, take me home, and spank me.

His full name, the Catholic baptismal name, was Francis Xavier
Aloysius James Jeremiah Keenan Wynn. On his driver's license it
said Frank Keenan Wynn. Born the only son of a Jewish vaudeville
star and an Irish-Catholic classical actress in New York on July 27,
1916, he became an actor himself, first in summer stock in the mid-
thirties and then on Broadway. By 1941, the year I was born, he
had been scooped into the constantly grazing maw of Metro-Gold-
wyn-Mayer, the biggest and most successful film studio in the industry.

Keenan Wynn became a contract player at MGM and began his
career playing the leading man's best friend. By 1947 he had made
over a dozen movies for MGM including, *For Me and My Gal* (1942)
with Gene Kelly and Judy Garland, *See Here, Private Hargrove* (1944)
with Robert Walker, *Ziegfeld Follies* (1946), *"The Clock"* (1945) with
Judy Garland and Robert Walker, and four movies with Van Johnson, *Weekend at the Waldorf* (1945), *Between Two Women, No Leave,*

No Love, and *Easy to Wed*, with Esther Williams and Lucille Ball. In my grandfather Ed Wynn's words, when Esther Williams dove into the pool, Keenan was the one who got splashed.

Once or twice a week, from the middle 1940s until he left the studio in 1953, he took me to Metro. He often went there, whether he was working that day or not, to get a shave from Joe, the white-haired Italian barber who operated the barber shop. There was also a manicurist in the shop and a shoeshine parlor directly across a short walkway.

I loved the shine parlor. One whole wall next to the three-chair stand was covered with comic books. Willie, the man who ran the parlor, used to save the latest issues of my favorites each week. My father would give me a quarter or fifty cents, and I would buy comics: Archie, Little Lulu, Mickey Mouse, Porky Pig, Superman, Captain Marvel, Bugs Bunny, Donald Duck, Tom and Jerry, Plastic Man, G.I. Joe, Tarzan.

I sat in a leather chair reading my comics and sniffing the rich chemical smells: the shoe polish, the waxes and dyes, the special black liquid Willie painted on the edges of the soles with a tooth-brush. These smells mingled with the alcohol, bay rum, and talcum powder from the barber shop, the clear polish and solvents from the manicurist's tray, and the smoke from a dozen cigarettes, pipes, and cigars. I never looked up from the pages, unconsciously mixing the stories in the books with the sounds of the customers' voices, the creak and the bang of the screen doors, the pop of Willie's rag, the shuffle of the brushes, and, those times I was allowed to sit in the high chair and get a shine, the soft luxury touch, the feel of Willie's hands on my shoes.

Having all that plus a half dozen new comic books in my pos-session was a compound ecstasy. For the rest of the day I would walk around with my head in an animated cartoon cloud, my newly polished shoes light as gliders and brown as my father's Dunhill briars, or impossibly black like the wings of a blackbird swooping low near the sidewalk, bearing me, like Mercury, a scant millimeter above the earth. Sometimes I had to be led, steered, or I would wander into walls, topple off curbs.

Famous people would stop and talk to my father. Hiya, Keeno! I'd be introduced. Ned, say hello to Greer Garson James Craig Clark Gable June Allyson Spencer Tracy Jimmy Stewart Donna Reed William Powell Katharine Hepburn Esther Williams Ricardo Montal-ban Walter Pidgeon Cuddles Sakall Lana Turner Judy Garland Leon Ames Rosemary de Camp shake hands look up gimme the comic book don't be rude. But at that very instant Pegleg Pete had Mickey and Ferdy and Morty tied up in the mine and Goofy and Pluto couldn't get the parachute to open. Or the Beagle Boys had just kidnapped Huey Dewey and Louie and Unca Donald couldn't get Unca Scrooge to pay the ransom or Gladstone Gander had just picked Daisy up in his new car driven over Unca Donald leaving tire tracks on his face and found a hundred-dollar bill plastered to the bottom of his foot and Unca Donald was trying to strangle him. Or Billy Batson, Crippled Newsboy, had just seen two bank robbers running out of the National City Bank and knock over an old man who was helping a woman with twins walk around an open construction site and they had all started to fall in and Billy was trying to say SHAZAM but he had laryngitis and he couldn't talk! And I've gotta meet Spencer Tracy? *Jeeeeeeeez.*

We would visit the soundstages, huge featureless blocks, fortresses with enormous soundproof doors. A red light turned on outside these doors warning us to beware, I supposed, the wrath of the inhabitant, almost certainly a giant, lest he chop off our heads for wrecking his shot. The light would stop. Now the giant would be at supper, or listening to the magic harp, maybe watching dailies. Quick, Dad! I would rush against the plunger that released the huge door, but it refused to budge. Then suddenly it would swing open with a *whoosh* as my father pressed his mighty hands against it from behind me. And then we were inside, and there was—another door! This took both of us to move, pulling on the long, metal handle. Another *whoosh* and, finally, the fortress was breached.

Inside the sound stage it was big, it was always big. It was as if space had been suddenly created, space that soared away from me. The walls stretched off on either side like the escarpment of some primordial valley. The ceiling . . . there was no ceiling. High above us, through a smoky haze I could see only miles of wooden catwalks draped with ropes, but no cats, great treeways hung with vines, the Lost Land of Paludon. Nearby there might be a *gryf* with its tricorned snout and armor-plated flanks. Later I would tame it and ride it, as Tarzan did, using only a small club and my incredible reflexes.

The haze hanging over us came from the huge carbon arc lamps that lit the stage, the distant swamp where great mud-caked saurians lapped silently through brackish pools. Huge tracts of the soundstage were dark and deserted. We would wind our way through this prehistoric maze of serpent cables and jungle pathways that led off into abrupt endings, the backs of scenery walls, a lonely phone, a fire extinguisher, or a room with a bed and a table, but no people. And then, disappointingly, the set, all lit and phony-looking with people swarming over it, hammering, smoking, talking on the phone, moving equipment, screaming orders. We'd always stop by the tall chairs where the actors, all wearing Kleenex in their collars, sat drinking coffee and studying scripts, or reading newspapers.

Makeup men and hairdressers would smile. Hiya, Keeno! Well, Neddy, what are you reading?

No, no, no, no, nothing, just Tarzan, nothing. Not even Tarzan. I didn't want them to know because they would say something about what's Johnny Weissmuller doing these days? I saw him at an auto-dealership opening in Long Beach drunk as a skunk, and I knew that Tarzan wasn't Johnny Weissmuller and he didn't get drunk and open auto dealerships; he was a real man who lived in Africa and could talk to the great apes and tame a triceratops. I would stand on one foot and then the other, fixing my eyes on the Kleenex, noticing the makeup stains, never looking into their clown-penciled eyes, and shake hands with Brian Donlevy Paul Stewart Mario Lanza John Hodiak Arthur Treacher Reginald Owen Warner Anderson Errol Flynn Van Heflin Janet Leigh James Whitmore you can read your comics later *sshhh* they're rolling everybody settle down *Quiet On The Set*! Bliss. A chair near a light. I could sit down and open Tarzan again and return to the real world, the Lost Land of Paludon, or Duckburg, or Metropolis, not this stuff, this hopeless fakery that passed for fantasy.

The commissary—my father liked to pronounce it the com-*miss*-siry—was the exact opposite of the soundstages. They could hear every noise you made on the soundstages. You had to sit absolutely still for hours. Sometimes I ran out of comic books and had to sit watching the same scene over and over again. You sighed and heads swiveled. You moved your foot and fingers flew to lips. You had to be quiet until you wanted to scream, to fling yourself beneath the silent wheels of the camera dolly; but in the commissary everyone talked at once and no one was quiet.

In here I could shout, incite to riot, and no one would bat an eye. No one could even hear me in this wind tunnel of churning mouths. The spring tide of voices was challenged only by the continuous clatter of dishes and silverware as busboys hurtled through the swinging kitchen doors shoving their busing carts ahead of them. The air was full of knives and forks, glasses, dishes, teeth, and hands. People were constantly waving and yelling from table to table; waitresses pursed their lips in concentration as they carefully threaded their way through the clogged spaces between the tables, their arms layered with trays of food and drinks. Real drinks. Sweated tankards of scotch and soda, mugs of bourbon and water, goblets of martinis. It was a show, and for me it was much better than the dreary, talky repetition of the soundstages.

Here, lubricated by the latest concoctions, Pimm's Cups, gimlets, and Moscow Mules, stars and supporting players alike leaned over and whispered their real salaries, their new billing status. Some came straight from the set in costume brandishing swords and whips, wearing six guns and wigs. Large, famous faces, gobs built for close-ups and layered in makeup leered down at me like the balloons at the Macy's Day Parade. "Hiya, Neddy, what're ya reading?" And here I got my revenge. I found I could speak and not be heard. I'd move my lips as if courteously explaining what I was reading, but what I'd be saying, very quietly so that I could hear but they couldn't was, Hi, Poopoo Face, hello Mr. Toy-tee Head, hello, Peepee Smell, Hi Miss Dog Dooty. Then I'd laugh and smack my cheeks, make farting noises, snort like a pig, pretend to die, bleed in my chair from a rubber dagger. What a funny kid, Keeno—be an actor someday. Yup.

"Mr. Wynn," the principal says. She grabs the edge of her desk and pulls herself to her feet. I can see the shoes cut into the flesh. She nearly staggers. Her mouth is a beige slit. My father walks into the room. Several other women are at the door. They smile swiftly at my father. He looks grim. Everybody flurries around the famous actor a moment, whispering his name to the newcomers filtering in from neighboring offices. Keenan Wynn Keenan Wynn Keenan Wynn. The principal basks in this a moment before turning her face toward the criminal who makes them all sick with his badness sitting in the chair. "Well, Mr. Wynn, I'm sure this is unpleasant for you," the principal says to my father. Then she hands me a tiny scrap of paper. Oh, please. And three crayons. Oh, oh no. It's as if they are gathered around me to watch me pee. ". . . as it is for all of us, surely. He hasn't filled out his deportment slip today yet. But I'm sure we all know what will be on it."

I toy with the green crayon a moment. Wasn't there a five-minute period there where I was kind of OK? Just a window of goodness, say, where I didn't try and strangle any bunny rabbits? Hopefully, I look up. The principal stares at the green crayon as if I had picked up a snake. I drop it instantly and pick up the black one. I look at my father and all I can see are his enormous meaty hands hanging at his sides. The big powerful porterhouse hands that breach the door to the soundstage, that ride the motorcycle, that drive the car, that chop the tree, that slap my . . . my . . .

I press down on the paper with the black crayon and the marks appear. One two three black marks. Shiny, like the wings of the blackbird. I glance out the window. Are there any birds there who will take me? Take me to their home in high treetops? My mother. I suddenly remember my mother will not be home. She has gone somewhere. I forget. Somewhere with Uncle Van. But why?

"I think that's a fair assessment of his deportment for today," says the principal. "Wouldn't you agree, Mrs. Gardner?" She turns to my teacher, who has shown up for the inquest. She hesitates.

"Yes. That would be a fair—assessment." She seems sorry now about her modern idea. I am very sorry about it. My mother. This would not be happening if she were here. I don't know why, but I know it would not be happening.

Then my father walks over and spreads his thick lamb-chop fingers and takes my wrist and pulls me to my feet. The last mile begins.

We drove. Black checks dappled the windshield, raced across my hands like tiny minnows. I tried to think of fun. I thought of the times at Metro when they would give up a whole screening room for me to watch cartoons. Walt Disney sent *Fantasia* over for me to watch with my father. Other times I would be all alone in the screening room watching Tom and Jerry, Droopy the Dog, Barney Bear, Woody Woodpecker. Once, in the screening room corridor, a long, carpeted corridor, very soft and quiet, Margaret O'Brien gave me a piece of candy. She was so beautiful, at eight years of age, that I, at four, was struck dumb. She smiled at me and blushed as she gave me the candy. For a moment she leaned against the wall. She had on a brown coat. Her smile was so radiant it seemed to tug at my neck, to warm my ears. I thought that I would like to follow her like a puppy, stay very near to her, to yip and beg for candy. I wept when her mother took her away.

I tried to bring the fun into my mind, but the fear lay in my stomach like hot iron. My father said little to me those afternoons as we drove home. It was enough to know I would soon be spanked. There would be no Margaret O'Brien there to smile at me and make me well. No cartoons, no Mickey, no Donald, no Droopy. Nothing but this enormous chateaubriand coming down on my pink buttocks.

When we came into the door June and the new nurse, Maria Holquin, a gentle Navajo from Tucson, would be silent. She would look at me longingly. It would be all right. Later, I'll give you a treat. June saved you a chicken foot. Don't worry, Neddy, don't worry. My father would pull me, too fast to keep up, through the house, my legs windmilling behind me like little propellers. I would already be screaming.

I began screaming the second we set foot inside the house, hoping once again to change the world as I had that day with Cocoa and the picture people. I screamed all the way through the kitchen, through the hallway and up the stairs. I screamed along the upstairs hall and into the master bedroom. The only sound in the room, in the universe now, was the sound of my screaming. Standing there in the middle of the bedroom, my father perched on the edge of the bed, I screamed as he pulled down my pants. I screamed as he bent me over his knee. I screamed as he raised his hand and brought it down. And then, for a split second, I paused: It didn't hurt. Right at first, that first fall of the hand, the first slap on my bare ass . . . was painless. Surprised, I stopped screaming. But then, in a matter of half a second, the pain was unbearable. I was always surprised then at how much it hurt. At this rude shock I cranked the scream up higher until it was a thin shell stretching across the sky, tenting the house, the block, the neighborhood.

I screamed at the empty closet in the empty dressing room, I wailed to the empty drawers, I appealed to the makeup case, the blouses, the sweaters that were no longer there. Only the smell remained. The smell of the angora sweaters and the powder and the perfume that could not stay the enormous flying roast at the end of my father's arm. His anger here was not only at me, but at her. Did he spank her? Is that why she ran away? Were we all bad? Bent over his knee, my underpants around my ankles, I watched the door to my mother's dressing room. She would not come out. I looked out the window. The pond was down there. Did it hear me? I'm coming, I thought. I'm coming.

When the spanking was finally over, it was over. No further punishment was offered. Instead, there was a reward. "You want some cookies?" my father asked. "Go see if Maria or June has some cookies for you." He was usually calm after a spanking. But sometimes I couldn't stop crying right away, a kind of regular, hiccuping sob would keep coming. That unnerved him. He would get angry all over again. I tried hard to keep these sobs from continuing. They disgusted him, and sometimes he spanked me all over again because of them. I held my breath. My body shook with each hiccup, but I made no sound. That was better. He seemed disconnected. His gaze wandered over to the empty dressing room door as if he had forgotten something. His hand massaged his finger. There was a wedding ring on it.

"Show me, Daddy," I said, careful not to hiccup. He pulled the wedding ring down his finger to expose the white, floundery skin which had been hidden by the ring. There was an indentation there. I thought of the principal's feet and touched the sunless skin. My father twisted the ring back and forth.

"I never take it off," he mused. "Your mother gave me this ring and I never take it off." He slipped the ring back in place and stood up. "If you like we can go to the Wellmans'."

"Can I play?"

"Yes." He bent and kissed me.

In the kitchen the women waited for the young criminal to straggle in from Golgotha. Poor Neddy, it must have been a terrible spanking. Yes, yes, it was. Can we do anything? Cookies and milk are best in these cases. And if I was lucky and we were having chicken for dinner, then June saved me a chicken foot complete with its toes and its lizardy yellow skin. I would take this foot outside and walk it along the railings and the tops of the walls.

I spent hours playing alone in the yard, catching minnows in the pond and laying them carefully on the bushes to dry out, maybe to get a tan. *Wham!* Oh, God, the flying roast! But . . . *wham!* The dead minnows drove my father nuts. *Wham!* They belong in the pond, they need water to live! *Wham!* Yes, yes . . . I didn't know, but now I do. Yes! I promise I promise I promise I'll be good. The yard, the friendly yard, was now a mine field.

Sometimes Dad took Tracy and me for walks on Chapparal, the street that ran along the eastern edge of our property. We had a new dog, Pledge. A gentle Belgian shepherd, Pledge sometimes was allowed to come with us in the afternoons. Tracy was walking now, but he was still quite small and needed to be lifted up and ridden on my father's shoulders from time to time. I was too big for that. I needed to be on the ground where I could take a stick and lop off the heads of any insolent poppies along the side of the road, dangerous plants that threatened us at every turn. I needed to walk on the road where I could kick stones and mash ant hills.

"Dada, can I ride on your shoulders, too?" Where did that come from? From my mouth? Too late to stop the words.

"Dada?" My father is incredulous. He mocks. "Dada, Dada . . ." Tracy, riding high above, chortles. A cheeky daisy nods at me from a garden. Whop! No more cheeky daisy. A smarty-pants rose bobs in the breeze. Whack! Just keep it up, Rosey, keep it up. At Engle Brothers Pharmacy I'll get a hundred comics and read them. I'll get a chocolate malt and drink it. We'll tie Tracy up to the bicycle rack, it's the law, you know, for kids under three, heh heh, and I'll get comics and chocolate malts for a year. All we have to do is cross Sunset Boulevard. That's all we have to do. "Can Pledge come, Dad?" Busy Sunset Boulevard.

"Too many cars." My father looks uncertain. He gauges the road.

"Please please please please . . ." Engle Brothers Pharmacy with comic books and chocolate malts. Pledge would love to come. I never see the car, Dad never sees the car, Pledge never sees the car, the driver sees only a brown shape jumping out on the road in front of him. I hear the screech, the high *kieeyeeyeeee*. Then I see the dog in the street lying down and making a horrible sound. She will not stop. My father's face is white with pain, anger, something else. He looks at me. People are looking. The car has stopped. Pledge's painful howls cut through me like a whip.

"Take Tracy home now!" shouts my father.

"I'm sorry, Daddy," I cry. It's not my fault. But, it is, bad boy, it is.

"You wanted Pledge to come with us," he says between his teeth. And now look. "Take Tracy home!" But you're the grown-up! Tracy is crying, too. I take his hand and we start to walk back down the once-happy flower-tossed street. Can I fix the daisy, repair the rose that lies in the weeds, dead for its impudence? I'm not the grown-up, I'm only the child. I'll never be the grown-up. Ever.

The dog was never the same. Weeks in the hospital, she came home meek and cringing. The veterinarian said that she had a constant ringing in her ears. She crouched at every sound. She was miserable. I was miserable. A dear aunt and uncle took her to live with them in Florida. I was dead. And still, my mother was gone.

Then, incredibly, easily, I would forget it all. I would spend days at Cissy and Timmy Wellman's house. Their father was William Wellman, the director. They called him Wild Bill, and in front of him even my father seemed smaller, less important. It was always the same. I would first go into the study where he and Dottie, his wife, would be sitting. I would say hello, shake his hand. He seemed at first always to be dour, a little angry. But then he would suddenly grin. After all, he had seven children and had not eaten any of them yet. They lived on a miniature farm in Brentwood only a few blocks from us. They had horses in stalls down in a canyon. There were chickens and ducks and geese, goats, dogs, cats. Elephants, I supposed, hidden in deep ravines, whales in the swimming pool. Why not? And one daughter, Kitty, who was more beautiful than anyone I had ever seen, even Margaret O'Brien. And there was Pat Wellman, the oldest, half girl, half horse.

Once Pat came to fetch me, the red-haired rancher's daughter on her horse, and I a Western hero, Frank McGillicuddy, was waiting in my chaps and boots, all rough and tumble, full of sand and grit. She rode into our yard and stood there, teetering high above my puny kingdom. I didn't know she was going to be on a four-legged boxcar. "Let's go, Neddy," she said, offering her hand to pull me up. But the animal had a head the size of a mailbox and eyes as big as Saturn, teeth like piano keys. Its nostrils flared at me threatening to suck me in like hair down the bathtub drain. No. I would not ride. Not behind her, clinging tight for all time. No. Not even if Kitty Wellman and Margaret O'Brien and Jane Fonda and the Ape Man himself were on the horse together. Not even then.

But most days I strode the prairies alone, and camped beside the pond, drawing pictures in the muddy bottom with a stick, and lying on the cool rocks behind the waterfall. I watched again for the fairies who were there, how long ago? A month? A year? A week? I smelled the moss, the maidenhair fern, the soft sweet-smelling grass that grew in the shade. I watched carefully. But no elves stirred. No gnomes. No leprechauns. She was gone, and she had taken the fairies with her.

We are in the kitchen. It's after dinner. June is at the sink, Maria sits at the kitchen table with me. My father walks heavily every night now. His face is red and big. He gets up at noon and doesn't speak to me until two or three. He drinks black coffee and eats burned toast for breakfast. He doesn't know it, but at night I see him in the living room in the chair. He sits and stares and drinks from a bottle he keeps by him on the floor. Tonight he comes into the kitchen. Under his arm is a small radio, which he plugs into the wall and sets down on the table. He turns it on.

A voice is coming out of the radio, one I have heard often. It has an edgy, racetrack whine: "Mr. and Mrs. America and all the ships at sea, let's go to press. . . ." His name is Walter Winchell, Dateline: Hollywood. I hear my mother's name. "Evie Wynn, former wife of actor Keenan Wynn, has married bobby-soxer idol Van Johnson in a civil ceremony in Juarez, Mexico, earlier today. They'll be going to Sun Valley for their honeymoon. When they return, sons Ned and Tracy will join Van and Evie in their new home in Santa Monica, California, a fantastic spread complete with a pool, tennis court, the works. Sorry all you heartsick gals—better luck next time."

It's like the spankings. At first there's no pain. Then it dawns on me that something bad has happened. I start to cry. My father comes over. His face has a crumpled look, lopsided, full of anguish. He takes my hand and places a dollar bill in it. "Here, son. That's a dollar," is all he says.

"Well, look at that, a whole dollar!" says June. Maria smiles brightly at me.

"My, my, a dollar. We better put that in your piggy bank," she says. My father unplugs the radio and leaves the room. I stare at my hand. There's a dollar in it. But what for? Did I do something good this time? Then why did Mommy leave and marry Uncle Van?

Maria picks me up and carries me up the stairs. I clutch the dollar tightly. Over my shoulder I see my father. He is sitting in his chair. If he gets up right now and takes me, we can go to Juarez Sun Valley and get Mommy back. Uncle Van won't mind. He'll give Mommy back to us once he sees how much we want her. Then he can come and visit. Then it'll be like before. I'll even give him my dollar. It'll be fine. But my father doesn't get up. He stays in the chair and watches me as we climb the stairs. I wave my dollar bill at him just before I disappear.

CHAPTER

The mountains were on fire. From our house, four miles away, we could see the glow that extended the sunsets and stretched across the ridges at night glowing orange and red, pulsing like a hungry caterpillar. By day, immense towers of black smoke hung over the ocean, and there was a fine layer of ash on everything, even inside the house. It was 1948. I was six and a half, and Topanga Canyon was burning.

On the third day of the fire I stood at my window after dinner and watched it. In my hand I held a model airplane, which I flew safely above the roaring blaze spotting people and cows and cats on roofs in need of rescuing. My copilot was Sky King, Jack Armstrong my all-American radio operator. We'd been flying through the raging fire storm for hours now. We were streaked with soot and bone tired, but there was a job to do, and we . . .

"Does it fly?" Ignore that. "Hey, kid, does it fly?" This is an emergency situation, mister, get off our frequency. I banked the airplane in order to avoid a windowsill that suddenly loomed up out of the smoke. And then I saw him. It was a boy. Standing across the fence by the garage was a boy.

"Yes."

"Then fly it," he said. Of course it didn't fly. It was made of metal. "Go ahead, fly it." In answer to that, I landed it on the windowsill and pursed my lips prissily.

"I don't want to fly it right now," I said.

"*Sure* you don't," he said. "My dad has one with a gas motor. He's giving it to me."

I looked at the boy across the fence. He was taller than I, older, thin like I was with brown hair.

"That's the Topanga fire," I announced.

"Well, *duh* now," he said. "Is that your house?"

"Yes," I said. He turned around and pointed to the house behind him and a little to the north.

"That's mine," he said. "You have a swimming pool, don't you? And a tennis court. I've been over there before."

"You want to come over and swim?"

"I've only swam there about seventy-eight times already. But OK. How old are you?" he asked.

"Six-and-a-half," I said.

"I'm ten," he said. "But we can play anyway." He looked at me and made a face. "Is your dad Van Johnson or not?" he demanded.

"He's my stepfather," I said. "Keenan Wynn's my father." I waited for the awe, the *homage*.

"Never heard of that guy. My sister's all big on movie stars, but I don't care about 'em one *iota*. They're all phonies anyway, not real people." I felt my skin prickle.

"They are so real," I said.

"*Sure* they are," he said. I swallowed and my eyes started to sting.

"My dad is real," I choked. "He lives in Brentwood."

"Well," he said, doubtfully, "maybe *your* dad's real, but the others aren't."

"What about Van?" I asked. I was whimpering now.

"OK, him too," he said. "Don't cry, OK?"

"OK." My mother came into the room. Quickly I wiped my eyes with my sleeve.

"Neddy, are you crying?" She knelt down. That was my cue. I started crying all over again.

"That kid said that movies stars aren't real." His mouth dropped open. I had betrayed him. It was a nice feeling.

"Guyyy . . ." he protested.

My mother laughed. "Some of them aren't, dear," she said. She turned to the boy. "What's your name?" she asked.

"Bobby Curry. I live over on San Lorenzo, it's the next street." He pointed to the fire. "Topanga Canyon burns all the time. I've seen lots of fires."

"How many?" I asked.

"Forty," he said. Then he looked at my mother. "Three." This revelation buoyed my spirits even more than the betrayal had. More fires to look forward to. Santa Monica was going to be great.

I lived at Uncle Van's house now. Or *Daddy* Van's. They had tried that for a while, but I wouldn't say it and they gave up. Their hearts weren't in it and he became simply, Van. The house itself was a sleek Deco/Moderne cube that my friend Jackie Hathaway called Uncle Scrooge's money bin. It was on a dead-end street called Kingman Avenue, a rustic cul-de-sac off Entrada Drive about half a mile from the beach.

How I got there was simple. One day I didn't get a spanking. I didn't even go to school. Instead, the nurse packed our clothes and we went outside and stood on the porch. There, in the driveway, were Van and Mom sitting in a brand-new 1947 Cadillac convertible. Midnight-blue with a tan top. It was a warm day, but Mom was bundled up in a new fur coat. Van had on shorts, a tennis sweater, and a camel-hair overcoat, which he always wore open. Everyone smiled a lot. Big whitewall smiles. Teeth bared to the gum line, lips white from smiling, Dad stood in the gravel drive, his hands on his hips, a pipe clenched in his mouth. He looked up at the sky and the trees as if he were about to announce the coming of winter.

"It'll burn off," he announced.

I ran past him and jumped into the car ahead of Tracy and the nurse. It was even better than Mom's closet. Not only could I smell her perfume again, but now it mingled with Van's Tabu, which he bought by the quart and splashed on like water. These exotic smells curled around the new leather seats and prowled my nostrils, exciting me until I reached over and pinched Tracy's foot. He yelped and I lay back and gazed at the shiny chrome struts that framed the canvas top. Won't this be fun?

"Are you OK, Tracy honey? Did something bite you?" my mother asked. Yeah. Something bit him all right. Powerful smells and quick, tiny violences. I sighed with pleasure.

This was the smell now. These were the people I would live with. Familiar, but not familiar. Tabu and Fred Perry, Mary Chess and Balenciaga, Cadillacs and tennis rackets, swimming pools and beach cabanas.

"Want the top down kids?" Van asks. Oh, yes. Can we? Please please please. . . . Van unsnaps the corners, pulls something under the dash and there is a whine. Suddenly the front of the top pops free from the frame of the windshield and starts to rise. Where is it going? Tracy is now screaming at the top of his lungs. My mouth is open, my buck teeth poised in rabbity wonder as I watch the miraculous electric top yawn above us like the prow of a sinking ship then fold and collapse on the back of the seat behind me.

"Like the Wicked Witch, Mommy, look!" I shout into the front seat.

"Wits!" screams Tracy. *"Ook!"*

"Tracy said wits, Mommy. What a dumb dodo. Wits wits wits . . ." I taunt him joyously.

"Now, Neddy, he's only two," she says. I wiggle uncomfortably. Want me to be good? Watch this.

"I'll teach him, Mommy, listen, *witch witch witch*," I say right in his face, my mouth open as wide as Monstro the whale. Tracy clams up and sucks his fist. As the top clears I can see Dad in the driveway again. He's pointing to the sky.

"It oughta be great at the beach," he says to no one in particular. "Very fancy car," he says a little louder, looking the whole time at the roof of the house. "Fancy schmancy." I notice his eyes are bloodshot. Suddenly he peels off his shirt, inflates his chest and starts rotating his shoulders. "Faaancy schmaaancy."

"Yeah. Isn't it, though?" says Van. It comes out bored, just the littlest bit what Mom calls snippy. Van barely looks at Dad, who stands in front of the car now, grinning hard, bare-chested and hairy.

"You look good, Keenan," Mom says. "Doesn't Keenan look good, Van?"

"Great," says Van. "Just great. Been working out, Keeno?" he asks, utterly without interest.

"Every day," says Dad. "Every single goddamned day." He massages his triceps. Will they play now? When the tour buses stop in front they always play. If Peter Lawford and Gene Kelly were here they'd play. The people on the bus would point and take pictures while the men took off their shirts and flexed their muscles and did cartwheels on the lawn and mugged and yapped like coyotes. I wish they were here, the tourists and Peter and Gene.

But Van wants to leave. He wants to be with Mom now, not Dad. We all want to be with Mom. She's a special prize, a reward, a treat like milk and cookies. Only you have to take her to your room with you and lock the door so no one else can be with her. That's how it's done. Otherwise, they'll want her and they'll take her and you won't get to be with her. I'm glad I know this now.

Dad finally drops his arms and lets the air out of his chest. "I'll come and see you tomorrow," he says quietly. *Tomorrow* is everyone's favorite word. And next week. "Next week we'll go to the studio and get a haircut."

"And comics?" I ask.

"Sure. Comics," he says. Then he looks up again. The sky is covered with gauzy clouds. "Today," he says, "today I think I'll get some sun."

There were no dramatics, no tears. This had all been arranged for a long time. My mother had fled twice before, once to Las Vegas taking me with her. There she had planned to get divorced, but finding she was pregnant with Tracy, she had relented. Then, after Tracy was born, my father, drunk and on a ten-day bender celebrating the birth of his second son, ran his motorcycle into a car turning left on Sunset Boulevard. That moment my mother was coming home with Tracy from the hospital. They say that the ambulances passed each other.

My father was in a coma for fourteen days. His jaw was wired shut for six weeks, and he carried a steel plate in his head for the rest of his life. My mother stayed with him for another two years.

As we drove away that day I got on my knees, turned around on the seat and stared back at my father. I was Cocoa, now. I was being taken down the street and Dad was there in the driveway watching. Good, I thought, good. As he grew smaller it came to me with great clarity: no more spankings. I was being delivered from the flying ham hock, the three checks, the principal of the Brentwood Grammar School. I was going to a better place, a much better place. I saw Dad look up at the sun once more. Then he waved the shirt at me like a flag. He shouted something. I think it was "tomorrow . . ." Then he disappeared from view.

And so it was that one day I left my father, the leading man's best friend, and moved in with my stepfather, the leading man.

It's dark, but I'm awake, and something awful is happening to the room. It's shrinking. I feel the ceiling lowering toward me. The chest of drawers, the chair, the table are all moving closer. I can barely turn my head to look at the window. The shade flaps. The man with the ladder is out there, the man from the back of the comic book. He wears a burglar's cap and a mask. He places the ladder up against the side of the house. It squeaks against the plaster as he climbs. He is climbing up to the window of the room where the little boy is sleeping. He is going to crawl in the window of the room where the little boy is sleeping and steal the little boy. His name is The Kidnapper, and he's going to walk right into the room and take the little boy away. But suddenly, one foot in the room and the other still on the top rung of the ladder, he is caught in the beam of a powerful flashlight. A vigilant neighbor has spotted The Kidnapper and trapped him in a bright beam of light, light that only comes from strong, dependable, law-abiding Eveready batteries. We have to have Eveready batteries if we don't want The Kidnapper to get us. I beg for these, even though I don't have a flashlight. I sleep with one clenched in my hand.

Other nights the room grows larger instead of smaller. The bed shrinks. This time everything is far away. Something from inside is coming out; huge pillars, thick, indistinct masses, blocks of impenetrable matter rise above me. The window is impossibly far away now, and no longer the object of fear. Now I wish I could get to the window, to look out, to breathe fresh air. In my stomach there is a desperate vacuum, a hole left by the things that have escaped outside. Now they have grown too big to get them back inside. I feel like throwing up. When I fall asleep I dream of tractors pushing huge piles of thick folded blankets into a pit. I am lying in the bottom of this pit. The blankets push the air out of me, smother me. It goes on for hours. Awake or asleep the nightmare revolves around me. No one can hear me. I'm a Big Boy now.

Tracy's room was next to mine. Sometimes I'd go into his room and wake him up. It was the only thing that would stop the terror. In the dark we'd play. I'd bounce toy cars off his head and he'd squeal with delight. Then, before I went back to bed, I'd ask him to go *dere-dere*. He'd roll and sing his little song and I'd finally be able to fall asleep.

Van and Mom rarely stayed home. They went out three or four nights a week, to parties and premieres. And every night before they left I'd wait at the top of the stairs, wait for the rustle of the Balenciaga gown, the Givenchy cocktail sheath, the click of heels, the *jing-jing* of Tiffany and Cartier, the waft of Mary Chess white lilac, wait for Van's big sunburned face and huge-shouldered jackets from Eddie Schmidt in New York, wait for Tabu, for red cashmere Forstmann socks from the London Shop nestled in black patent leather pumps with satin bows from Carroll & Co., wait for them to arrive at the top of the stairs on their way to somewhere I couldn't go. And when they got there I'd start crying. Every night I'd cry and beg them not to go. Mom would kneel down and hug me and tell me she'd be back soon. But I no longer trusted her to come back. Then Van would kneel down and pat my head and tell me that I could sleep in their bed. I'd watch, sobbing, as they went down the stairs, my mother tossing running orders to the nurse and the maid as she went about dinner and bed and radio and lights out and clothes for tomorrow. Finally Tracy would come and put his arm around me and tell me it would be OK. He'd be fretful and agitated until I stopped crying. Then we'd play until he went to bed.

Sometimes we'd play miniature golf. I'd be the golfer, he'd be the golf club. I'd swing him around by his ankles until I managed to drive his head into a cabinet or a piano bench, at which point the game would automatically end. He'd start crying, the nurse would rush in, and we'd both be sent to bed. I'd go to Van and Mom's room and fall asleep after listening to *Sky King* and *Red Ryder* and *The Cisco Kid, Bulldog Drummond, The Fat Man, Let George Do It, Fibber McGee and Mollie, Jack Benny, Amos 'n Andy, The Shadow, My Friend Irma, Life with Luigi, Straight Arrow, Captain Midnight, Jack Armstrong All-American Boy, It Pays to Be Ignorant, Can You Top This?* and "Tales calculated to keep you in"—*Suspense*. Later, when they came home, Van would pick me up and carry me across the house to my room. These times were the best. Half-awake, nestled safely against Van's broad chest, I would be spared the dreams and hallucinations. I was no longer afraid.

Most summer days I'd play with Bobby. Our relationship was different from any I had had before. For one thing, his parents were not in the film business and did not socialize with my parents. We weren't friends just because our parents were; we chose each other, and we needed no one but ourselves. From the first day we met we created a world in which our friendship existed as a third person, another boy who accompanied us everywhere. The function of this invisible boy was to act as a silent go-between, to carry thoughts and feelings between us without our needing to say anything. At times I felt as if there was no difference between Bobby and me, that there were no borders, no discrete physical characteristics that could keep us from flowing together at any time, like little bike-riding amoebas, changing bodies in midair, changing hearts and digestive tracts and bones and blood, each becoming the other as we floated above the neighborhood on the soft sea wind of our summertime.

We went on hikes to the beach when the fog was so thick that it lay in fat bundles on the sand, and the ocean ten feet away was a veiled, hissing snake that chased our ankles and gobbled the flat stones we fed it. Or we climbed into the nearby foothills to a secret cache of old abandoned houses where we broke what windows were left and peed into the cracked, empty swimming pools. We kicked down the crumbling walls and smashed bottles on the bare concrete slabs where neighboring homes had never been built. A ruined fantasy, this dissolving grandeur was all that was left of some developer's dream. Bobby said the man who had built the homes had ended up living in a tiny apartment in Hollywood during the Depression. There one night, pining for his lost Arcady, he had shot himself in the mouth. But instead of dying, he'd simply lost half his face and now he roamed the hills sleeping among his idle walls and lingering stairways, watching us with his single eye, sniffing the air with his single nostril. I was fascinated. But I was also a fearful timid mama's boy, a crybaby afraid of everything, and Bobby was trying to show me a different way to be.

He took me to a secret cave in the shady sycamore woods of the Hills Brothers' estate. The coffee family's huge property lay on the other side of a wall at the end of both our streets. The first time he boosted me over the wall, I stood there bravely in the crisp, shin-deep sycamore leaves until I saw a car coming along the private road, then I bolted for home. He took me to the Criterion theater for my first movie without parents, but I wouldn't go into the bathroom there so we had to leave. He showed me how to use a pay phone, but when I put in the nickel and the operator came on the line, I couldn't speak and Bobby had to complete the call. He took me on the bus, but my hand was gripped so tightly on my carfare he had to pry it open and take the money and drop it in the whirling coin collector while people behind us shouted to hurry up and I stared, mortified, at my shoes. He showed me how to catch a frog and put it in Old Mean Walter's gardening glove, but when the little scratchy toes of the frog tickled my palm, I yelped and threw it into the bushes.

Eventually, I lost my fear of the sycamore woods and learned to hide in the leaves when a car went by. I learned to hold a frog and to climb down into the stream that ran out of the Riviera Country Club golf course and disappeared somewhere beneath the street. There, growing just beneath the surface of the running water, were little clumps of watercress, which I would pick and bring home to Elsie the cook who would garnish the plates for the evening meal with it, or break it into a salad. I learned to retrieve golf balls, put them in a vice, and peel the coverings off until we got to the miles of wound rubber bands inside. I was still too scared to approach the golfers and sell them back for a nickel apiece, but I was becoming bolder and slightly less terrified.

Sneaking around the course one day, Bobby warned me about a gang of pachucos whose territory we were on. They were called the White Fence gang and they also liked to get golf balls and sell them to the members. He told me that once he had been captured by the White Fence gang and tied up and tortured at knife point. They had a secret place in the Riviera where they kidnapped little boys and held them hostage. But, he said, we could probably get away with it. If we saw them, just run.

That day we found about six balls. I was very excited, concentrating on the hunt. After an hour or so we got separated. I was alone on a small dirt track that was used as a maintenance road when I saw them. About six kids, all pachucos. One of them had a hunting knife in his hand, exactly as Bobby had said. Instantly, every pore on my body sprung a leak. For a long moment I stood there, transfixed, staring at the boy with the knife. He was older than I was, old enough to have some little wisps of black hair on his upper lip. They were skinny and sparse, and for some reason I became absorbed in this detail of his face. When he grimaced the hairs shifted and wiggled like little wires. Instinctively, I imitated him grinning like a chimp, pulling my lips back tightly over my teeth.

"Hi," I said.

"Hi," said the leader, pleasantly. Then he bared his teeth even further and licked at some of the longer hairs.

"I'm playing with Bobby," I offered.

"Gee," he said, "that sounds nice." I nodded eagerly. "What you got in your hand, Paddy-boy?"

"*Um. . . .*" I stared at my hand and drew a blank. What? "Nothing," I said. Who is Paddy-boy? Then a form rushed past me.

"Run!" it shouted. "Run!" It was Bobby. I turned apologetically to the gang leader.

"Good-bye," I said, politely, remembering the lessons my mother had taught me. "I have to go now." You don't just leave a room without excusing yourself. It puts others in an awkward position.

The leader actually nodded pleasantly for a split second. Then he frowned and stepped toward me. I started to run.

Bobby was about ten yards ahead of me. He glanced back. "Drop the ball," he screamed at me. "Drop the damn ball!"

"Drop the ball!" I yelled back. "Drop the damn ball!" The wind whistled by my ears. We ran across the fairways, through the sand traps, across the greens, and through the hole in the fence. "Drop the ball," he screamed. "For chrissake drop the damn ball!"

"Drop the ball," I replied, dutifully. "For cries ache drop the damn ball!" We ran through the Hills Brothers' woods past our cave where we stored matches and candles and sat around burning roots and talking about forest fires and Japs. "Drop the ball," he pleaded. "Drop the frigging damn ball!"

"Drop the ball," I screamed. "Drop the friggydan ball!" I was getting hoarse from all this screaming. We climbed the last wall and jumped into Bobby's yard, dashed inside and up the stairs to Bobby's room where model planes hung on strings from the ceiling and fluorescent paint on the walls glowed in the dark and used-car batteries sat on the floor wired and ready for the electrocution of flies and spiders and a mouse if we got lucky (we never did), and war-surplus flashlights and compasses and shortwave radios and canteens littered the bed and closet and shelves. We flung ourselves, panting, onto the bed. We lay there for several minutes catching our breath. Finally Bobby sat up.

"Boy, that was close," he said. "Those guys would've killed us if you hadn't dropped that ball. They'd have tied us up and taken us to their hideout and . . . hey . . ." He grabbed my wrist and turned my hand over. In it, clinched in a death grip, was the golf ball. "Jesus, Mary, and Joseph," he said, which was the only way we could legally say Jesus—then he started to laugh. He took the ball from me and tossed it against the wall. "Let's put it in the vise," he said.

"Yeah. Then go to my house and get root beers," I said.

"Yeah," he said.

"Neat, huh?" I said.

"Neat," he said.

Summer was over, and I was shocked to find that I was actually expected to go to school again. I thought we'd settled all that. It had to be a mistake. I thought I was supposed to play for the rest of my life. I had already been to school, it wasn't terrific. It had to be an experiment, like trying to get me to call Van "Daddy Van." But it wasn't. They were completely serious. I had to go to school again. Not only that, but I would have to go to school for *many years to come*. Probably until I was *eighteen years old*. It was *the law*. Worse, I didn't get to go to school where Bobby went. He was going to a

public school, but I had to go to *private school*. I was shattered.
Bobby had told me that private school was the ultimate humiliation
for any real kid. Real kids went to public school.

Van and Mom took me that first day. They drove me up the
Seventh Street hill where Bobby and I had had to walk our bikes
because it was too steep to ride. We turned left on San Vicente and
drove toward Brentwood; Bobby and I always went straight down
Seventh Street into Santa Monica when we went to the Criterion or
the Aero without our folks like the other real kids did. My parents
would drive me up to the school in a Cadillac, but Bobby would go
to his school on the bus with the other real kids who would throw
sandwiches at each other and blow off firecrackers in their lockers.
I was being condemned to be a movie star's kid, a rich kid who had
to go to school with other rich kids. That was bad, but that wasn't
what really bothered me. The old fear was back; it had found me
like a dog sniffing a trail of sweat. A lump of terror that rolled and
burned like a little Greek fire inside my stomach, it would have been
there no matter where I went to school. Would there be a principal
here? Would they make me evaluate my own deportment? Would
Dad be waiting when the school day was over to take me home and
spank me? And what about the other kids? *They* frightened me the
most. The other kids. Rich or poor, they scared me. Why did school
have to have other kids in it? I lay on the floor of the car and held
my stomach.

"You'll love this school, Neddy," my mother told me. "It's gorgeous. It's just like being home. They have creative playtime and
clay modeling and even a horse and a queen of the May." Oh, boy.
A horse to torment me further with its huge Jupiterian eyeballs and
piano-key teeth. Great. And what's this ominous-sounding thing
called creative playtime? We never had anything like that at home.
But I didn't answer her. I was resigned. I knew fresh horrors were
being prepared and the little fire would burn more brightly. I was
growing up.

The school they took me to was on San Vicente Boulevard near
Twenty-sixth Street at the border of Santa Monica and Brentwood.
It was called Brentwood Town and Country School, and it seemed
that many of the same children I had known before went there. It
was not always clear whether I was actually meeting the same children I had known before, or whether I was meeting new children
who only reminded me of children I had known before. In that
summer I had gotten some strange kind of amnesia and had actually
forgotten everything, including how to write. I had to learn all over
again.

Often, when I saw certain children, I thought they were the
same ones I had known at Brentwood School, but I couldn't be sure.

Their faces *looked* the same. Maybe I had met them at a birthday party, one of the many arranged by all the famous parents at which I met children like Christina Crawford and Bobby Walker, Jr., children I very rarely saw, but who I was supposed to know.

I am three or four years old. I am dressed in a little short-pants suit with a bow tie, and I clutch a present in my hands that I would as soon be opening myself. "Go on, Neddy," my mother urges. She gently shoves me forward. I'd rather just go watch the elephant or the camel or the clown or the magician or the hundred other things that are going on outside. But first I have to give this present to someone called "the birthday girl." Where's the birthday girl?

"Where's the birthday girl, Joan?" my mother asks. The lady in front of me at the door leans forward and smiles. Her mouth is a huge scarlet chasm that nearly bisects her face, her eyes are outlined in finger paint, and her eyebrows, two huge dark caterpillars, are definitely done in crayon. She is how I would paint a face in my coloring book. This face fascinates and terrifies me at the same time; it seems as if each section of it is alive and under the control of a different operator. I recognize her as an actress like the ones my father introduces me to on the set at Metro. All she is missing is the Kleenex at her collar. Her name is Joan Crawford.

"Oh, she's been very difficult today, Evie," Joan says. "She's been sent to her room. She can't come down and join the party with the other little boys and girls until she apologizes. So Neddy will have to give her present to me." The lady sticks out her hand, but I refuse to give her the present. My mother has instructed me to give the present to Christina.

"I'm supposed to give it to Christina," I say firmly. Joan smiles.

"Well, Neddy, I'm afraid Christina's been very bad and can't come down to accept it, although I'm sure she'd like to." She reaches for the present again, and again I refuse to give it to her.

"I'm sorry, Joan, but I've told him that he must give it to Christina," my mother says. Her voice has gained a slight edge that wasn't there before.

"Well, Evie, I'm afraid that's just impossible. Christina's simply too stubborn to enjoy a beautiful birthday party like this. So all the other little boys and girls, all her little friends, will just have to enjoy it without her. But I'll see that she gets her present when she apologizes."

I look at my mother and then at Joan. I don't want to give the present to this woman. I don't know Christina, but I want to give the present to *her*, whoever she is. I also want lemonade and cake and ice cream and a balloon.

"I tell you what, Neddy," Joan says. "Why don't you wave Hi to

Christina and show her the present, then she'll know you brought it to her. She's right there on the balcony." Joan points above me to the second story.

I turn around and look up. Standing there on a balcony in a pretty little party dress is the saddest child I have ever seen. I stare at her.

"Wave to Christina, darling," my mother says, and I wave. Christina raises her hand slightly and wiggles her fingers. A tiny smile flickers on her face and dies. "Surely, Joan, she can come down and join her own birthday party. She couldn't have been *that* bad," my mother says. I can plainly hear the distress in my mother's voice. I am now alarmed. This woman, Joan, sends shivers down my spine and awakens the Greek fire in my belly. In an instant I have understood everything. I start to cry.

"Do I have to take a nap here?" I ask through my tears. I'm thinking of being placed in this huge house in a distant room with this woman standing at the door. My mother kneels and hugs me.

"Of course not, Neddy," she says. "Now why don't you go ahead and give the present to Joan and she'll give it to Christina later." Behind me all the other children are riding on the elephant or the ponies, eating the ice cream and cake, and getting balloons from Bozo the Clown. There is a merry-go-round and a Punch and Judy show and a Ferris wheel. If I don't get to these things soon, they may disappear. The hell with the birthday girl.

"OK," I say and hand the present over to Joan. In an instant I am free of the birthday girl and her mother. Once, as I am watching the Punch and Judy show I turn and look at the balcony. Christina is still there. Around me at the party there are a hundred other children. We don't know each other, and none of us knows Christina.

Debbie Daves was different. She was my girlfriend. And even though I didn't remember where I knew her from, I knew she was my girlfriend. Didn't we get in trouble together at the other school? Or was that another Debbie, or was that a girl whose name wasn't Debbie, but who looked like Debbie? Whatever the case, our relationship had become severely strained after an incident that occurred on the playground that first year at Town and Country. It was at the instigation of one of the teachers who thought it was a good time for us to learn how to defend ourselves. Since it was an impromptu decision, bare knuckles would be the style. The teacher who decided on this as a new creative playtime activity was not the same teacher who had, at the other school, decided to let us evaluate our own deportment, but probably a cousin of hers.

Naturally I refused. This was not a skill I felt compelled to learn, and certainly not during creative playtime. What happened to the famous clay modeling, the terrific horse, the Queen of the May? I resisted this new certified fun through a whole list of opponents and about six other fights in which two kids got bloody noses. Finally, the list had been whittled down from Teddy Armbruster, to Stephen Loesser, to Debbie.

"Come on," said the teacher, "you're not afraid to fight a *girl*, are you?" He said it with such disdain that it seemed unthinkable that I should refuse this golden opportunity. The other children picked it up and started shouting at me. But I *liked* Debbie. "Look," said the teacher, putting his face inches from mine, "if you're too big of a baby to fight a girl, then I guess we'll just have to put diapers on you and give you a bottle." The other children all started shouting and jeering. Even Debbie looked at me and hitched up her jeans. OK, I thought. Debbie. I should certainly be able to beat up Debbie.

Debbie's father was Delmer Daves, the director, and it was a well-known fact among actors' children that actors could beat up directors. This was confirmed for me by Sean Flynn who told me his dad, Errol, often beat up directors without a second thought. My own father, I imagined, beat them up regularly before taking off his shirt and getting some sun. Or perhaps in lieu of getting some sun—I wasn't quite clear on that part of it.

There were exceptions, of course. No actor could beat up Timmy Wellman's dad, Wild Bill Wellman, for instance, or Jackie Hathaway's dad, Henry. But most of the other directors like Mary Seaton's father, George, or Tommy Capra's father, Frank, were thought to be physically inferior to actors, and they weren't considered to be particularly brave either. So it was axiomatic, I reasoned, an actor's son should be able to beat up a director's daughter. It was only later that I found the opposite was, in fact, the case: Directors had always been tougher than actors and beat them up from one end of Hollywood to the other; from Romanoff's to the Brown Derby, from Ciro's to the Mocambo, actors were seen flying out of doors behind the ample fists and steel-toed boots of wild, two-fisted, brawling directors. However, at the time I thought the odds were stacked in my favor. I couldn't lose. I was primed for victory, on fire for pugilism. All at once it was something I simply had to learn.

Once I was sure of my opponent, I dove right in. I began with a flow of taunts generally impugning all directors and their offspring while windmilling my arms in a threatening and intimidating manner. Debbie stood uncertainly, looking at me. Was I sure I wanted to do this? In reply I increased my rpm. My arms were a blur; I was a dervish, a human eggbeater. Debbie looked at the teacher. Are we really supposed to do this? I could sense the fear in her heart. Just like a director's daughter to shrink from a fight. At that point I rushed her.

By all rights I should have won that fight. My arms were moving and she was looking the other way. But at the last moment she shrugged, drew back her fist and hit me on the bridge of the nose. I stood for a moment, wavering. The blunt pain of being hit traveled around my face to my ears and back again. My head rang. Mom? Everyone was laughing. My eyes filled with tears. I ran over to the edge of the playground and fell into the patch of ivy growing there along the fence and wept.

The next day I changed girlfriends. I decided that my new girl-friend was Betty Lynn Dupy, who would never have considered punching me in the nose. And anyway she had better knees.

We are in the second grade. It's nap time, and each child has a cot and a blanket. We lie in rows pretending to sleep, but I don't sleep. Instead, I watch Betty Lynn Dupy on the cot next to me. She shifts slightly and I can see her legs peeping out from under the blanket. When nap is over she will fold the blankets while the rest of us go out on the playground. The playground is not my favorite place. In fact, the playground is purgatory for me; I have learned to hate recess. I decide that I will volunteer for blanket-folding after nap. Then, when the rest of the kids go to play, Betty Lynn and I will be alone. I actually think all this out. Even though I'm not clear on why I want this situation to occur, the very thought excites me.

Once everyone has gone, and Betty Lynn and I are alone, I feel my pulse banging in my throat and a hollowness in my stomach. I don't know what it's from, but it has something to do with being near Betty Lynn. As she stands there in front of me in her little plaid skirt and Mary Jane blouse, her blond hair combed and brushed, her white shoes scuffed, one of the straps broken, I finally do it. I fall to my knees and clasp Betty Lynn's legs in my arms and hug her against me. She stands there willingly, unprotesting. She says nothing; there is no reprimand, no tears. She doesn't seem to hate it or to like it particularly, she just accepts it. For what seems like a thousand years we remain like that, I on my knees, she standing there calmly looking around. We're two tiny tortoises, baby lobsters attached for the winter. I am seven years old, and I know that I want to do this until I'm at least fifteen. Then the teacher comes. The teacher always comes. She looks at us a moment. Then she claps her hands and I leap to my feet. Instinctively, I know it was bad. Instinctively, I also know that I will do it again every chance I get.

CHAPTER

4

Women dominated my life from the beginning. I was always either in the care of maids or governesses, or running amok, rampant and spoiled among my parents' actress-friends. I had always been excited by the presence of these women, performing, clamoring, baying for their attention. From the time I was three or four years old I was used to being fondled and kissed by women like Marlene Dietrich, Jennifer Jones, and Claudette Colbert. Lana Turner and Betty Grable, frisking at our pool, had held me in their laps, encouraging me to lie across their sunny thighs. Once, when my mother and father were still married, Ava Gardner had come to our house with her new husband, Mickey Rooney, and even at that age I was awestruck by her beauty.

I was playing on the floor, and when she walked by me and I felt the breeze of her dress, the hair on my arms stood up. I could hear the swish of her stockings and smell her powder and cologne. There I was, eight years from puberty and already horny. For one brief instant I could see up her dress, see the tops of her stockings, the utopian gams, the garter belt, the underwear. She squatted down beside me, her dress billowing out like a parachute, and gazed into my face. She was almost too beautiful to look at. She touched me and my skin jumped. Then Mickey came over and stood nearby smiling down at us. "Is he your husband?" I asked her.

"Yes," she said.

"He's too short for you," I said. Everyone laughed at the clever child. But it was done; I was addicted. The combination of beauty, perfume, silk, and nylon had made me a junky.

As I grew older I remained the clever child appearing, usually unbidden, at parties to sing songs from movies, especially movies Van was in like *The Duchess of Idaho*, or to do whole routines I had memorized from "Bozo the Clown," or to perform the entire recording of "Sparky and His Magic Piano." The crowd, stoned to the eyeballs on Moscow Mules and Dewar's White Label, whistled and stamped its extravagant approval. Guests, I decided, like nothing better than to have the party monopolized by the precocious children of the host and hostess.

When the guests became drunk enough, my mother herded them down to dinner. Then I would try and get Tracy to come with me into the living room where all the half-filled glasses of liquor and stubbed-out cigarettes remained to be cleaned up by the maid. Quickly, one by one, I would taste the different drinks. Tracy, worried that the maid would catch us, would finally run back to his room, but I stayed as long as I could in this bright place with the crystal glasses and sparkling ice and the phonograph music, and one after another I would drink the drinks. They tasted awful, but I never stopped trying. If I could learn to drink them, maybe I could go to the parties; I would put on a big-shouldered coat and patent leather pumps with satin bows and go to the parties with Mom and Van. Then I would not only continue to do the much-in-demand "Sparky and His Magic Piano," but probably add "Sparky and the Talking Train" to the repertoire. And I would laugh very loudly and clap my hands crossways like a grown-up, and look up women's dresses and bathe eternally in their enraptured attention.

Much of this was either in a conscious or unconscious imitation of Van. For one thing it amused him, and amusement was tantamount to acceptance. Other than the approval of the women, I sought his approval most, and I figured that acting like him would gain that approval quickest. So I mimicked everything from his attitudes to his laugh.

Van was famous for his exorbitant laugh, a high-pitched, open-throated peal that soared above the crowd like a carillon. It started as a long *aahhheeeee* that lasted for two or three full seconds and then began oscillating like the shrill *kwheeah-eeeah-eeah-eea* of a hyacinthine macaw. That endorsement by Van was the hallmark of our house. A moody, temperamental man, if he was laughing we were safe. My behavior, then, became centered upon being funny, light, and entertaining. Problems belonged to my mother, to what Van called her "department." "That's *your* department, Evie," he would yell, spotting a problem, and then storm out of the room.

Van was the master of The Huff. If there was the slightest hint of trouble with one of the children, or with the house, the car, the servants, the delivery of the newspaper, the lack of ice in the silver ice bucket, the color of the candles on the dining-room table, Van immediately left the couch, the dinner table, the pool, the tennis court, the party, the restaurant, the vacation, and strode off to his bedroom, hands raised above his head as if he were stopping traffic, to avoid what he called a "scene."

It was always chilling; often it was ludicrous. If a Huff originated in the pool, for instance, he had to pull himself out of the water and walk, dripping wet, across the deck, up a long flight of broad stone steps, across another patio, into the house, through the entry hall, up the stairs, across the living room, which nearly spanned the whole second story, and into his own bedroom. He had to do this without calming down, otherwise he wouldn't have been able to perform the coda to this performance, the Slamming Door. The Slamming Door was the conclusion to The Scene and all part of the Huff.

Van was good for a good time, but he was not good for a bad time. Or even for a mildly uncomfortable one. His tolerance of unpleasantness was minuscule. If it wasn't funny and rewarding instantly, it was hell on earth. I learned a lesson from this, and it was the worst lesson I could have learned: It worked. If you don't get what you want instantly, throw a fit. This behavior dovetailed perfectly with my own natural inclinations toward retentive infancy, and I practiced it fervently. At times my fits ran concurrently with Van's Huffs, scenes flew like confetti, and my mother's department grew into a bureaucracy.

My mother's chief role at these times was to act as if nothing had happened. There would be a few minutes right after one of Van's dramatic exits where everything was quiet. Guilt seeped like poison gas from person to person. Somebody had made Van angry. I'd look at Tracy, we'd both look at Mom. She'd glance briefly at the upstairs window. There was sadness and regret in her face. I'd feel awful, whether or not I'd been to blame. "Is Van mad, Mommy?" Tracy would ask.

"Oh, no, darling," she'd say. "He's working so hard at the studio. . . ." Then she'd fluff the moment back up like a pillow. "Well," she'd say, bright as Mickey Mouse, "who wants a 7-Up?"

She was good at what she did. As a mother she was unstoppable, a determined disciple of the child-rearing gurus of the day. If she read somewhere that a certain procedure should be followed, she adhered like St. Augustine to the Word of God. The single towering example was toilet training.

Good doesn't cover her dedication here. *Ardent* comes to mind. My mother was the DI of toilet training. It began with the exhortation, on a daily basis, to produce solid matter, and not to leave the bathroom until you did. Our family pediatrician had told my mother that a child's entire medical record was revealed in its crap, and so a schedule for the pickup and delivery of stool samples was instated. There were hours spent sitting on "the duck," or "the horsey," small portable toilet seats with little wooden heads to hold onto so that we wouldn't fall through and drown. As I got older, the duck was dispensed with, but not the sessions. Sometimes my mother would find it necessary to come in and cheer us on, to "grunt" and "try hard." This lay a solid foundation for such apparently disparate problems as hemorrhoids and compulsive labeling, not to mention a lifelong performance anxiety. But I would rather have spent ten hours a day riding the duck than having to endure its alternative, the enema.

There was no cute little representative of the animal kingdom on this medieval device, with its slick, shiny orange bag and hose. It hung behind the bathroom door like a rubber cat-o'-nine-tails waiting to scourge our intestines with warm water and baking soda. If we failed to manufacture a respectable heap, my mother would lift it off its hook and the next half-hour someone would pay the price for his meager output. Hiding it did no good; she had a backup. It lay in a box in a cupboard in her bathroom and was sprinkled ritually with talcum powder to preserve its supple ministry.

No amount of begging or pleading could move my mother: She was slavishly attached to the doctor's will. Lying face down across her lap, the growing pressure making me certain I would spray the room at any moment, I would beg her to stop. Tears, screams, threats, nothing could stay this vulcanized reign of terror. She had great compassion in most things, but every now and then her natural inclination toward mercy was overridden by a greater imperative, in this case, Dr. Bernstein. Dr. Bernstein had dedicated his life to the invasion of the human body. His motto was: If there isn't already a hole there, make one. And stick something in it. Preferably something foreign and uncomfortable. It was he who had instituted the weekly stool samples and suggested that enemas were beneficial adjuncts to peas, carrots, and lima beans.

The enema treatments lasted, incredibly, until I was eleven years old. Then one day, in absolute, rigid refusal, I succeeded in ending this particular form of humiliation forever. My mother stood at the door with the bag in her hand, shocked and angry, as I faced her, defiant in my Jockey shorts. I was tearful and trembling, amazed at my own determination, but I would not allow her to give me one more enema, even if it meant that I would die from departmental overload.

My mother was suddenly uncertain. Enemas had become emblematic of parental control; they were given on principle rather than out of sound medical necessity. I had begun to understand this, but my mother either could not or would not acknowledge this fact, and I couldn't gain a position through reason. It was as if it had never occurred to her that there might come a time when it would be inappropriate to give an enema to her son. The ghosts of a generation of doctors stood silently behind my mother watching to see if she could uphold the traditions of blind obedience to current dogma, or if she would capitulate to the cornered rat of a growing boy who sought to overthrow established practice.

My only recourse was rebellion. I found that it was possible to win a standoff if I were sufficiently enraged and had some sense of righteousness on my side. Also, I was just too goddamned big. She evaluated the situation quickly and decided on the spot to save what parental authority she had remaining for other things. The enema bag passed unlamented into the archives of childhood where it rested, sanctified no doubt, under a layer of talcum powder.

For several years it was possible to walk through the kitchen of our house and see anywhere from one to three jars on top of the refrigerator with selected turds leaning against the sides like tired little soldiers. The jars were carefully capped and labeled with the particular child's name and awaited only delivery to the doctor, who had ostensibly demanded this ritual collecting in order to ascertain our pathological destinies. I don't know why the refrigerator was the way station for this cargo. Possibly because it was in the kitchen, and the kitchen was the exit to the garage. This was certainly better than the front-hall table, but it had its drawbacks. For one, it was not altogether appetizing, and for another, Van used it for a quick escape in case he was in a particularly overwhelming Huff.

It's Thanksgiving. For days everyone has been discussing the enormous quantities of food that we will all consume. I am not what my mother calls a "good eater." I can barely choke down the bread on half a sandwich. Still, I try to join the general excitement and anticipation of the event. I smile weakly when told for the eleventh time how there will be buckets of mashed potatoes sloshed with gallons of gravy, Sierra Nevadas of dressing drifted against slump-stone walls of sliced turkey, volcanic cones of peas and lima beans drenched in calderas of butter, and cranberry sauce, delivered by dump trucks, smeared over everything. I imagine all this food will be troweled into me and then packed down by street pavers in lead-soled shoes.

I begin to see Thanksgiving dinner everywhere. Clouds in the sky are mashed potatoes rolling over me; palm trees become huge drumsticks leaning toward me in the wind; at a construction site, caterpillar tractors push acres of stuffing into piles that will be used to bury me. At night my pillow is lumpy with peas and lima beans. By the time Thanksgiving Day arrives I'm so nauseated that I have to stay in bed. I lie facing the wall all day until the dreaded meal is over. This happens two Thanksgivings in a row.

On the third Thanksgiving the languid stench of roasting turkey fills the house. Even in my bedroom I can smell it. People arrive and I hear them exclaim how delicious it smells. I battle a surge of nausea. There are a dozen guests this year including Jackie Hathaway and his parents, Skip and Henry.

Jackie has come into my room to ask me to please come downstairs, it'll be fun—when Skip strides in. Grasping Jackie's wrist, she announces that I'm just a spoiled little bastard who shouldn't be allowed to get away with it, and if I were her child, I'd sure as hell be in my suit and bow tie and sitting at my proper place at the dining room table sick to my stomach or not sick to my stomach, at which point she yanks Jackie off to the groaning board.

Up in my room, rolled in a ball, I can hear the dinner going on. The guests sound happy, their glasses rippling with cider and wine, their silverware busily sawing through the slabs of mortared grub. The spoiled little bastard doesn't feel happy. I don't mind being spoiled, but I hate nausea and I hate being ignored. There's a war going on inside me. Although I feel constantly like throwing up, and I've been feeling that way for days, there's no way I can make it through this meal from a distance. I lie there until I can't fight it anymore; I'm going to throw up, and I'm going to take some people with me.

I get out of bed, but instead of going to the bathroom, I go downstairs to the dining room. There, in my pajamas, holding my hand over my mouth, I appear like an apparition at the foot of the table. A couple of the people who see me smile tentatively, turkey straggling from the corners of their mouths, a patina of gravy glossing their chins.

"Look," says Jackie, "Neddy must be feeling better." When he speaks, the fully-churned, technicolor meal peers at me from inside his mouth. That's all it takes. Like a fire hose, I vomit right there on the hardwood dining room floor. It splashes and bounces all the way through the kitchen door and stops, steaming slightly, an al-luvial fan of upchuck. For a moment everyone is stunned. Then Henry Hathaway explodes.

"This kid ran downstairs to throw up in the *fucking dining room? Jesus Christ!* . . ." he shouts.

"Don't say Jesus Christ in front of the fucking children, Henry!" screams Skip. She hates people to say Jesus Christ. Jackie has ex-plained it to me. She's a Catholic and it's bad for them to say Jesus Christ. They have to go to Hell.

Van flings his napkin over his food and leaps from the chair. He can't stand throw-up; it makes *him* want to throw up. *Eugghh eugghh eugghh.* Panicky, he starts to kack like a cat with a hairball and runs from the room, but he makes a big mistake; he takes the kitchen exit. When his leather-soled shoes hit the barf slick it propels him right through the door. He grabs the door jamb and pivots into the kitchen, and there they are: three little khaki-clad sentries lined up on top of the ice box. As I am rushed upstairs and maids swoop with buckets and mops, I hear him screaming my mother's name. Even on holidays her department is open.

While that may have been a watershed of attention-getting for me, the spotlight had already shifted earlier that year to my baby sister, Schuyler. Born in January 1948, she changed the balance of power in the house radically, something I instinctively felt the first time I saw her, the day they brought her home from the hospital.

As it is, I didn't really see her, rather I saw the ambulance, and I saw my mother, very weak and smiling, being wheeled through the front gates on a gurney. I saw a nurse in a starched white uniform and a bundle of pink blankets in the nurse's arms. I saw flashbulbs popping as magazine and newspaper photographers gathered on the sidewalk in front of the house and took pictures of the pink blankets. Two fans, twin sisters who haunted our front gate and were obsessed by movie stars, Van in particular, were there thrusting little knitted baby booties at the blankets. Somewhere in that bundle of blankets was my new baby sister—I could see the little peaked cap on her head.

I'd already tried to climb into the pram they'd bought in England for her, but I was too big for it. I'd combed every inch of the enormous new bedroom they'd prepared for her looking for toys. The room was bigger than Tracy's and mine combined; there was a crib with pink lace ruffles and a lace canopy, and drawers full of little pink clothes and the closet full of little white shoes, but the only toys I could find were baby toys, things that hung on the crib rails and spun around and squeaked. They didn't really interest me, but toys were toys, so I demanded them for myself. It was pointed out to me, quite fairly, that I had a roomful of toys. "Enough," I was told, "for any little boy to have." I became sullen. Didn't they understand? My entire nervous system simply could not accept the concept of enough. Enough was deprivation.

My mother had complications after her third cesarean operation, and in fact her life had been in danger several times during her recovery. Even after she returned home it would be weeks before she was up and around again, and there would be a full-time nurse there taking care of her.

I responded to this callously, swaggering about the house loudly, entering her bedroom and flinging myself down on her bed demanding to see the scar on her stomach. Meekly, she would show it to me. Raw and big and crossed with stitches, it had become infected and was slow to heal. But I didn't care. A coldness had grown in my own stomach. I hadn't asked her to keep going to the hospital and having children taken out of her stomach, had I? It wasn't my fault. Why had she done this again? Wasn't Tracy enough? Wasn't I enough?

I was sitting in my mother's dressing room on the second floor watching the procession as it came through the gate, down the steps and toward the house. It was time to dash downstairs and perform the New Baby Dance. Time to clap my hands and beg to see her, to hop around eagerly at the sight of her and maybe start teaching her some of the things I'd taught Tracy, like how to play cars in the dark. But first I had something to do. I had to open a jewelry box my mother kept hidden on a shelf in her closet.

This was a box I had opened many times before. There were many little treasures hidden in this box: mostly coins and bills from foreign countries, coins that my parents had picked up on their frequent trips to Europe. There was one bill in particular I'd had my eye on for a long time: a twenty-dollar bill from the Territory of Hawaii. As I watched my sister being brought through the gates it came to me that now might be the time to take it. I lifted up the top tray, reached inside and pulled out the bill. I quickly stuffed it in my pocket and put the box back into the closet. Then, with the bill breathing gently against me like a tiny bird, I went downstairs to *ooh* and *ahh*. Bring all the babies you want home, Mom. And make sure you have plenty of money on hand, because it'll cost ya.

Schuyler was the instant object of attention in the house. She was Van's first and only child and she was the apple of his eye. She was plump and blond, healthy and happy. She was there to be fondled and bounced and kissed and dressed in eighteen petticoats and made to look like a storybook doll, like Scarlett O'Hara, or Maggie O'Brien, or Van's latest leading lady, Janet Leigh. Schuyler's role was more complex. She was, among other things, to be the antidote for Van's own miserable childhood.

Van was born in Newport, Rhode Island, on August 25, 1916. His father, Charles Johnson, was a cold, humorless Swede, a plumber who had been forced to raise his son alone after his alcoholic and profoundly miserable wife, Van's mother, had deserted the family when Van was a boy. The resentment and hatred that surrounded his relationship with his father had hurt Van to the point that he could barely tolerate mention of either parent. It was shocking to me to hear him say that he hated his father. I had never heard anyone say that before. When I asked him about growing up he would look at me and make a face. "You don't wanna know," he'd say. When I asked him about Charles he'd make his *eughh* sound. "Horrible man," he'd say, pronouncing it *haar-able*, "an awful man." About his mother he would not even utter a single word.

Once, after Van had become a star, he had invited his father out to California. He took him to Chasen's for dinner. Once inside the chic steak-and-chili dive, known for its New York cuts, Dave Chasen's special chili, and sky-high prices, Van tried to convince his father to go ahead and enjoy himself, order whatever he wanted. Tight-lipped and grim, the old man ordered a tunafish sandwich. Van was beside himself. He begged his father to have something else, something "better." But Charles wouldn't even consider it. He refused to eat anything else. Tunafish. That was what he wanted.

Plain honest food for a plain working man, not all this flashy Hollywood crud. None of this fancy steak business for him. No sir. Van was devastated. He had wanted to show his father that now, after years of a gray, loveless, miserly life, he was a star, he could afford steak, and the old bastard had beaten him down one more time

Van had worked hard at achieving his place in the MGM star shed. Leaving his wretched life in Newport behind, Van had made it into the chorus lines of several New York shows including Leonard Sillman's *New Faces of 1936*, and George Abbott's *Pal Joey*. At night after the shows, he haunted the "21" Club, standing with other star-struck kids to watch the flow of celebrities in and out of the famous restaurant. To him they represented the epitome of *suave*, the beautiful life. It was exactly like life in the movies, and it was what he had always wanted.

Ten years later he was living in his own movie; it was clean, shiny, well lit, and in Schuyler he had cast a role, a role essential in any good, heartwarming Van Johnson movie: the juvenile lead.

Schuyler was to be many things for Van. A chance to revise his own growing up, to create a fable wherein the child he never got to be now grows in an environment that provides it with everything it could possibly want. No privation, no hardships. She was to be the barometer of his success, the indicator of his escape from the cramped, Calvinist environment from which he had sprung. But most important, she was Proof. Proof to millions of American men and women that the freckle-faced boy they had watched in the Army uniform in *Thirty Seconds over Tokyo* and *A Guy Named Joe* and *Command Decision* was everything he appeared to be.

Appearances were everything. This was another department of my mother's, perhaps the most difficult and least rewarding of all her departments. Making sure appearances were kept up was a full-time job. She made sure I was always aware that people were watching us, and that we should always be very careful of what we said and did. She showed me a copy of *Confidential* magazine. In it there were pictures of Mom and Van and Dad. The story was about two famous Hollywood stars who had been the best of friends. The two best friends and the wife of one of them formed an inseparable threesome. They went everywhere together. Then the wife divorced the one star and married the other one. This was called gossip, my mother said. But, I thought, didn't that happen? Isn't that what they did?

Yes, she told me. But it had all come out wrong and she and Van and my father had been made to look bad. Really they hadn't done anything terrible. It happens every day. People divorce and remarry all the time. If Van or Keenan had just been Joe Blow, nobody would have cared.

Joe was a famous character in our house. Sometimes he was referred to as Joe Schmoe, or Joe Blow from Kokomo. I asked Van where Kokomo was. He said it was a Podunk somewhere in Indiana. A Podunk? A Burg. Jerkville. Ah, like Duckburg where Donald lived, or Smallville where Clark Kent grew up? Now I was getting it. If Dad and Van were just some Joe Blows from Kokomo, then nothing would have been in the magazines at all. The magazines evidently cared little for Joe Blow.

But for Keenan Wynn, Ed Wynn, and Van Johnson, the rules were different. They were famous people, and the magazines were very interested in them. Joe Blow himself was very interested in them. In fact, Joe's wife is the one who bought the magazines.

Being the son, grandson, and stepson of famous people, I figured the rules might be different for me as well. Now it was becoming clearer. Perhaps, if I had been Joe Blow, then nobody would have made such a big deal out of the fact that I threw away my report card, tipped my desk over in arithmetic, and pooped in my pants during hide-and-seek then threw the dirty underwear behind the bookshelf so that they had to get an exterminator in school because they thought a mouse had died inside the wall. A light was dawning. All my troubles were solely because I wasn't Joe Blow.

I took the family's mandate and applied it personally. And I began to look for Joe everywhere. Was he the guy working on the house down the street? The guy in the gas station? The guy making hamburgers for the members at the Westside Tennis Club? The towel boy in the locker room at the private beach club we belonged to, Ocean House? Will I be a towel boy when I grow up?

"No, honey. You're not some Joe Blow. You're handsomer than Jimmy Stewart. You'll be a famous actor someday. Or at least a famous lawyer like Greg Bautzer," my mother said.

"Be a producer!" shouted Van with a grin. "They make all the moola."

"Actors make a lot of moola, too," my mother said softly.

"Why does Butch Jenkins get to be in a movie with Van?" I hated the cocky little red-headed jerk. I hated the way he got to be with Van all day on the set like he was Van's son or something, and made a lot of moola, and everybody thought he was so great. "I want to be in a movie with Van."

"Well, dear, you have to learn to be an actor first," my mother soothed.

"OK," I said. Then I thought about it. "Do I have to go to school?"

"Well, you can have an acting teacher," she said.

"Oh," I said. "Like Mr. Galloway?" Mr. Galloway was my piano teacher, a mild-mannered man who played "Rustles of Spring" for me and had big, soft fingers. I liked Mr. Galloway.

"Sort of," she said. "We'll send you to New York and you can study with Uta Hagen." Study? Uta Hagen? Her name brought to mind thin, stiff fingers. I tried another tack.

"Does Butch Jenkins have to go to school?"

"He has a tutor on the set with him every day," Van said. "He has to go in his dressing room between takes and do arithmetic." Oh.

"Can we go to Ocean House?"

I'd let it alone until the next child actor was in a movie with Van, then I'd start in all over again. Next time it was Liza Minnelli, who was in *The Good Old Summertime* with Van and her mother, Judy Garland.

"How come Liza gets to be in a movie with Van?" I asked. "Is she an actress? Does she go to school?" I began to pout.

"Liza's just a baby, Neddy," my mother said, "and she's only in the last minute of the movie."

Then it was Dean Stockwell.

"How come Dean Stockwell gets to be in a movie with Van?" I whined.

"He's a child star, for chrissake," Van said. "Tell him, Evie. Tell him about child stars."

"You don't want to be a child star, Neddy," she said.

"Yes I do," I said. Of course I wanted to be a child star. What child didn't?

"No you don't. They have a few years and then they're through. Look at Shirley Temple. Maggie O'Brien. Their careers are over."

"What about Dean Stockwell?"

"He'll be selling shoes by the time he's eighteen, fer cryin' out loud," said Van. "Tell, him Evie. Be a producer. They make all the do-re-mi."

I wandered around that year making life hell for everyone. Nothing pleased me. Even seeing Jan Sterling's bazooms when she was changing in the pool house didn't help. I played halfheartedly with Tracy and cheered silently after Schuyler locked herself in the bathroom for six hours. I practiced arson with Jackie Hathaway and Bobby Curry, destroying a toilet to get the hang of it and then setting fire to the vacant lot across the street.

It had started as a day of simple match burning. Bobby and I each had stolen some wooden matches and we were experimenting with them, lighting them and throwing them on the ground. It was another hot, tinder-dry summer. The lot directly across the street from my house was actually the side of a steep hill, baked hard as a clay pot from the sun and covered with brown grass. One of the matches caught a little clump of this grass. We watched enthralled, paralyzed by the beauty of the flames as they began to spread beyond the edge of the circle we had drawn in the dirt with a stick. In minutes a quarter of an acre was burning, and the fire was racing up the hill toward the houses above on San Vicente Boulevard. Bobby ran one way, and I ran another.

The fire trucks came. Three, four, five of them. They filled the street, their red paint bright, their huge diesel engines shaking the ground. The firemen shouted and dragged hoses up the hillside beating at the fire with shovels and spraying the trees and nearby rooftops with huge jets of water.

I watched from my mother's dressing room both excited and scared. What would they do to me? Would they put me in jail? Would they send me to reform school? That's when I realized once and for all that I was different. Whereas Joe Blow's kid would have gotten in a lot of trouble for setting fire to the hillside, that wouldn't happen to me. When the firemen came to the door to ask my mother about the fact that the neighbors had seen Bobby and me in the lot, she lied as I knew she would. She told them her children were at the beach.

The firemen looked doubtful. My mother stonewalled. She knew what would happen. Things like this get in the paper, in the scandal sheets, and it wouldn't look good. It could also affect where Tracy and I lived. Headlines marched past her eyes: STEPSON OF FAMOUS MOVIE STAR TURNS JUVENILE DELINQUENT. "NO FATHER IN THE HOUSE," SAYS SCHOOL PRINCIPAL. CUSTODY BATTLE LOOMING. L. B. MAYER VOICES DISPLEASURE WITH STARS' PRIVATE LIVES. The publicity wall would be breached, and that would never do.

Eventually, the firemen left. The most important thing had been accomplished: damage control. My mother was torn between horror and triumph. On the one hand her son was a budding human torch, on the other hand no one knew it but her. Solution? She took Jackie and me to the beach. Lesson learned: Burn down the neighborhood in the morning, ride the waves in the afternoon. I was developing a great fondness for *Confidential* magazine.

Then my mother discovered the twenty-dollar bill. I had very carefully hidden it behind some books, but my mother, like others of her species, had X-ray vision.

"I found it," I said, like any natural-born liar. The brazenness of it astonished us all, even me. For one thing, being from the Territory of Hawaii, it was distinctively different from ordinary U.S. currency. It could only have come from one place, my mother's jewelry box. But I had seen how my mother had buffaloed the firemen. I had seen her stand fast and deny her child's involvement. So I tried to buffalo the buffalo. "I was playing by the new house and I found it." The air went out of my mother for a moment. Her son, her little fire-setter, was now a thief and a liar.

She showed me the jewelry box, but I pretended to know nothing

about it. I stonewalled. Her recourse was one of enlightened par-
enthood: She pretended to believe me. She was giving me a chance
to tell the truth. The problem with that was I had already begun the
lie, and the lie had taken over. It excited me. It entangled me. I
owned the lie, it was mine, and I now began to defend it.

"Where did you find it?"

"By the new house," I said. I was referring to a house under
construction down the street. "A workman probably dropped it." I
was learning to use good old Joe Blow for lots of things.

"Just back from a Hawaiian vacation, no doubt," she said.

"Yeah," I said. Boy, she was making this easy for me.

"Let's go to the house and ask them if any of them dropped the
money," she said.

We went to the building site. The workers were nonplussed at
my appearance. Yeah, they'd seen me around the site. No, they'd
never seen the bill, No, none of them had dropped it. I shrugged. I
didn't realize it, but by now the lie owned me. "I guess it just must've
got there somehow," I said. Just flown out of the clouds on some
Hawaiian trade wind.

We went back home. My mother was very quiet. When we got
inside we went upstairs. Would she call Dad? He had a new wife, a
woman named Beetsie, a pert, horsey blonde whom my mother
detested and avoided as much as possible. But Beetsie or no Beetsie,
she was certain to call him this time. His job had devolved to the
point that he was now strictly the bearer of the flying ham hock.
"I'll call your father and he'll come over and spank you," was the
usual threat. But she didn't mention him. Instead she sat down and
looked at me.

"I know this money came from my jewelry box. Van and I got
it last year in Honolulu." She let that sink in. Couldn't have been
that Hawaiian twenty-dollar bill. I *found* that one. We faced each
other, buffalo to buffalo. "Well," she said, tapping her fingers on the
mirrored tabletop. "We'll just put it in the bank for you for college."
Putting things in the bank was the ultimate solution for things that
my mother didn't wish me to have. I imagined that the bank housed,
in addition to hundreds of dollars of mine, pocket knives, bubble
gum, comic books, chemistry sets, cap pistols, guns, and motorcycles. That's where everything went, including, evidently, the stuff I
stole. You could steal, but it would all go toward your college tuition.
I fidgeted, played with my belt, kicked my shoes against the chair
leg. Now what?

"What's wrong with you?" she asked. "I've never seen a child
like you." I searched my mind. I could feel that we were at a cross-
roads. A question like "What's wrong with you?" has to be answered
very carefully. What should I say? If I say I'm sick, she'll call Dr.

Bernstein. Dr. Bernstein will either have her fill an available hole, or he'll come over himself and make one with one of his needles. Nope. I'm not sick.

"I'm bored." It popped out. I'd heard Van say it. It was adult to be bored. Smugly, I congratulated myself. The Quiz Kid, the Answer Man.

"You're bored?" she was incredulous. "How can an eight-year-old boy be bored?" I sighed wearily.

"Eight going on thirty-eight," Van shouted, networking briefly with my mother's department. Inspiration struck. Blaming someone else usually worked. So I decided to blame her.

"You never plan my day," I whined.

My mother's eyes opened like wildflowers after a rain. Instantly I knew I had said the wrong thing. If I could have swallowed the words I would have. Her mind was racing with possibilities. Was this the answer to the dilemma of her lying stealing arsonist son? He was bored?

"Oohhh . . ." she said, "I see. I never plan your day? Well . . ." All my senses were alert. Which way was this going to go? Acting lessons with Uta Hagen? Arithmetic with Butch Jenkins? Worse. It took a few days. Lots of phone calls. But it was worse.

"Captain Nast's Boys' Club." My mother's smile was calculated to sell, and if that didn't work, it didn't matter.

"What's Captain Nast's Boys' Club?" I asked. My arms were prickly with worry. His name was even more frightening than Uta Hagen.

"It'll be fun. You'll love it. It's just like summer camp." Uh-oh. She slid that in beautifully. I hadn't even started to recover from the goose-stepping Captain Nast yet.

"What's summer camp?" My voice was getting weaker and weaker, like a radio transmission from a distant galaxy.

"First, starting Monday, every day after school, you're going to get on a bus with two dozen other boys and play football and baseball and other wonderful fun things that boys do," she said with that coconut-cheeked smile I had come to fear. What other fun things? A little bare-fisted boxing, perhaps? I put my hand on my stomach. "Then, next summer you're going to Catalina Island Boys' Camp. They have archery and sailing and horseback-riding. . . ." I'll be crushed by a horse, then I'll drown. The Greek fire flared. "And Jackie Hathaway is going with you. Sean Flynn is going. All your friends will be there."

"Will Bobby be there?"

"I don't think so," she said. As I suspected. A camp for rich actors' kids. "You won't be bored," she said. And you won't steal and light fires. You'll learn discipline.

"I'm already not bored," I said. "I'm over that. I'm completely not bored." Can we cancel these plans? Jeez. One little brush fire, one little burglary. . . . "I can play with Tracy. I won't take his toys. I won't pinch him. We'll just play. Very quietly." For years, if necessary. But my mother was in another world, transported on her new magic carpet of ideas.

"And when you come back from summer camp," she said, letting it build, "when you come back from camp, we'll be all moved into the new house." Wait a minute, wait a minute. . . . "No more of this awful fog," she said looking up.

One of my favorite things about Santa Monica was the fog. It drifted overhead, often no higher than my bedroom window, light wispy clouds that seemed only a few feet off the ground, close enough to touch. "We're going where the sun shines every day," she said. "And where they have the best public school system in Southern California." Oh, well . . . what better reason to leave Paradise?

"New house?" I was now only a remote beep barely audible above the background noise of the cosmos. Boys' Clubs, Summer Camps, New Houses. . . .

"Yes," she said. "We're moving."

"Why?" I was nearly in tears. I'll never light another fire. I'll never steal another dollar. "Why do we have to move? I like it in Santa Monica. Why do we have to move?"

Because it was ordained. It had come in a dream. Angels and chariots had descended. There was no why—it was self-explanatory. We were moving to the land of milk and honey. Across Egypt. Across the Jordan. Across Town.

"We're moving to Beverly Hills," she said.

It didn't register. What was the big deal about Beverly Hills? I'd been there many times. Dr. Bernstein's office was there. Mom's hairdresser was there. She went there for lunch and shopping. Most of Mom and Van's friends lived there. So what's the big deal?

I looked up. A seagull passed overhead, flying inland. There must be a storm at sea, I thought. That's what everyone always said when the seagulls headed inland.

Jackie and I are all ready for camp. We have on our designated denim pants and our blue sweaters with a big gold "C" on the front. Our regulation footlockers and regulation dufflebags are packed, and Van has loaded them in our car. Skip and Henry and Jackie wait out on the street in their car. We are going to San Pedro to board something called a water taxi that will take us across the channel to a place called Howlands' Landing on the island of Catalina.

Everyone is happy, excited. Skip has only called Jackie a little sonofabitch twice and me a little bastard once. And she hasn't said *fuck* at all. As I am about to get in the car, I glance across the fence. There, on the other side, just as he was on that day three years ago, stands Bobby.

I dash over to him. "I'm going to Catalina to camp," I say. "We have to go on a boat."

"Well, *duh*," he says. "I've only been there about forty-seven times myself."

"Is it neat?"

"It's pretty neat," he says. With his finger he traces the outline of the "C" on my sweater.

"Then we're moving to Beverly Hills," I say.

"That's not so far," he says.

"You'd probably hate it," I say. "It's all full of rich people and movie stars."

"Movie stars are OK," he says. "It's not your fault your dad's a movie star."

"Yeah. Will you come over when I get back?"

"Yeah," he says. "I'll ride the bus. It's two transfers. Simple Simon." We stand there looking at each other.

"Neddy," my mother calls. "We have to be on time or they'll leave and you won't get to go to camp."

"You better go," Bobby says. I turn away and start back to the car. "Hey," he calls. I stop and look back. "Remember those pachucos in the golf course?" Yeah, I remember. "Those guys weren't really pachucos. That was Mike. He's a gardener with his dad. He's friends with Gordon." Oh. "We were playing a joke on you. But you did good. You thought they were real pachucos. But you kept the golf ball." I nod. Van honks the horn. I lift my hand.

"See ya," Bobby says.

"See ya," I say. Then I return to the car and climb inside.

As we drive out of the driveway Bobby cups his hands around his mouth. "Don't forget how to ride the bus," he shouts. "And don't burn down the island!" I nod vigorously and make a big clownish display of picking my nose right at him out the back window. Quickly, he jams his finger in his nose and does it even more disgustingly, falling to his knees and grabbing his wrist. Van spots it in the mirror and howls with laughter, "*Aaahhheeeee....*" I scream with delight. At the last second, before we turn the corner, Bobby lifts his hand and waves.

CHAPTER
5

The old man is waving his cigar as he talks. He always has a cigar in his hand, it seems, and he smells of a combination of talcum powder and H.Upmann Monarchs. Even in his bathing suit, an old-fashioned one with a cloth belt and a striped top, current when he had been a big Broadway star thirty years earlier, even in his old Roaring Twenties' beachwear sitting by the pool on Oakmont Drive in Brentwood in the fifties, he smells that way as he waves his cigar in the air.

"Your father," he says, "drinks too much." I glance at my father, who lies on a chaise lounge, his trunks rolled up so he can get more sun on his legs. He covers his eyes with his hand and groans.

"Jesus, Pop," he says.

"I've been around it all my life. It killed your mother and it's gonna kill you, Keenan. God knows it'll probably kill me and I hardly touch the stuff." The old man glances at me. "Remember, Neddo, moderation in all things." I nod sagely. I never disagree with my grandfather. "Your father doesn't do anything in moderation. He drives too fast, he drinks too much, he spends every dime he makes on booze and motorcycles and dames."

"Christ, Pop," my father groans again.

"And he thinks he owes them everything when they walk out on him, too. He can't wait to reward them for their disloyalty. Your mother got the best deal any dame ever got. I love your mother, Neddo, but Keenan's my son. He didn't have to make that kind of a deal. You'd think he's the richest guy in the world . . . or that I am." My father takes a deep breath, purses his lips and blows a thin stream of air past them. It's a habit, a tuneless whistle, a quiet complaint; maybe this'll blow over. Not while I'm around it won't.

"Mom says he hardly ever pays her the child support," I pipe up, shiny as chrome.

"Jesus, Ned," my father says and gets up from the chaise and begins scratching his chest with both hands.

"That's because the latest one got it all."

"Beetsie didn't get it all, Pop," my father says, his voice rising. Now he's agitated. What he wants is a drink. He glances longingly at the empty glass on the deck by his chaise.

"He buys her a racetrack and barns and horses so she can run off with that dancer, what's the guy's name? . . ."

"Dan Dailey!" I squeak. My father sags. Dan Dailey's name has hurt him. The whole conversation has hurt him. My grandfather plows ahead.

"A hoofer! I hired and fired 'em by the dozen in my shows. She'll be crawling back in a month. Don't eat your heart out, Keenan. Remember what Earl Benham used to tell me when I was going crazy over Frieda—picture her sitting on the toilet with diarrhea. How attractive is that? It's hard to have a broken heart over a woman with diarrhea. I'm sorry to be so crude, Neddo, but that's the point, y'see. When your cock rules your conscience you need strong medicine."

"Ned," says my father, "why don't you go and play, go explore. There's an orchard down below, right Pop? Walnuts or filberts or something."

"But I want to swim some more first." My father blows another tuneless whistle. My grandfather starts pacing. He and my father are walking up and down on opposite sides of the pool. My father's head is back, his arms outstretched as if by some miracle, bourbon will pour from heaven. My grandfather conducts an unseen orchestra with his cigar.

"Walnuts. Can you believe that, Keenan? Joe E. Brown sure lives like a swell, doesn't he? Walnut groves. A mansion with walnut groves, and he charges me a fortune to rent it. I'm not interested in the walnuts, Joe, I told him. I can buy them at the market. They come with the property, Ed, he told me. For a guy whose whole idea of comedy is opening his mouth and showing his tonsils, he sure lives like a swell." He shakes his head, stupefied at the nature of his art. "Comedy," he says.

He was born Isaiah Edwin Leopold, Izzy to his friends and family, in Philadelphia in 1886. His father was a milliner, a comfortable middle-class Jewish hatmaker, and when his son ran away to become a comedian he was horrified. "What will people say?" he asked Iz. It was a disgrace to have a comedian in the family. My grandfather offered to change his name. Grandpa Leopold thought a moment and shook his head. "What if you make a hit? No one'll know you're my son," he said.

Izzy changed his name anyway, splitting his middle name in two, and as Ed Wynn he became a star, first with a partner named Jack Lewis in an act they called "The Rah Rah Boys," and later as a solo. He made the big time when Florenz Ziegfeld put him in the *Ziegfeld Follies of 1914*. "Eddie Cantor," he told me years later, "keeps talking about 'Flo,' about how close they were. It's 'Flo' this and 'Flo and I' that. Eddie Cantor, a man with no talent whose idea of entertainment is rolling his eyes and moving his hands in circles, never called him Flo. Eddie Cantor never called him anything but Mr. Ziegfeld."

"What did you call him, Grandpa?" I asked.

"*I* called him Flo," he said. Then he thought a moment. "But only after he was dead," he added.

Ed Wynn became a star in shows such as *The Grab Bag, Simple Simon*, and *The Perfect Fool*. These were shows in which he not only starred, but which he had written and produced as well. They were hits, and *The Perfect Fool*, a clownish idiot dressed in baggy pants, outsized shoes, and a funny hat became his first widely known persona. Later, in the thirties, dressed in a red fire hat, he became known as the Texaco Fire Chief on the radio. In three years in the middle of the Depression, Ed Wynn made one million dollars from *Texaco Fire Chief* alone. He did it by appearing on the airwaves one hour a week and doing the following:

> **WYNN:** Tonight's opera is called "Within The Law." The hero comes from Syracuse, New York. You can tell he's from Syracuse because his legs are full of Syracuse veins . . . . The boy is dishonest so he decides to join a nudist colony, that way he figured the cops couldn't pin anything on him . . . . In the first week he runs away from the nudist colony and they mark him absent without leaves . . . . As he has no clothes he sneaks into a lady's backyard and steals a garment from her washline—it's his first slip. To disguise himself he grows a moustache. It's an installment moustache, a little down each week . . . . He meets a Chinaman who offers him some laundry whiskey. "What's laundry whiskey?" he asks. The Chinaman says, "One drink and it take you unaware. . . ." He gets arrested. The judge says, "The charge against you is getting drunk with a Chinaman—what is the Chinaman's name?" The hero says, "Yo Ho." The judge says, "Six months." The hero says, "Six months? For what?" The judge says, "Yo Ho and a bottle of rum." Play that, Don.

This was in addition to the money he was making the six remaining nights a week as the sole star and part owner of *The Laugh Parade*, a show he had created and made into a hit despite terrible advance notices.

Worried that he had a flop on his hands, Ed Wynn bought up 90 percent of the seats for the first week of his Broadway booking at the Imperial Theater and gave the tickets to several friends of his, among them the heads of Macy's Department Store and the Ludwig Baumann store. He then asked his friends to give the tickets to all

their employees, and he also instructed the advance-ticket sales
clerks to tell people there were no more seats available "at present."
Of course, the house was packed all week with grateful, friendly
faces, faces stretched thin by the Depression and eager to laugh,
happy to have one night of their lives turned into magic, to be able
to sit in the completely unaffordable $5.50 orchestra seats for noth-
ing, courtesy of the Fire Chief, The Perfect Fool himself. Word
spread, and in days, people were clamoring to get tickets to *The
Laugh Parade*. The show ran for 102 weeks, making it a certified box
office hit. "Henry Ford explained it to me one night," he said. "It's
how he got people to buy the Model A."

It's no wonder Ed Wynn was happiest when he was in a theater
and on stage. He was most comfortable when he was in costume,
and it was where his real success was achieved. Life at home was
another story altogether. "To tell you the truth," he said, "I never
wanted to be a real person."

When I knew him first he was well past his heyday. He had
made a short-lived comeback in 1950 on television, in *The Ed Wynn
Show* on CBS. It was canceled after the first year. He then went to
NBC where he was one of four rotating stars on *The Four Star Revue*,
along with Jack Carson, Danny Thomas, and Jimmy Durante. Later,
his career had a resurgence with such shows as *Requiem for a Heavyweight*, and films like *The Great Man* (1956); *Marjorie Morningstar*
(1958), *The Diary of Anne Frank* (1959), and *Mary Poppins* (1964).
It was in this period, from the fifties until he died in 1966, that I
knew him best.

He rented the house on Oakmont with the walnut grove from
Joe E. Brown for a year or so before buying a house of his own
down the street on Rockingham Road. He lived at the time with his
third wife, Dorothy, a sweet, dazed alcoholic, and her son, Jay, a
boy about Tracy's age with red hair whom my grandfather, in a
blaze of benevolence, had adopted, much to my father's chagrin.
There was a silver lining in this, however: It was something my
father could disapprove of, and disapproval was an industry, where
my father and grandfather were concerned. "Where do you think
the kid got the red hair?" my father mused. "Do you think Aunt
Dorothy got the name of that trumpet player?"

We went once or twice a month to visit "the old man" in his
current grandeur, faded to be sure, but only by comparison. The
Rockingham house was huge and dark, a Spanish mausoleum, my
father called it. "Just the sort of place he'd buy," Dad said. "Something to depress his friends with."

Although the house at 441 North Rockingham was a mansion
by Brentwood standards, it was a scaled-down version of the home
he had owned in Great Neck, Long Island, a vast, echoing dungeon

called Wyngate. There he had lived with his first wife, my grandmother Hilda, my father, and a half-dozen servants in the twenties.
He had appeared to the local WASPs as a curiosity, an upstart Jew,
an absurd, levantine Gatsby living among the people he had always
envied and admired. "I was accepted by all the swells," he liked to
boast, "Jews and Gentiles alike. I was invited to all their homes. And
in the theater I was the first Jew to cross the line into the mainstream
vaudeville houses." Now he lived in isolated splendor with his sod-
den, bedraggled flapper and her confused and unhappy child.

Aunt Dorothy was a classic Ed Wynn wife. An around-the-clock
drinker, she must have been something of a beauty twenty years
earlier. She still retained the mannerisms of the looker: the sidelong
glance, the batting eyelashes, the shy, submissive voice, the white-
blond Jean Harlow hair. Around the house she wore long, satin
peignoirs and high-heeled, ankle-strap pumps. When she was awake,
which was rarely, she could be seen wobbling precariously across
the polished terrazzo floors clutching in her pale, spidery fingers a
tall tumbler of vodka lightly colored with orange juice. She was like
a tattered nymph, a crepuscular presence who made brief entrances
around dusk, bid us good day, and then retired to her bed.

There was a Fourth of July when we went to Grandpa's. I was
allowed to invite a guest, Penny Roach who lived down the street.
Her father was Hal Roach, Jr., a producer, and her grandfather was
Hal Roach, Sr., whom I revered as the producer of the films of Laurel
and Hardy, as far as I was concerned, the funniest men who ever
lived.

Penny was beautiful. She was as tall as I was, with deliriously
long legs, blond hair, and rakish blue eyes. Once, we had been allowed to spend almost an entire day together at Grandpa's house
when no one but the cook and the maid had been there. I had
managed to grope her and press against her in the pool for hours
without anyone stopping me. She was a robust, athletic girl and she
didn't seem to mind the tussles and the body contact. I was looking
forward to many more hours of sweaty wrestling with Penny, but
at the last minute her mother called saying she couldn't come.

I was disappointed, but my father had brought something for
me to play with that dispelled any mood of perverse rottenness I
was gearing up for: a Bangsite cannon. It was a miniature siege gun
that used a low-yield gunpowder, which, when mixed with water
and ignited by a spark, exploded with a truly ruthless noise. It would
hiss and make a sound—*fffuh*—then it seemed to pause momen-
tarily, change keys, hike up about two hundred decibels, and then
explode. It actually went *fffuh-BLAM*! Jets of flame shot at least ten
inches out of the barrel, smoke poured from every crack, and it left
your ears ringing. It was the greatest toy I had ever had. I shot it

off continuously for at least four hours. *Fffuh-BLAM! Fffuh-BLAM! Fffuh-BLAM! Fffuh-BLAAAM!*

Finally, around two o'clock, the curtains on the upstairs master bedroom windows parted, the glass doors opened, and slowly, gingerly, Aunt Dorothy stepped out on the balcony. She stood blinking in the sunlight and gasping slightly as if she had just stepped onto the surface of Uranus and found the air was really methane gas. She was wearing a salmon-colored silk nightgown with a marabou collar and sleeves, pink pumps with frou-frou on the toes, and in her hand she had her ubiquitous sixteen ounces of vodka and orange juice. Next to her, in a sconce on the wall, my grandfather had placed an American flag which popped and snapped vigorously in the breeze. For a moment she stood there by the flag, a patriotic tableau from the Jazz Age.

"Aunt Dorothy," I shouted, "come down and see our cannon!" She teetered slightly in response. Then she looked down. A slow smile parted her lips, painted red for the occasion, probably with a roller. She raised her glass. When she spoke her voice sounded like wind chimes.

"Hello, children," she sang. Then she looked at Grandpa. "Ed," she said, "this flag is quite loud." Then she turned and went inside. That was the last we saw of her that day. My father glanced at my grandfather. Grandpa's head was whipping back and forth like a metronome.

"Hey, Grandpa," I shouted. The Aunt Dorothy part of the day was over with, and now it was time to shoot my brother with the cannon. "Hey, Grandpa, do we have any corks? This cannon'll shoot corks," I said, dragging Tracy in front of the barrel. My grandfather turned to me, his eyes widened in a rare moment of irony and mock indignation.

"Corks?" he asked. "In this house?"

Once, when I spent the night at Grandpa's, Aunt Dorothy came to my room and got into bed with me. She cuddled up behind me, cooed to me, and held me in her arms. I was ten or eleven at the time, and I started to get an erection. This was a fairly recent phenomenon for me and something about which I knew absolutely nothing. In fact, the first time it happened, I thought I'd somehow swapped dicks with a troll. We had been staying at Carter Burden's house in Lake Arrowhead, and I had managed to slink into a nearby guest room and subdue the thing. The experience was so rewarding I even tried to let Carter in on this little secret, but Carter, a chubby little goody-goody, stuck with the grownups while I "napped" in the other room.

My mother was suspicious of this. For one thing, I had always hated naps, and I was way too old for them now anyway, yet suddenly I needed several a day. Finally, during my fourth nap, she walked into the room to see if I was OK. I smiled reassuringly and nodded, keeping my hands absolutely still beneath the covers. She stood there for a moment taking in the situation, then pursed her lips and launched a non sequitur. Non sequiturs were one of my mother's strengths. They allowed her to face life and yet maintain a graceful distance from it. "Good," she said, chipper as a bluejay, "later we'll go in the speedboat with Carter." Then she turned and walked out.

After that she left me alone during these crucial rest periods. I later learned that the official name for this importunate Cyclops was "boner," and I paid close attention to it, becoming something of a professional napper.

When Aunt Dorothy snuggled up to me, I had no idea of why she was there except that she was lonely and drunk, an occupational hazard in that household. Instinctively, I responded to her loneliness with a wave of empathy, but her yawning needs were way beyond me. She required more than anyone could ever provide, and it frightened me. And besides, I was scared she would see my boner and tell Grandpa. This fear soon resolved itself in a pubescent fantasy.

First of all, she wasn't my *real* grandmother, I reasoned, unclear on why that should make a difference. And sure she was old, maybe even fifty. But to me there was no such thing as too old or too anything as far as sex was concerned. If I'd known how, I'd have fucked a tree, a door, a llama, anything as long as it was either unconscious or too dumb to know the difference. Aunt Dorothy fell somewhere between the two, and as she lay there it struck me that I would like to put my hand between her legs.

A turmoil erupted inside me over this. Could I touch her, or was I just supposed to lie there and see what she wanted to do? She began kissing the back of my neck. In the dark I couldn't see her, but I could smell the perfume and the vodka. It was a smell well known to me, an early, proto-sexual signal I had received from some of my mother's actress friends who would stumble from time to time into my room during one of their many hilarious cocktail parties. Nothing overtly erotic ever happened, but these women had projected the same confused mixture of desires that Aunt Dorothy had, a powerful combination of wantonness and tenderness, of lust and the need simply to be noticed, to be given credit for their existence. It was as if they felt safe showing this to a little boy, a little boy who wouldn't respond carnally as the other males in their lives did.

But this little boy knew. Maybe not how or why, but I knew, and I was stirred, terrorized, excited. She kissed and stroked me for about five minutes. All the while I struggled with my feelings. This was arousing, but I knew somehow that it shouldn't have been. A grown woman, drunk, in my bed. And my grandfather's wife at that. Could I touch her? Could I lift up her peignoir? Would my boner come into play at any point? Then, quietly as she had entered, she got up and left. I heard the clinking of the ice in her glass. "Goodnight, Neddy, darling," she said from the door. And then she was gone.

My father was acutely sensitive to the status we occupied as the sons of famous people. He had been in a lifelong rebellion against his father and what he perceived as a neglectful presence, the man who signed the checks but gave nothing of himself. His mother, Hilda Keenan, had been a beautiful, effervescent Irish-Catholic girl when she had met Ed Wynn. She was an actress, energetic and talented, the daughter of a famous Shakespearean actor named Frank Keenan.

Frank Keenan, a contemporary of DeWolfe Hopper, Sarah Truex, and Tyrone Power, Sr., was what my father referred to as a "furniture actor," meaning that he was often so drunk on stage that he had to hold onto the furniture in order to keep himself from falling down during a scene. He was also blatantly anti-Semitic, and his daughter's romance with this nervy Yid, a *parvenu* and a slapstick comedian to boot, was anathema to him. Frank Keenan later came to respect and value his son-in-law, if not to love him, but his daughter, used to a life of creativity and excitement, ultimately wilted in the hothouse environment Ed Wynn provided for her. She died in my father's arms when she was forty-nine, of malnutrition and alcoholism.

During my father's entire childhood, Ed Wynn had been a munificent panjandrum, a grand and distant poobah sitting in judgment on him and his mother. He had never experienced the closeness with his father that he had craved. The money was no compensation, and he had grown up with a deep, smoldering resentment against the older man. In a way, he felt that Ed Wynn, not alcoholism, had killed his mother, essentially through absence and neglect. There seemed to be nothing that his father had not been responsible for, and the dominion his father held over him and his own life was so complete that he had called his own autobiography *Ed Wynn's Son*.

In my case, determined to spare me the pain he had endured, he bent over backward to provide me with ready-made excuses; it seemed he felt the need to lay the groundwork for failure. I think that he found me something of a sissy and a mama's boy, which I was, and maybe he wanted to keep me from being totally lost to him. Or maybe he was just embarrassed at having such a puny, geeky son, what he probably saw as a limp-wristed, buck-toothed, borderline fairy, so he was ready with a prepared statement which he repeated every time we went anywhere together. Within moments of introducing me to someone, he would tell them that although he had had it tough, being Ed Wynn's son, *his* son was *triply* cursed by his family status. "Before anyone asks Ned how he is," my father would say, "they ask him how his father is, how his stepfather is, and how his grandfather is."

Instinctively, I hated this litany, but I didn't know how to object, or even why I should. At first I would simply stand there nodding and grinning like a fool. After all, it was perfectly true, people did greet me that way, and it seemed to please my father immensely just to say it, as if he had just voiced a monumental truth whose airing left him somehow lighter and more whole. Also, I didn't like to interrupt my father when he was on a roll. He was a commanding actor, and it was mesmerizing to listen to him speak. When he talked, he automatically performed. He made the simplest statements either terribly amusing or vastly important, so adroit was he at manipulating his tone and attitude.

As a child I had always accepted my status as being perfectly natural. I was even proud of it. But after years of listening to my father say what a lousy situation I was in, I found myself resenting people for their breach of manners. And after a while the idea of being constantly overlooked became addictive, like a drug. I got used to it, and in the end I came to embrace it. It was part of me, and it evolved into a quiet, internal alibi.

Whatever the roots may have been for his overly protective posture, it was very crucial to my father to keep it up. Perhaps he was apologizing for himself, something he did often. Or maybe he was determined to keep me from being the victim of impossible expectations; but in so doing he created a different set of expectations: I learned to expect that allowances would be made for me.

In a family where one or more members are rich and celebrated, it is simply impossible to avoid being singled out by other people. In their own ways, both he and my mother tried to ameliorate this situation. My mother did so by sending me to boys' clubs and summer camps where she hoped I would learn to be like other children. My father's means of accomplishing this democratization and virilization of his son was to take me to what his friend Jimmy Backus referred to as "low crotch" events: motorcycle hill climbs, midget auto races, boxing matches at the Hollywood Legion Stadium. Of course we always had the best seats, passes to the pits, knew all the drivers, went into the fighters' dressing rooms. I got to eat richly poisonous hot dogs, pee in filthy men's rooms, and, after the events, sit in the local dives with my father while he stood rounds of drinks and accepted the glad-handers, stuffing ten-dollar bills into the pockets of old punch-drunk fighters and broken-down race car drivers. I loved every minute of it, but I wasn't fooled. All these attempts at creating a "normal" life for me were wasted. I knew that I wasn't a regular kid. There was too much, text and subtext, telling me I wasn't. And to confuse things further, Van, the only constantly present male, was exactly the opposite.

Whereas Keenan Wynn yearned for acceptance by the "regular guys," to be considered cool down in the pits with Joe Blow, Van Johnson yearned for the antithesis—for specialness, for isolation from the herd. With Van I lived in Beverly Hills, if not exactly in the lap, at least in the hip pocket of luxury. With Van I went to Sun Valley at Christmas and learned to ski, taking private lessons, never classes, from my own personal instructor twice a day. With Van I sailed to Europe first class on the *Queen Elizabeth*, dressed in black tie every night for dinner, and ate with the captain; and in London I was privately tutored before being sent to a snotty boys' school in Zermatt. I spent my summers at the Hotel Del Coronado, ordering hamburgers and room service and tennis lessons and signing my name to the check for everything I wanted. All of these were things my father had done in his life, had found vitiating and insidious, and from which he now wished to distance both himself, and me.

My grandfather's attitude was one of benign ambivalence. He thought of Van as the genuine article, a true movie star, and as such incalculably caught in the web of stardom. Much about that he found good, and unavoidable. He appreciated the perquisites of stardom, and he was an advocate of the things that money could buy. "When you cry," he told me, "it's easier if your tears fall on Persian carpets."

All in all he seemed to be happy that Tracy and I lived with our mother and stepfather rather than with his son. But he also knew that Van's career, like any performer's including his own, was at the mercy of the public fancy. He knew that at any time the whole thing could simply collapse. And he felt that Van did not properly appreciate that fact.

Ed Wynn's basic advice was simple. "You need two things to succeed in life," he said. "Persistency, and a goal." Good advice, I thought. My only problem was that I had no goal and didn't know how to go about getting one.

If I had been able to articulate it at the time, I might have said that my goal was never to grow up. I was actually physically frightened of becoming an adult. I could not conceive of a gradual body change through growth; instead, I imagined it as being an instantaneous corporeal transformation in which my child's body would stretch and stretch until one day, suddenly, it would explode like popcorn and turn into the body of a man. Clearly, something like that would hurt. I didn't want anything to hurt.

I had an overwhelming impulse to avoid anything that implied even minor discomfort. Initially, it must have been part of the natural inclination of any organism to get away from pain. But with me there seemed to be no middle ground: Either something felt great, or it hurt like hell. I had no tolerance of even the slightest adversity, because I was certain that greater pain lay ahead. This pain, be it emotional or physical, seemed to be concomitant to achieving adulthood, and therefore I wanted no part of it.

As an adjunct to this fear of growing up, I had no special hankering for taking consequences. The last place I wanted to be was anywhere in the vicinity of a reckoning. I had become the worst of both my father and stepfather without inculcating any of the best of either. I either wept and whined like my father, or I tantrumed and pouted like Van. While both of these men displayed more than their share of childish behavior, they were also artists and as such were given extraordinary latitude. I was just an exposed nerve in sneakers. At the first inkling that things might not be going my way, I went right to my peak reaction: anger, tears, or flight. Over the next ten years, my parents, in an effort to give me some direction, turned me over to various sets of authorities at various institutions. Summer camp was the first of a series of cures.

"I'd let her give me a hand job."

"I'd let her give me a blow job."

"I'd let her give me a hum job." The object of our largess was Doris, the camp nurse. Doris was married to Bart, the head wrangler, a grim, taciturn cowboy who looked like Jack Elam, stank of horses, and smoked hand-rolled cigarettes which he held forever in the corner of his mouth until they burned down and went out just before they singed his lips. In complete contrast to her husband, Doris was sexy, athletic, and nice. Also, she was the only young woman in the camp, and, more important, she wore shorts. Her status as queen of our mummy bags was unchallenged. I was one of the youngest in this bunch at eleven, and I'd never heard of a blow job in my entire life, much less a hum job, but I was gaining all kinds of direction at Catalina Island Boys' Camp.

Catalina Island was a stripped-down, rural paradise in the early fifties. From out in the channel, a cold blue-black stretch of water boiling with stingrays, sharks, and moray eels, the island appeared to rise like a massive brown boulder, all rock and dirt. Actually, it was covered with dense, impenetrable chaparral, and overrun with rattlesnakes, rabbits, wild pigs, goats, and tarantulas. Standing barefoot on the dock on a still, ninety-degree afternoon, dodging the flopping, snapping eels and lobsters as they were dumped from the camp's illegal traps, the air smelled strongly of salt water, dead crabs, seaweed, diesel fuel, outboard motors, and body odor. A hundred yards inland, dodging the hooves of the fly-tormented horses or hiking through the burr-infested underbrush, it smelled of dust, leather, canvas, manure, garbage, rotting lumber, and body odor.

At Howland's Landing we had no hot water and no electricity, except in the kitchen and the infirmary. We slept in bunk beds in barrackslike wooden-sided war surplus tents, took freezing-cold showers on foggy June mornings, were stung daily by armadas of jellyfish in the Pacific Ocean, battled with squadrons of bayonet-stingered yellow jackets over our powdered eggs and Spam, baloney and Wonderbread, hot dogs and succotash, and drank fly-encrusted chartreuse-colored Kool-Aid, which we called bug juice. Once a week we had a scoop of vanilla ice cream with Bosco on it served in thick china coffee mugs and looked forward to it.

We hiked all over the island, to the Isthmus, to Little Harbor, and once, all the way to Avalon where we saw a movie with John Wayne about the Fighting Seabees. At the Isthmus there was a tiny country store and several primitive pay phones. It was rumored that there was also a whorehouse left over from World War II and that the counsellors stole skiffs and snuck down there at night. I remember sitting with another camper and staring at a dilapidated wooden shed for an hour, hoping to catch a glimpse of a whore. All we saw was a lizard which we cheerfully murdered.

At the store we bought candy bars and gum with our allowances, made obligatory calls home, shouting that we were fine, waiting in agony as our parents shouted back to us things we couldn't hear, dying to hang up so we could chew the gum, hoard the candy, and hike back to camp where we could have our cuts and bruises patched up by Doris.

"I'd let her give me a rim job," said Mike Metzger, finally. It was the most mysterious job of all, and no one tried to top it. Mike lit up a cigar which he had stolen from his father and brought to camp. He was a senior camper, nearly fourteen years old and he knew everything. "Her bush isn't thick enough," he added, blowing a cool stream of blue smoke at the stars. "I like a woman with a thick bush." What did bushes have to do with sex? Was it camouflage or something? "You can tell if they have a thick bush by the way it puffs out their bathing suit. Women with thick bushes like sex better. In fact, they can't stop once you get them started. Claymore's mom has a thick bush. I saw her in a bathing suit last year at Parents' Day. She's probably helplessly fucking Mr. Claymore right now." John Claymore was another senior camper. There was no animosity between Mike and Claymore. The remark was made as a clinical observation, and Claymore took it that way.

"My mom's a whore," said Claymore casually. "At least that's what my dad always says. 'You fucking whore,' he calls her." Mike nodded.

"They're the best kind," he said. "She probably fucks like a bunny." Then Mike turned to me.

"What kind of bush does your mom have, Wynn?" I squirmed. Everyone was suddenly looking at me, waiting for me to speak.

"Big," I said. "Huge." A forest, trees, a veldt, a fruited plain. Everyone nodded in appreciation of my mom's bush.

"Is she coming on Parents' Day? Is she gonna wear a bathing suit?" Bob Irvine asked.

"She's in the south of France with my stepfather." It was always the south of France, never Europe. Unless it was Hawaii, or Mexico, which was known as Acapulco, or Southampton, which was what they called Long Island. Each year it was different.

The conversation swerved to stepparents. Half the boys had at least one.

"My stepfather's an asshole."

"My stepmother's got huge tits."

"That's why your dad married her. Stepmothers always have bigger tits than mothers."

"It's not how big they are," said Mike, "it's which way the nipples point, up or down. Stepmothers' nipples always point up."

"My dad and stepmother are coming, though," I said, trying to keep the conversation on me. "She's real pretty and she's only twenty-one." Everyone whistled in appreciation.

"Has your stepmother got a big bush?" asked Mike.

"What's your dad do?" a kid asked.

"My dad's a mechanic," I said.

"He is not, he's a movie star," sneered Claymore.

"Yeah, but he's not stuck up like Sean Flynn," said Dick Tarnautzer. "Sean Flynn's stuck up."

"Sean Flynn's dad is a homo. My father told me so," said another kid.

"Is Errol Flynn a homo?" Mike asked me. I thought it over.

"Yeah," I said. I didn't know Errol Flynn and wasn't very clear on the homo thing either, but I knew that if I had said no it just wouldn't have been as good an answer.

"What do homos do, anyway?"

"Bump dicks," said Irvine.

"Well, *duh*," Mike said, wearily. It was hard to be the fount of knowledge twenty-four hours a day.

"Ask Miner," said Dick. Everyone guffawed.

George Miner was a kid in our tent who always wet his sleeping bag. He had to hang it on the fence every morning to let it dry out, then he slept in it again that night. Three weeks into the camp season and it could walk to the fence by itself. Every summer for four years it was touch and go as to who would be put in George's tent. No one wanted to sleep in the same tent with him because every morning it was the same: A dozen campers would stumble out onto the campground holding their noses and coughing and rolling around in the dirt while George emerged with his sleeping bag and walked to the fence and spread it out. It never dawned on any of us what an act of tremendous courage it was for George Miner to return to that camp year after year. All we knew was that George must be a homo, because only homos, when they weren't in the bushes bumping dicks, wet their beds.

I spent four summers from mid-June to mid-August on Catalina Island. Once I successfully got out of boxing and horseback riding, by crying, of course, and refusing to participate, I actually garnered a small amount of self-confidence at the camp, despite myself. I earned merit badges in hiking and sailing and swimming, riflery and archery. My constant terror abated a little. At first I had been homesick, but I made friends. There were the kids in my tent plus kids I already knew like Jackie Hathaway, Sean Flynn, and a rolypoly kid named Joe DiMaggio, Jr.

Joe was expected to be the best softball player of all the campers, but because he was only average, he was razzed. Even though I was supposed to be his friend, I found myself standing on the sidelines razzing him with the rest of the campers. It made me feel slightly ashamed because I had often been challenged to perform like my father or Ed Wynn, and I knew what it was like to be in Joe's position. But after being chased at every recess around every playground in Southern California, pushed and pummeled in every line, having dirt thrown in my face, my books thrown on the floor, my bike knocked over, being tripped, jeered and laughed at, it all boiled down to—better him than me. I knew what happened to kids who were different, so I denied my feelings of kinship. Joe DiMaggio, Jr., was just a fat kid who couldn't play baseball very well. George Miner was just a bed wetter, and Sean Flynn was a stuck-up movie star's kid.

I was determined to fit in. Life wouldn't be so painful, I thought, if only I could fit in. And fitting in meant sharing the prejudices of those I wanted to fit in with. I was learning the art of social camouflage. For me, it was being funny or fast.

GRAHAM: What's it to be tonight, Chief?

WYNN: Graham, tonight's opera is the only gangster opera ever written. It's called, "He Couldn't Get a Doctor, So He Had to Kill Himself." As the curtain rises we see the gangster's baby boy pulling the legs off a centipede. He wants to see how many he has to pull off before he can make a worm turn. . . . He picks things up quickly—he got the seven-year itch and scratched it away in three years. His parents are in the iron and steel business—his mother irons and his father steals. The father enters. He's a tough gangster—in fact he's so tough that if he wants hot water he takes a mouthful of cold water and sits on the stove till it boils . . . the kid says, "Pop—how old is Mom?" and the old man says, "When I married her she was twenty-five, but I think she was marked down from thirty-eight. . . ." the wife enters with the doctor who is there to look at the baby's throat. "Say *ahh*," the doctor tells him. The old man says, "What are you trying to do, make a sissy out of him? Don't say, *aahhh*, say *awww*. . . ." The doctor turns to the wife and says, "Be careful with this child, there are measles in port." The father says, "If there's measles in port, we'll give him sherry." At that moment a terrific storm arises and a flash of lightning is seen. The doctor says, "Do you think that lightning hit near hear?" And the father says, "I don't know, but your pants weren't on fire when you came in." The wife says, "Doctor, have you got fire insurance on those pants?" The doctor says, "No, but I hope my coat will cover my loss. . . ." Play that, Don.

CHAPTER

6

When I came home to the new house in Beverly Hills at the end of that first summer, I found the streets went east and west and north and south; all the kids knew all the rules to all the games; and the social ante was sky high. Whatever I might have learned at camp, whatever self-confidence I might have shakily acquired over the summer, went right down the drain the first day I entered Hawthorne Grammar School.

Nothing I had learned at camp could have prepared me for the sophisticated children who lived in Beverly Hills. It was as if a manual had been handed to them at birth, they had memorized it, and now they were operating on a plane of self-assurance and poise that I couldn't begin to match.

It wasn't just money. Although most of the children had parents who were very well-off, if not arrantly loaded, I had that advantage as well. It was more a kind of deep-seated savvy, an effortless aptitude they displayed within their social precinct. They knew who they were and where they fit in, and that put them hopelessly beyond me.

Although I had frequently been around my parents' famous friends, that was no preparation. Most of them were exciting and excitable artists, insecure and manic by turns; they were never completely sure of themselves. They were beautiful, funny, exotic creatures with constantly shifting moods and readily accessible feelings. I could relate easily to them.

These children, on the other hand, acted as if they owned the world. Their parents were at the top of the food chain. They were wealthy merchants and manufacturers, political movers and shakers, film industry executives, social behemoths all. These were the children and grandchildren of the Jews and Gentiles my grandfather had strived to emulate. These were the swells.

Their parents owned businesses that I had never even considered before. It had never occurred to me that other people had manufactured and distributed the things that I possessed. I had imagined all my life that the movie business was somehow responsible for all the *stuff*, that the world of things had been created at Metro, in the prop department, and then apportioned to the rest of the planet through the conduit of imagination and the Saturday matinee. Now I learned differently.

In Beverly Hills the world of things was divided up between these two groups: The Jews seemed to have proprietorship of all the clothing, jewelry, furniture, appliances, and cut flowers; the Gentiles owned construction-and-paving companies, oil wells, car dealerships, and, it turned out, the President of the United States. One of my sixth-grade classmates, Steve Pauley, told me his father had "put Harry S Truman in the White House." News like this left me mute. I didn't know how to appreciate it. Was it a good thing? I didn't know. Apparently, Steve's father traded off with his friend Hank Salvatore's father, who put Dwight D. Eisenhower in the White House. If I ever needed to know who our next President was going to be, I only had to ask the guy sitting behind me in Geography. Another classmate at Hawthorne was Lindy Wasserman. Her dad was the head of something called MCA and his name was on all Van's checks. What was MCA, and why did our money come from there?

These children moved in a separate universe. Their parents were rich and powerful, much better I found out later, than being merely rich and famous. Their parents weren't employees like my father and stepfather, their parents were employers. People like Van Johnson and Keenan Wynn worked for people like Lew Wasserman and invariably voted for whomever people like Edwin S. Pauley or Henry Salvatore put in front of them.

The school was split pretty evenly among Jews and Gentiles. In fact, we took Jewish holidays as well as Christian holidays, much to my delight and my mother's horror. Beverly Hills was so Jewish, my mother took one look at the names in the phone book, got as far as the Cohens, and sent Tracy and me immediately off to All Saints' Church, an Episcopal redoubt, presumably to be inoculated against the dreaded onset of our genetically inherited predisposition toward Jewishness. Suddenly my mother, a completely nonreligious person, was pushing the Prince of Peace.

In my earlier life, in Brentwood and Santa Monica, God was for bedtime prayers. A lenient, laissez-faire attitude prevailed. But once we were moved into the big Spanish house on the corner of Foothill Road and Lomitas Avenue, she circled the wagons. It was All Saints' Church, and step on it—and don't bring them home until they've been baptized.

Van, a WASP's WASP, dutifully trundled us off to All Saints' every single Sunday for years. I was baptized and confirmed in the church, served the Mass as an acolyte, and spent many sweaty, tumescent hours burrowing among the sleeping bags with exotic blond and red-headed Episcopalian girls in the back of the bus on long, dark, church-sponsored snow trips. I had never even set foot inside a church before we moved to Beverly Hills, and now suddenly we were devout goyim. The irony was that I had to go to Beverly Hills to become a Christian. Paul was struck on the road to Damascus; I was struck on Camden Drive.

My ignorance of social customs among children was vast and unfathomed. I was great around adults, and I much preferred them to children. For years I had moved freely among my parents' friends. It was nothing for me to sit at the bar in our house in Beverly Hills and chat with people like Judy Garland, Rosalind Russell, James Mason, Deborah Kerr, Jack Hawkins, Ronald Colman, Tyrone Power, Janet Leigh, Gene Kelly, Frank Sinatra, Peter Lawford, and a dozen high-powered agents and lawyers, producers, and directors. But put me with a bunch of contemporaries, and I was fish food.

"Hey, Spazz, you don't even know what a batting average is."
"I do too."
"OK, if a guy's four-for-nine, what's his batting average?" We are standing on Rexford Drive near the bike racks after school. There are two awful times at Hawthorne: recess and right after school. I am trying to bluff my way through this one. My tormentor is a kid I grew up with. His name is Chris Whorf, and I have known him since kindergarten. His father, Richard Whorf, is a director and an actor, a friend of my parents. Now Chris calls me Spazz and wants me to tell him what four-for-nine means.

Spazz fits me. I am tall, gawky, uncoordinated, and afraid of the ball. With good reason. No matter how hard I try to catch it, it hits me in the face. Any ball, it doesn't matter. Soccer balls, baseballs, footballs—they chase me across the playground like heat-seeking missiles, thread their way between my hands and hit me in the face.

"Four-forty." Steve Pauley and Ricky Cohen are whispering a number to me. "Four-forty. Just say four-forty." They stand right next to me urging me to say these numbers. But I'm so out of it that I don't even know that a batting average is expressed as a number. For all I know, a batting average is green.

"Hey, Spazz—why don't you admit you don't know what a batting average is?" But I know better. I have learned not to admit to ignorance of any kind. To know, or to pretend to know, is the key to this daily social lottery. Success in this crowd is measured by an attitude of easy familiarity not only with things like sports and sex, but with business and religion as well. He could have said, "Hey, Spazz, what's a ten-year cash-deferred debenture?" or, "How many candles on a menorah?" and no one would have blinked. The fact that I didn't know a batting average from a stock quotation was partly the result of growing up at Metro. My father never played baseball with me. In fact, the only thing I'd ever seen my father pick up that was remotely round was a highball glass.

"Goddamnit, Ned, say four-forty." A small crowd has gathered. There is a group of girls watching. Sonny Tomblin, Amanda McCoy, Barbara Covey, Gretchen Boldman, Terry Adams—the cutest girls in the school. Now it becomes suddenly clear: They have come to judge me. My masculine potential from this day forward is in the balance. If I don't answer this question correctly, I will never have sex with any woman anywhere. I will be blackballed. In bedrooms across America, bedrooms I will never see, women will say, "He didn't know the answer to four-for-nine—don't fuck him."

Steve kicks me in the ankle. "Four-forty!" He's practically spitting in my face. I take a chance.

"Four-forty," I blurt. The girls cheer. Four-forty is the answer?

"Pauley told ya," Chris says disgustedly, and walks away. But I have passed a test. I will not live a life devoid of sex after all. But I still have no idea what a batting average is.

The experiment in public-school education lasted three years. It would have lasted four except for another experiment in the seventh grade: military school. This mild parental fugue became fashionable for a period during the early fifties among certain of the elite of Beverly Hills and Bel-Air. The object was something called discipline. Discipline was a buzz-word in the fifties, and I was one of those children deemed most definitely in need of it.

I'd already seen some chilling experiments in discipline among some of my friends, and I wanted no part of it. By far the worst were the beatings inflicted, by their fathers, on several boys I knew. One day at Danny Milland's house, his father, Ray Milland, had burst into the room and started smacking Danny around for no apparent reason. Danny was very big. Taller and heavier than his father, he could doubtless have broken Ray Milland in two. He pleaded with his father to stop, apologizing for whatever it was his father was angry about and covering his face while Ray, with his closed fists, hit him again and again in the face and screamed at him, "You goddamn little fucker who do you think you are!" I remember clearly the sound of the older man's fists on his son's face. The thick, blunt, dead noise it made, not like a slap at all.

Danny was a soft-spoken, good-natured kid. He could be smart-alecky, but he wasn't even in the same league with me as far as that went. Smart-aleckism was my forte. My father was often drunk, and he could be obstreperous and very physical. Would he do that?

Seeing fathers punch their kids had a very weird effect on me. Somewhere along the line I had begun to lose empathy with other human beings. I had become so utterly self-obsessed that all I was aware of was either my own pleasure or my own pain. While it scared me, because of the implications for me, it also excited me. I had an uncomfortable itch to see more of it, just so long as it wasn't directed my way. When Dad and Mom made the joint decision to send me to military school in the seventh grade, after two years at Hawthorne, in order to teach me some discipline, it seemed a reasonable alternative to having my face beat in.

Harvard Military Academy was "under the auspices of the Episcopal Church." I didn't know what that meant, but I felt somehow that it ought to ameliorate some of the more fearsome aspects of whatever constituted the military element. I thought of the kindly Rector of All Saints' Church, Kermit "K.C." Castellanos, a round, cheerful, crewcut Italian from Boston, a man of God who genuinely loved children and his Creator with equal fervor. I pictured someone like K.C. smiling, praising God, lining up the blondes for the church trips, and, since it was military school, patting our heads at rifle practice. Harvard would just be All Saints' with guns.

As with every other school I had ever attended, I was in trouble from the moment I got there. That first day, dressed in my full army cadet uniform with my cap and insignia and regulation everything— shirt, tie, something called a "spiffy" which I had on upside down with the little metal points at my throat, Eisenhower jacket, webbed belt, brown shoes, brown socks—I stood on the corner waiting for the school bus, the Greek fire glowing a cheery-orange in my gut. As soon as I got on the bus I was confronted with an old problem: being the new guy. I was grabbed, tripped, kicked, punched, my books were thrown to the floor, and my lunch was stolen. By the time I got to the school, I was a mess. For being out of uniform, I got three demerits.

No matter how hard I tried, I couldn't get the hang of things at Harvard. I'd learned how to fake it at camp, and I'd learned how to fake it at Hawthorne. It had taken me two years to recast my personality into a more acceptable mode in order to gain a measure of approval at school.

Becoming a complete phony had taken a lot of work, but it had its own rewards. I'd gotten to where I was asked to play football after school with Steve and Ricky and David Miller on Steve's lawn. I had a girlfriend, Terry Adams. I could slow dance, I could make out. Once I even managed to make a completely unconscious force at third by having my glove in the right place while I stood there daydreaming. The ball missed my face, hit my glove, and stuck. The cheers on the sidelines were deafening. I signed autographs. Now I was being asked to redo the entire operation.

No amount of ego reconstruction would have worked at Harvard. I was an utterly hapless cadet. Being much taller than my classmates, I was placed in C company with boys in the eighth, ninth, and tenth grades, boys who were merciless. Still taller than most of them, I was the target, I stood out. I was given the record number of demerits ever given to a seventh-grader. There was only one kid worse than me: Vernor.

He had problems I could only dream about. He was short, adenoidal, and wore thick glasses. In that respect he was an average dork. But he also had an outstanding partiality to pointed objects being pressed against his rectum. He was able, evidently, to satisfy this urge by sitting on pencils. In class, on the bus, in shop, wherever fate would find him, Vernor was trying to shove something up his ass. The other cadets gave him various sharp objects to see which he preferred, arrows, sticks, dowels, spoons, but in the end, it was pencils. I kept thinking, where was this guy when my mother went into an enema frenzy?

Vernor took a lot of the heat off me. Compared to him I had no pathology to speak of. Once they had thrown my homework around the bus, squashed my sandwich, stolen my cookies, and spit into my thermos, they turned their attention to Vernor. Whenever Vernor was around I tried to use the opportunity to bully him a little so I could fit in with the other guys. But in a school made up largely of bullies, it was hard to make an impression short of permanently maiming your victim.

The best I could have hoped for, realistically, was toadie. The elite at Harvard were autocratic snobs, and they thrived on toadies. But toadying could be dangerous, too. The seniors wore real sabers on their belts, and when they grabbed any luckless underclassmen after lunch for a few quick torture sessions, they used the flats of these sabers to thrash them. Presumably, this activity aided in their digestive processes.

They prowled a fenced-off jurisdiction called the Senior Enclosure, a kind of free zone for criminal assault. The unfortunates they grabbed were usually toadies, as they were the only ones who would venture near the area, usually looking for someone to please. Once in the Senior Enclosure, there was no redress. They were allowed to beat and pummel the younger boy until they had either ruined his uniform or his schoolwork and made him cry, or until a bell rang summoning them to Centurion 101. Toadies weren't murdered. That was their break.

"Wynn!" I had become Wynn. I never heard my first name uttered at that school. Other children I knew there were Hathaway, Melcher, and Wellman. Jackie, Terry, and Billy weren't anywhere to be seen.

"Wynn, report to Captain Russell on the double. Now! Move!"

Captain Robert C. Russell, Professor of Military Science and Tactics, was the military head of the school, called the Commandant. There was also a nonmilitary headmaster, Father Chalmers. Father

Chalmers was an Episcopal Reverend, a man so white his lips seemed to have a slight blue tinge. He gave thoughtfully intoned sermons at Chapel twice a week and smiled his azure smile at the neat rows of cadets in the pews. His world was orderly beyond reproach. Father Chalmers had the kind of demeanor that said that he was unacquainted with the unpleasant aspects of his school, and that he really only wanted the boys to be happy and to glory in the well-groomed nature of the Heavenly Spirit.

There was also a student Commandant. His name was Cooly Butler. He was a popular student, looked up to by all the cadets. He was about to hand over the office to a boy named Jergens, heir to the hand lotion fortune. Of all the boys in the school, Jergens was one of the least liked. In fact, whenever the school was lined up for battalion inspection, a chant would begin in the ranks: "Jergens eats it, Jergens eats it . . ." Everyone was careful not to move his lips. It was impossible to see anyone doing it, but the chant, done to the tune of the Lava Soap commercial ("L-a-v-a, L-a-v-a . . ."), was clear and unmistakable. Eager to fit in, I would take up this chant along with the three hundred other boys while Jergens, strutting in front of us with his student colonel insignia and his saber and his white gloves, would cock his head and glower.

This had been going on for years before I had even arrived at the school. I certainly had no quarrel with Jergens, and I didn't really know what it was that pissed everybody off about him so much. I didn't know him, and therefore had no reason to dislike him. In fact, I thought he was pretty decent for a swaggering, undersized, vainglorious prig, and of course I revered anyone who didn't throw me into the dumpster during gym.

On the parade ground the day of Jergens's installation as *Oberstkommandant* of the student body, the chant began anew. I joined in cheerfully. Chanting "Jergens eats it" was a way for me to be a part of the group, to belong, and besides, it was kind of festive. For some reason, perhaps because Jergens was unduly attentive that day, swooping from rank to rank during inspection like Henry the Chicken Hawk, everyone suddenly stopped chanting at once. Except for me.

I was in that same trancelike state I had been in the day at Hawthorne when I made the force at third. I was drifting on the mantra: Jergens eats it, Jergens eats it—sing-songing, drifting, free of the pain in my back from standing for an hour at attention, free of the headache and the faintness from being in the hundred-degree weather of the San Fernando Valley in full-dress uniform while another boy fainted dead away two ranks in front of me, free of the shoulder-crunching weight of the M-1 rifle and the searing skillet-hot metal butt-plate that rested in my grimy, gloved palm. Suddenly

Jergens was in front of me and I was saying "Jergens eats it," right in his face.

"Wynn, report to Captain Russell on the double. Now! Move!"

Captain Robert C. Russell, PMS&T, had ended his career in the army by becoming the commandant of a rich kids' military school in Studio City. I don't know if this was how he'd seen himself the day he entered Officers' Candidate School, but this is where he was. When he looked at me, a teary-eyed, sissified little rich brat who got caught chanting some idiotic phrase about another sissified little rich brat, he was staring his career apogee in the face. At that moment the full import of where he had ended up must certainly have hit him squarely. He tried to care. He strode up and down behind his desk making all the requisite threats. He called my parents, told me I'd be kicked out of school, I'd be lucky if I could ever again look anyone in the face, I'd lost all pride and honor, etc. He managed to work up enough righteous anger to spray me with spit several times.

I was truly stricken at the gravity of my offense. I wept and pleaded to be allowed to make up for my monstrous iniquity, to apologize to Mr. Jergens, to crawl in the dust and beg forgiveness. Satisfied I was properly cowed, he gave me two hundred demerits.

A demerit required one half hour of marching after school in a muddy pasture behind the gym. Two hours a day of this meant that I would miss the bus, and that my parents would have to drive over to the valley to get me in the dark for the next two months. My parents lost interest in the discipline experiment soon afterward. The next year I was back in Hawthorne.

There were no more elves in mossy dells. Fairies no longer peeked from behind pomegranates. My mental wonderland, steadily eroding since early childhood, had been shattered by the onset of puberty, and I could no longer call up my private world as I could when I was younger. Objects, once as fluid as space, had gained an unrelenting obduracy, and their human counterparts, the rules and the concepts of others, especially children, had encroached upon my life so forcibly that the held breath of my incunabula was squeezed from me like a tiny, mournful wind.

In its place was a new and urgent upheaval: pubic hair, erections, a shrieking, cracking voice, dandruff, B.O., zits—my body was in eruptive rebellion against the comfortable terrors of childhood. The popcorn was popping.

In Beverly Hills I had been ineluctably thrust into a hostile universe driven by unfathomable social demands, paralyzing appetites, and sweating palms. Desperately, instinctively, I had begun, as an adjunct to my latest personality overhaul, to seek out those things which created that durable physical reality I saw others using with such great success. Could I run fast, jump high, catch a ball, comb my hair right, wear cool enough clothes, say the right things to girls? Especially that.

Where I had once been allowed to play, unrestricted, among the bodies of women, I was now forced to leave their skin alone, to learn instead a complicated new scenario based on connivance whose sole purpose was to inveigle, con, worm, cajole, beguile, and hoodwink females into letting me for one second, for one minute, for one hour, do the things I had always done on the laps and legs of beautiful actresses and more, only now there was a new and monomaniacally obsessed purpose.

"Let's just go over that wall and explore."

"No."

"C'mon. There's a squirrel."

"No." We're walking near a vacant lot on Sunset Boulevard. There is a low stone wall and a patch of grass beneath some fir trees. I've just got to get her in there. I pull a Three Musketeers bar out of my back pocket. I've been sitting on it since fourth period.

"I know," I say brightly, waving the warm, squashed chocolate bar. "Let's have a picnic." She wavers. This is invention at work. She wrinkles her brow.

"No."

Her name is Carla and she isn't going for it. She's tall and blond and just the slightest bit airy. Her current attitude is perplexing because in Literature this same girl allows me to feel her up. I sit in front of her, and she parts her legs to let me put my hand up as far as I can without falling backward out of my chair. It's awkward but effective. I leave my hand between her thighs, my arm twisted and extended back and under her desk for forty-five minutes at a stretch, my other hand holding open Sir Walter Scott's *Lady of the Lake*. Of course, the blood soon leaves my whole arm and I can't feel anything, so I might as well have my hand between two bricks, but this is, after all, the eighth grade, and opportunities for sex being what they are, I have to strike swiftly and often.

"Ned Wynn . . ." The teacher, Mrs. Kauffman, is calling on me to read. This wouldn't be so bad except that we have to go up to the front and stand, facing the class, in order to do it. I quickly slip my hand out from between Carla's knees. Around me everyone is grinning.

"Me?"

"Is there another Ned Wynn in the class?" Snickers. Slowly I drag myself out of the seat. I have made a grave miscalculation: My boner is facing down. It's bad enough when it's up, but down it's impossible to hide.

Boner-hiding is a skill all its own in the eight grade. Any boy seen walking with his books in front of him, across his fly, better be hiding a boner, because otherwise he'll be pegged a homo. It's common knowledge, printed somewhere in that manual, and I'm still doing makeup work. As it is I can't hold my book down far enough, my boner is creating an awning somewhere near the bottom of my pocket.

"I'm wise to the rise in your Levis . . ." Amanda McCoy chants as I pass her desk. Amanda gets her poetic predilection from her father, Horace, whose book, *They Shoot Horses, Don't They?*, is famous in our class. No one knows what it's about, but its title is ruthless and obscure, and it lends a kind of danger to Amanda. Next to her Nortie Styne smiles knowingly at me. His father is Jule Styne, the songwriter, and Nortie, suave, good-looking, and knowledgeable, tells me he has felt up half the girls in the class and gotten bare tit off the other half, all to his father's "Three Coins in the Fountain."

"Are you having difficulty finding the front of the class, Ned?"

"No, ma'am," I say. Slowly I walk down the aisle between the desks. Toward the front, Guy Webster is coughing into his book, trying to hold in his laughter. Guy's father is also a songwriter, Paul Francis Webster, and Guy has been knocking off Beverly Hills High School girls using "Thee I Love." I wish my dad wrote songs.

I get to the front and stand, my back to the class. I begin to read, " 'At length with Ellen in a grove/He seemed to walk, and speak of love; . . .' "

"Why are you addressing the blackboard?" Oh, Jesus.

"Huh?"

"Excuse me, Mrs. Kauffman?"

"Excuse me, Mrs. Kauffman?"

"Why are you addressing the blackboard? Please turn around and face the class and read." I start to turn, being very careful to hold the book down as low as I can. The book at arms' length, I bend slightly at the waist and peer at the pages. This is not having the effect I want it to have. Instead of hiding anything, the book looks like a serving platter with a curious hors d'oeuvre on it.

" 'She listened with a blush and sigh,/His suit was warm, his hopes were high. . . .' " Steve Pauley barks.

"Is there something wrong with your eyes? Why are you holding the book so far away?" Guy Webster explodes. To cover, he pretends he is having a sneezing fit. *Whooaaacheee!* . . .

"Guy Webster, report to the infirmary. Go on, Ned." Guy caroms off the walls and through the door. I can hear him shrieking in the hallway, bouncing off the lockers.

" 'He sought her yielded hand to clasp,/And a cold gauntlet met his grasp:/The phantom's sex was changed and gone,/Upon its head an helment shone; . . .' " Steve Pauley and Ricky Cohen are next to go. Sneezing and coughing, their faces are scarlet.

"Ricky Cohen, Steven Pauley, report to the infirmary. Continue, Ned."

" 'Slowly enlarged . . . to . . .' Excuse me, Mrs. Kauffman, what is *an helment*?"

"*An helment* is a helmet. Read until I tell you to stop, please."

" 'Upon its head an helment shone;/Slowly enlarged . . . to *giant . . . size . . .* ' "

Whoooooaaaacheeeeee! The entire class comes down with a cold at once. Books fall to the floor, desk tops are banging up and down. Mrs. Kauffman has lost control entirely. I stand before them, laughing helplessly.

"Ned Wynn, report to the principal's office."

Each time I got into trouble my father was sent for. In this way I saw a lot of him. There was a watchful truce between my mother and Van, and my father. In an effort not to disrupt our upbringing too much, my mother had allowed for a liberal and open visitation. I went for occasional weekends and stayed with him wherever he happened to be living, which in the early and middle fifties was a house on Fontenelle Way in Stone Canyon, a beautiful winding street in Bel-Air.

Tracy and I usually went separately. My father felt that he could give more attention to each of us one at a time, and my mother wanted to keep a closer watch on my brother. She felt that while Tracy could be saved, I was a goner. I'd spent too much time with my father already.

What she most objected to about Dad were his drinking, his motorcycles, and his low-crotch friends. She might also have been affected by his excessive nature. He was always too much of everything, especially too stingy (to us), and too generous (to his low-crotch pals). He was constantly getting involved with people in dubious business ventures, usually one form or another of a motorcycle shop. He wanted desperately to have his own grease pit where he could sit around with guys whose crotches required sub-basements, and smell the gasoline and the oil, and drink and lie about motorcycles.

If nothing else, my mother had once loved him for his potential, what she saw in him that she could improve. Now that he was hopelessly beyond her influence, she tended to recall his negative aspects more clearly. In fact, he was a mixture of things: wit ("Let's bring Aunt Dorothy a case of her favorite wine. What do you think that might be, Blue Nun?"); optimism ("I think the work I've done in this show [*Orca, Piranha, Shack Out on 101*, etc.] might just be the best I've ever done. Something's bound to happen from this . . ."); peevishness ("I'm always in the middle—I just don't make enough goddamned *money*—I can never get ahead. . . ."); misinformation ("Use hot water in the ice trays—it freezes faster"); and bluster (". . . I said to him, 'Duke, I'm no Communist. . . .' and the Duke by God backed off.") He attracted all kinds of people to him. Most were simply after a soft touch, some were genuine friends. My father accepted most of them without question. None met with my mother's approval. She didn't even need to meet them to know.

"Guess who came over to Dad's this weekend, Mom?"

"Let me guess—Bugsy Siegel? Argentine Rocca? Caryl Chessman?"

"*Ma-ahm*—no—an actor."

"Leo Gorcey? Huntz Hall? Louis Quinn?"

"Louis *Quinn*!" Van shouts this from two rooms away. "Jesus. I *love* Louis Quinn!"

"Marlon Brando," I say.

"*Hmph.*" Hmph?

"*Ma-ahm*—Marlon *Brando*."

"I heard you."

"But, Mar-lon Bran-do. He came over on his bike."

"You didn't ride motorcycles over there, did you?" Now she has something to discuss.

"No, Mom, I didn't ride motorcycles over there. Jeez. But Bud —that's what everybody calls Marlon—Bud's bike stalled and he *pushed* it all the way up Dad's driveway. An Ariel Square-Four! He's the strongest guy I ever saw."

"I don't want you riding motorcycles over there."

"Guess who I met at Dad's this weekend, Mom?"

"Mmm—let's see—Slapsie Maxie Rosenbloom?"

"Very funny. I met Lee Marvin."

"He's going to be very big!" Van shouts this from the backyard. "Very very *big*!"

"Not if he spends much time with your father, he's not."

"He's got a Triumph 500 cc Trophy Dash like Dad." Whoops. Don't mention the . . .

"Did you ride motorcycles over there?" Jesus.

The careers of both my father and stepfather had continued in a comfortable arc. Between 1950 and 1954 Van made fourteen pictures including *The Big Hangover, Go For Broke, The Last Time I Saw Paris, Brigadoon,* and *The Caine Mutiny.* He was a big star, and he was making close to half a million dollars a year.

During the same period, Dad, who liked to rename the films he was in to suit his attitude about them, was making things like, *All the Brothers Were Valiant* ("All the Brothers Were Ferblunget"), *Kiss Me Kate* ("Kiss My Kootch"), *Code Two* ("Code Jew"), *Fearless Fagan* ("Fearless Faegeleh"), *Desperate Search* ("Desperate Crotch"). Some films he liked, or at least had fun doing: *Royal Wedding*, with Fred Astaire and Jane Powell, in which he played twin brothers, one of them English; *Kind Lady*, starring Angela Lansbury, Maurice Evans, and Angela's mother, Moyna MacGill, in which he played a killer; and his personal favorite, a little-seen nor long-remembered bit of *film noir* called *Holiday for Sinners*, with Gig Young and Janice Rule, in which he played a prize fighter who goes blind.

In 1953 Dad decided to leave Metro and become a free-lance actor. Television was coming into its own and there was enough work for him to do quite well without the steady income from MGM. Still, never in all the years I knew him, did my father ever express satisfaction with the amount of money he was getting. In his worst years he still managed to make a hundred-fifty thousand dollars, yet he constantly complained that he was the one, as he put it, "in the middle," and that the multifarious demands of life were so consuming that he would never see over the edge, never get ahead.

"Just like his father," my mother would say. "Cries poor, just like Ed Wynn."

His feeling seemed to be that the world was pressuring him in some puzzling and eminently unfair way. He seemed to feel that he could never satisfy the myriad demands that were crushing him. He needed help to bear his life, and I was one of his sherpas. His favorite expression was, "Do me a favor, willya, kiddo?"

"Do me a favor, willya, kiddo, and tell your mother it's been slow since I left Metro and I just don't have that kinda cash. . . ." Or

"Do me a favor, willya, kiddo, and go back to camp this summer. It'll make you mother happy, and it'll get me out of a jam. . . ." Or

"Do me a favor, willya, kiddo? Don't tell anyone we stopped off for a few drinks. It'll just start a whole routine."

I stopped off for a lot of drinks with Dad from the time I was five or six and I sat on a barstool reading Donald Duck and Archie, until I was well into manhood and I sat on a barstool reading Donald Duck and Archie, and drank with him. One of his favorite hangouts was the Retake Room, a typically dark, studio bar behind Metro on Washington Boulevard; it was the first real dive I was ever in. The bartender was a man named DeeDee, and every day after getting his shave at Metro, we'd stop at the Retake Room to "say hello to DeeDee." Sometimes Dad would start off British.

"Deedee, my good *chatelain*—a demijohn of vodka, with just a *soupçon* of vermouth—there's a fellow."

"Keeno—what the fuck is a *chatelain*?" Dad would peer at DeeDee behind the bar.

"The guy who owns the booze."

"Ok. Uh—now what's a *soupçon*?"

Or he'd start off Yiddish/German/Trans-Caucasus.

"DeeDee, *mein gut man, ein flasch vodka rocks mit ein tvist, bite*?"

"How do you want that, Keenan, in a demijohn?"

People always recognized him and chuckled at all the accents he could pull out of a hat. My father knew very few of these people by name, but, amiably, he always pretended to recognize them.

"Keenan, remember that picture we worked on with Clarence Brown?"

"Ohhh, by God, suuure. . . ." Who in the hell is this guy?

"'Member that actress—the blonde with the . . ."

"Yeah, the blonde with the knockers. . . ." Any blonde with knockers.

"Did you, ahh? . . ."

"Nah. . . ." Well. Maybe.

The cook would make me a plate of greasy french fries and I'd settle down in a sticky, squeaky naugahyde booth with my comic book stack while my father stood at the bar and regaled the barflies with stories and jokes. He was usually the biggest celebrity in that bar. Mostly it was a watering hole for grips, electricians, and scenery painters as well as the occasional editor and camera operator. Most actors, afraid of their reputations, or perhaps desiring a nicer place to drink, would avoid the Retake Room. My father hadn't much regard for reputations. His or anyone else's. And as far as a nice place to drink went, a shot of liquor was a shot of liquor. Who cared if they had potted plants?

I thought it was a pretty great bar to be in myself, and at fourteen I was counting the days until I could sit on the stool and order a vodka martini. I liked the stale odors of booze and disinfectant, the sound of DeeDee walking back and forth on the wire rug, the silent piano with the perpetual layer of dust on the top, the harsh white sunlight that blasted through the front door and died about three feet from the first stool. It always amazed me how the sun didn't penetrate the Retake Room, even with the door open. The murk was too ancient, or maybe the sun had respect for the hangovers in there. Later, when I drank on the naugahyde-booth circuit, I found that the sun steered clear of all of them. It's something for which a true drunk is always grateful.

It was in this bar that I got a taste of booze without drinking. I liked the easy flow of false camaraderie. There were ready-made pals in this place. Could I learn to be pals like that? It looked easy enough. I wouldn't really need to *know* anyone. It was all faces and voices and laughter. I was struck by the fluid way in which my father could slip on an entirely different personality when he was drinking. He had friendships that started and stopped right there.

"So, Keenan, how'd you make out the other night?" The man who is talking is a slightly paunchy stuntman. He's a heavy drinker, and it's starting to show.

"Oh, Jesus. . . ." My father groans and shakes his head.

"You looked like you were feeling no pain. . . ."

"Stoned . . . like, numb. . . ." He downs half of his drink, bends over, and slams his fist into the bar. "God *damn* that's good."

"Did you see the broad? Went into the men's room? . . ."

"You're kidding. . . ." I try and stay absolutely still. I'm about to hear something wonderful.

". . . into the men's room, with the guy, right—what's his name—Frank?"

"Oh, Jesus—Frank?"

"The guy used to double Franchot Tone. They're in there—I don't know—how long they in there, DeeDee?"

"Ten minutes—fifteen."

"They're in there fifteen minutes—he comes out—no sign of her, right?"

"Jesus Christ. . . ."

"No sign of the broad. He sits down and orders a drink like nothing's going on, right? I say, 'Where's the broad?' What broad? Like he's six feet past bombed. What broad? So *I* go in, right?"

"Oh, shit—*you* go in? . . ."

"Fuck yes, *I* go in—DeeDee . . ." The stuntman circles his hand indicating a round of drinks. Dad shakes off the gesture and indicates they're on him. "Thanks, Keenan. I go in and she's in there. On the toilet. And there's this *schwartze*. You know the guy. He went to UCLA. Plays in those Roman movies. Big sonofabitch. He's got his *schwantz* out. It's *this* fucking long. *Umm* . . ." Suddenly the man notices me. He glances questioningly at Dad. Dad grins.

"Ah, he's heard everything—right, kiddo? Shit. He's heard it all." Yeah. So let's keep talking.

"Anyway," the guy says, "ya shoulda been there. It was unbelievable. So, Ned—you gonna be an actor, too?" Hey! What happened with the *schwantz* and the *schwartze*?

DeeDee was an example of the unique friendships my father had. I never saw DeeDee anywhere but the Retake Room. It was as if he grew there, a thin, sparse reed of a man who could move several feet to the left, and several feet to the right, and that was it. I heard my father talking on the phone with DeeDee once or twice, to wish him happy birthday, and once I actually saw him standing outside in the sunshine. There was something tasteless about it, as if I shouldn't have caught him like that, white-skinned and blinking, he looked as if he'd just had his clothes stolen. Dad maintained a warm and friendly association with DeeDee for years based entirely on the ordering of drinks. The bar was like a separate world, a haven, and in the back of my mind I knew it was a place I would fit into immediately.

Years later I return to the Retake Room to have a drink, and DeeDee is gone. I sit on the bar stool and look out at the heat shimmering on Washington Boulevard. One of the same faded bar-flies, her makeup peeling off like plaster, sits at a stool near the front. I smile at her and she looks down at her hands. Maybe she isn't one of them after all. My stomach is clenched. I feel a little gypped. I look at DeeDee's replacement and think, if I come back here every day for a week, this guy'll be my pal. He'll remember me, he'll even know my drink. He might even call it "the usual." Or better, he'll simply smile and nod when I come in, realizing instinctively what kind of night I've had, get a glass and pour me a double, place a napkin in front of me, and set the glass down with a wink and a little slap on the bar top. He reserves that slap for the regulars, the people he really likes. I'll shake my head ruefully and buy the house a round. The woman will tell everyone how she remembers me from when I was a little kid. It'll be just like my dad and DeeDee. One week, that's all it'll take. I think about it for a while. I have one drink, and leave.

CHAPTER

7

I sit down hard on the sand. It shakes me so my teeth bang together. My cheeks are loose. My tongue is thick and wooly and this makes me talk funny. I'm laughing. It's very funny sitting here on this little beach behind the hotel. And very friendly. I've got lots of friends reeling and stumbling on this beach with me. Their faces come and go. Where is that fucking bottle? Earl? Where's the fucking god-damned jesuschristing bottle? Earl's face rolls up in front of me like a humpback whale, grinning, and then the bottle pops to the surface. Popov. I grab it and tilt it into my mouth. The vodka pours in and a little animal instantly clutches my throat, but I don't mind. When I first did it the animal tried to climb back out and I nearly puked. But now, all I feel is the rake of its claws going down. I like it. It doesn't hurt anymore than falling down does. The lights across the bay in San Diego glimmer like Christmas. What a lovely beautiful place. I'll think I'll stay in this new and beautiful place forever.

Earl and I work at the Hotel del Coronado. Earl's dad is the head cabana boy at the hotel pool, and Earl is his assistant. I work as a counselor at the hotel day camp taking care of the guests' children. Which is awkward because my parents are guests here, too. In fact, they got me the job.

Harvard Military School had taught my parents the meaning of discipline better than it had taught me. And now this job was sup-posed to teach me the value of a dollar—something my parents already knew and which I was never to learn. It was another pose, the rich-kid employee. I didn't mind it so much, but it made the real employees very fidgety. They thought I was some kind of spy for management.

The previous summer I had worked with our gardener, Jim Beers. Of course my mother had given him extra money with which he had paid me. I knew this, but I was supposed to pretend it was a real job. So I hosed-down driveways, clipped hedges, rode around in Jim's truck with him, learned to run his new Toro power mower and how to shift a three-on-the-tree Chevy transmission, and overall made his day about an hour-and-a-half longer than it would have been if he'd done it all alone. These summer jobs of mine were hell on the people who worked for my mother.

We slide into town, drunk and adult. Earl nearly falls down twice. Cars filled with Coronado High School girls pass and scream to us. We're drunken heroes. Trail blazers, icons, champions. Kids, smashed in public. Hello, ladies, I'm fifteen and drunker than shit. We laugh so hard we have to stop and lean against buildings. Everyone is staring at us. The local cops keep driving by. Finally they stop us. Earl whispers to me, "Act sober." You bet.

"You boys been drinking?"

"No, sir," says Earl. We both stand there waving like wheat in the field.

"No, sir," I say. Absolutely right. Totally clear. Little soldiers. I look at Earl. One eye is about a quarter of an inch lower than the other. His face is beet red, his cheeks sag. The cop nods.

"You boys better get some coffee. Earl, you better not be drinking anymore. I don't want to have to tell your dad. And you, Son," he turns to me. "What's your story?"

"Nothing, sir. No story." Stand up straight. Stand up.

"Your folks know you're down here?"

"Yes, sir." Pronounce each syllable. Pronounce.

"That your dad in that *Men of the Fighting Lady* picture?"

"Yes, sir." What picture was that?

"You see that Bob?" He turns to his partner. "*Men of the Fighting Lady*? This kid's dad's Van Johnson." I don't correct him. Bob nods, extremely bored.

"Get some coffee, Johnson. You too, Earl." The cops squint hard at us and drive away. We're too clever. Too good. Coffee. Why not? God, we're suave.

A car pulls up with four girls in it. Locals. I know them from the beach and the hotel pool. One of them has been dragging my heart around in her purse all summer. Cheryl. Her face shows adult concern, her short shorts show plucky thighs, tanned and downy. She comes up to me and puts her arm around me. "You need some coffee," she says, smiling at me. This girl has never put her arm around me before. This is getting more adult by the minute. Her perfume hits me and mixes with the Popov. Old signals, new messages. Getting drunk seems to have switched on the concern buttons in all the girls. Remember this.

"Get some coffee, Johnson," Earl howls.

"Coffee," I say, grinning idiotically.

"You *guuuys* . . ." Cheryl squeals, practicing her concern-voice, "what have you been drinking?" Only she says, dring-*keeen*. She sings it, stretching out the vowels alluringly. Thirty years later this language will be called Valspeak. But now, I hear it for the first time in Coronado, California. It's adorable, this girl language. I can't get enough of this delicious affectation. And isn't that just the slightest hint of something like admiration in her voice? It's cool to be drunk. It's beyond cool.

"It's world," Earl says to me.

"World," I say.

We were men that night. I was fifteen years old, Earl was sixteen. Attack of the Fifty-Foot Teen Men. Everything that summer was cherry and world. It was a Bill Doggett-Honky Tonk summer. Annie Had a Baby that summer, probably by Old Dan, the Sixty-Minute Man. Oh, yeah. "Fifteen minutes of squeezin', fifteen minutes of pleasin', and fifteen minutes of blowin' my top, bop-bop-bop. . . ." We hot-wired cars and took joyrides on the Strand, sometimes all the way to Tijuana. Sometimes we took Earl's '50 Ford. He'd let me drive, even though I didn't have a license. Sometimes we stole a car, but we always brought it back. Earl showed me how to take the tinfoil from a pack of cigarettes, fold it, and press it between the two ignition wires to make contact. Sometimes I held the foil, sometimes Earl held the foil. Then we drove for miles, one of us bent over holding the wires together. Sometimes we went to parties. Hank Ballard and the Midnighters. I could dance. I could even sing. I was learning to be a chameleon, to blend in with any society. All I had to do was learn the words, the songs, the clothes, the attitudes. I was getting to be a regular social behemoth.

My mother had become one of the most influential hostesses in Beverly Hills in the fifties. Her only rival was Edie Goetz, Louis B. Mayer's daughter and the wife of Bill Goetz, the head of Fox. Ever since the Santa Monica house they had been friends and attended one another's parties. My mother and Edie seemed to switch off, each having a party every other week. Some of these parties were informal, some were black-tie. All of them involved having dinner at some point. They were big, loud, fun. The same people, for the most part, made the rounds of these parties. My father called this the "A" group.

"What group are you in, Dad?"

"I'm in the 'B' group. But, I plan on using the entire alphabet."

There were no Marlon Brandos or Lee Marvins at my mother's parties. It was all strictly high-crotch.

Who's got the scotch? Judy? Scotch and water for Judy, scotch and soda for Roz, hell, everyone drinks scotch. "Ned, a vodka martini . . ." That was either Helmut Dantine or Jean-Pierre Aumont. What did Greer Garson want?

"Scotch for Liz, honey. Rocks, with a splash." It's my mother's voice. If I just poured scotch in every glass, no one would give a shit. I hate scotch, but I sip each drink anyway. Wouldn't want to give anyone a bad drink.

I look straight out at the surging crowd in our living room, and I see Elizabeth Taylor talking to Van. The blood rushes to my neck. She looks at me and I can't swallow. How can this woman look like that? She has replaced Ava Gardner in my heart. I don't know why people say her eyes are violet. They aren't violet. They're the color of the skin of an eggplant. Aubergine. Garnet. Rubies hewn from the Hall of the Mountain King. Only women and fags talk about her eyes anyway. It's the tits. Oh, Jesus. The tits.

"You remember Neddy, don't you Liz?" My mother draws Liz to the bar. Everything hisses as she moves: the silk, the nylon, the elastic underneath; and the tits, each one alive, jiggling, reaching out, playful little beings, snuggly little dears. I wonder: Do they think? She sticks out her hand. I could do it, I could reach out and squeeze her tit, but instead I shake her hand, and then, incredibly, I feign boredom.

"Neddy," Liz says. "Of course, I remember him. You came to our house in Malibu. Remember? When I was married to Michael? My, you've grown. So handsome, Evie." She smiles radiantly at me.

I remember her, all right. On the beach in Malibu. Michael Wilding's house. They had just married. I was standing on the edge of the waves. Tracy was playing in the sand. Schuyler, still a baby, lay like a white muffin on a blanket. Liz walked along the shore and stopped near me. We both threw rocks at the water. She was seventeen and I was eight. There had never been a seventeen-year-old girl like her before on Earth. This much was apparent to everyone including Wilding who looked like the cat who swallowed the canary. We only stood there for a minute or two, throwing rocks. I picked up a flat rock and skipped it across the top of a wave. She wanted to know how I did that. I attempted to explain skipping rocks, but suddenly, without a word, she turned and dashed back up the beach to her husband. Fuck her if she doesn't want to learn how to skip rocks.

"Um, yeah. . . ." I say, looking around as if I have an important message to deliver anywhere else but to Elizabeth Taylor. "Who ordered this scotch and soda, Judy?" That'll get her. She'll be jealous of Judy. My aloofness will attract her. What twenty-five-year-old movie star, for whom world rulers would gladly eat a pound of dirt in exchange for fifteen seconds alone with one of her nipples, wouldn't be attracted to a zit-faced sixteen-year-old kid with the kind of seductive indifference I could affect? I'll pretend I'm looking for Judy Garland, the woman I *really* love.

Judy is standing on a coffee table with Roz Russell. They are performing a duet. Cole Porter is playing the piano. "Night and day, you are the one . . ." Roz, taking the black-tie invitation seriously, has arrived wearing a black tie, ruffled shirt, shorts, and heels. Judy, at the brief peak of her whole roller-coaster night, raises her skirts and kicks. I see her husband, Sid Luft, watching. He will leave long before Judy does. Liza, Lorna, and little Joey are waiting at home. But Judy will not leave until very late. Then she will return to our house because Sid will not let her in. This is the way they play it. Later that night Judy will come into my room and complain bitterly about Sid. She'll sit on the floor and smoke. I will hear the ice clinking in her glass, see the orange tip of the cigarette light her face, not happy anymore, but bent, sagging with drunkenness, streaked with mascara. The sonofabitch locks me out of my own goddamned house! Self-righteous sonofabitch!

I try and sympathize, but actually, I sympathize with that son-ofabitch Sid. Judy's drinking is legendary now. She's out of control, a bad drunk. I agree with her as long as I can stay awake. Finally, she wanders downstairs. My mother puts her to bed on the couch in our living room. The next day the whole house is as quiet as a tomb. The maids are tiptoeing around because Miss Garland is asleep on the couch. The whole house is tiptoeing. Even Van, who is slipping out to play tennis with James Mason, is tiptoeing. No vacuums are running. Sid has called fifteen times. Everyone is whispering. Judy is running our household from her stupor. I don't forget this lesson: Royalty is forgiven everything. If there is an error in my thinking, it is that people love Judy Garland in spite of her excesses; I think they love her because of them. This kind of thinking does not prove fruitful.

Surreptitiously, I make myself a bourbon and 7-Up. No one at this party drinks bourbon. Bourbon is my father's drink. I drink in honor of my uninvited father and all those in the uninvited "B," "C," and "D" groups who are sitting at the Red Log or the Little Club, the Fox and Hounds, the Bat Rack, or the Cock 'n Bull.

Liz finally takes her drink and drifts away. I have scored big with her all right. She'll undoubtedly think of me for the rest of the night. I live entirely in my head: Wouldn't that little bitch in Coronado—Cheryl, the one who liked me for twenty-four hours—just shit if she knew that Elizabeth Taylor thought I was handsome? The thought keeps me going for hours.

This mental sex was a survival technique honed to perfection at boarding school. After Hawthorne I had been sent to Webb, an all-boys' school tucked up in the foothills somewhere between the San Gabriel and San Bernardino Mountains. Below us were nothing but miles of orange groves, above us, snow. Webb had a high level of academic excellence, and I learned a great deal there. But my social skills, such as they were, had deteriorated even further among the sage, orange blossoms, and mesquite. In this bucolic setting I had become used to a strange and monkish life. Here we went to chapel five times a week, classes six days a week, played sports, and masturbated three times a day. Our visual aids were generally the pictures in cached sex magazines like *Escapade, Cavalier*, and *Nugget*, whose pages became so laminated with semen they could have been used as wallboard. Or they were the mental pictures we had of women we knew. I was luckier than most because I knew women like Elizabeth Taylor. Either way it was a bleak sexual landscape.

The extent of our socializing at Webb was to sit at a table in the dining hall with the family of one of the masters and try and imagine frottage with either his prune-faced wife or one of his rhino-haunched daughters. It was Victorian. A woman's ankle, thick as a football, was the object of pornographic frenzy.

Much of the sexual frustration boys felt at Webb was converted into aggression. In order to forestall this aggression when it turned my way, the only thing I could think of was to emulate the bullies. I was a coward. If they were hammering some poor kid, I never interfered. And sometimes I joined right in.

Bob Roos came from a wealthy family of clothiers in San Francisco. He seemed designed for the kind of cruelty that is offered at all-male boarding schools. He was a little kid with thick glasses and a dorky personality. He could be humorous and dark, shy and aggressive by turns, a smart kid who sometimes acted dumb. He could be incessant, always interjecting, sticking his face in, jabbering manically. He could also shut himself away in his room and not talk for days. I understood this moodiness implicitly, but I never allowed my recognition to show.

Roos had two enthusiasms outside his studies: baseball and theater. He was too small for sports, but Les Perry, the athletic director, made room for him on the "B" team anyway. His tenacity and desire counted for something with Les, who had compassion for spazzmos like Roos and me.

I had a room next door to Bob. Although I teased him some along with the other kids, I was a new boy myself and not yet into the flow of casual torture that I would learn the following year. Nonetheless, I found Roos to be a constant source of annoyance which, at Webb, doubled as entertainment.

"Wynn—you got the assignment for history? I forgot the assignment. What's this—where'd you get this?" He had burst through my door without knocking and picked up my favorite copy of *Peep Show*, a particularly sophisticated magazine in which most of the women were photographed wearing carpenter's aprons and bending

over holding various-sized wrenches. The articles had titles like,
"Greta Doesn't Monkey Around" and "Mona Lays More Than Carpet." My favorite feature, "Wet Thighs, Blue Skies" had been completely obliterated during a previous loan-out.

"Roos, put that down. Don't ever come in here without knocking
again, you little rat-faced asshole. No, I don't have the assignment,
so get outa here."

"Hey, this is neat—"Livia's Lascivious"—can I have it? Are you
going to try out for the play?"

"Goddamnit Roosy, boy—am I gonna have to kill you?"

Roos flashed a sudden grin. Sometimes, when the lights were
gleaming off his glasses and he grinned, he looked like a little elf,
or a Martian. Or a Martian's pet. At those moments it was hard to
hate him. I never knew that the Greek fire that burned in my stomach
every day also glowed fiercely in his. It probably wouldn't have made
any difference if I had. I'd spent a long time learning not to feel
other people's anxiety. I had to concentrate full-time on my own.

"Here, did you see my mitt? Don't let Rogers see it, he'll wreck
it." Kem Rogers was Will Rogers's grandson. He lived across the hall
and had a running feud with Roos over just about everything.

"Nice, Roosy, boy—now you wanna get the piss outa here so I
can study?" What I wanted to do was beat off. It had been a good
three hours since I had last done so, and I was getting horny.

"Aren't you coming to the tryouts? Isn't your dad an actor? How
come you're not in the play?"

"I don't want to be in the fucking play. Why aren't you opening
a department store? Dickface."

"I got on the baseball team today. Coach Perry said I could
play."

"Who gives a fuck, Roos?" I jumped up and shoved him out the
door. He slammed into the wall across the corridor. This brought
Kem out. We tossed Roos back and forth between us for a while
like a medicine ball. He just laughed. Nothing we did to Roos that
day seemed to upset him. He was in an uncompromisingly upbeat
mood. He was in the play, he was on the team. All his dreams were
fulfilled.

That night Bob Roos hanged himself in his room. He took his
belt and looped it around his neck, tied it to the pipes near the
ceiling, then stepped off a chair. Mrs. Sumner found him the next
morning when she went to inspect his room. I had heard absolutely
nothing through the thin plywood walls. I wondered why I hadn't
heard him choking or kicking the walls. Didn't dying people do that?

It was typical of the nature of boys' schools that none of the
students seemed particularly sad about Roos's suicide. If anything
we were grateful to him for breaking up the routine. We were so

tracked in our daily lives that anything that caused a disturbance was welcomed. Our callousness was neutral and without rancor. We were too young to treat death with respect. We were just little animals feeding and sleeping and wanting to rut. Roos had simply dropped out of the herd, a smaller animal that couldn't keep up.

But I couldn't get the image out of my mind of him hanging there by his belt. I searched for a feeling, but all I could find was morbid fascination. Suicide was monstrous and final—I knew that because I had been told. But my own response was fear mixed with envy. Roos had taken control of his life. No one could make him do anything anymore. At least he didn't have to be *here* anymore.

I thought of Roos as having been very brave, while I was afraid of both life *and* death. Suicide was a very enticing idea to me, the ultimate act of defiance. But I also knew that, much as I might have liked to kill myself, I would never have the nerve to do it.

I had had my first real drink in the summer of 1956, and now, that fall, I went on my first trip to Europe. The combination was unbeatable. At fifteen I was drinking in bars in Europe like a man of forty.

Van was making his first movie in two years, a film with Martine Carole called *Action of the Tiger*. I didn't know it at the time, but his career was faltering. We still had plenty of money, and no one seemed to be worried. No doubt, back in Brentwood, Ed Wynn was looking out a window and rolling his cigar in his teeth. He was worried, but then, he was always worried.

We sailed to England on the Queen Elizabeth. We traveled in First Class where it was black-tie for dinner every night. I copied what I thought was the proper attitude for such travel from Freddie Bartholemew's spoiled rich kid in *Captains Courageous*. I swaggered along the rolling decks smoking Players' cigarettes and small cigars called Between The Acts that I had bought in the ship's kiosk. I went to the ship's gymnasium and had massages and steam baths with British and American industrialists and imagined myself on an equal footing with all of them. I drank and danced in the ship's nightclub with the daughters of Greek shipping magnates and Canadian cookie tycoons and pretended to be an American college student on his way to study at Oxford, and everyone pretended to believe me. The whole trip was like a time-out from life. Everyone was entitled to a time-out, of course, but I had begun to prefer the time-outs to the game.

In London, we had a flat at 44 Mount Street in the heart of Mayfair. I was enrolled in a tutorial school called the Davies Academy in South Kensington. Every cold gun-metal-gray morning, I would be up and out and on my way to school by seven o'clock.

Sometimes I'd actually go to class, but most times I'd only go for an hour and spend the rest of the time riding around London on the buses or the Underground. I learned absolutely nothing at the Davies Academy except how to start the little gas fire in the classroom. There, in front of the hissing orange flame, I huddled with my teacher, an impoverished young man who taught me English history. I found that he was grateful if I bought him some tea and cakes, so rather than the lesson, we'd often go to a warm restaurant in Knightsbridge near the Underground and I'd feed him with the allowance my mother gave me.

I had never seen anyone as poor as that teacher. He was a bohemian Micawber straight out of Dickens. We'd walk to the restaurant in the bleak snowy light, and he'd wave his hands excitedly, his fingers poking through the holes in his gloves, skirmishing with the snowflakes. He'd recite his knowledge of the English kings and poets, constantly tonguing the curling ends of his wispy beard from his mouth and blowing clouds of steam into the air. I enjoyed these moments the most. I wasn't learning anything, but I was enjoying the theater of education.

One day I met my teacher in the classroom and told him that I wasn't coming to school anymore. My mother had decided to send me to school in Switzerland. To my surprise he was very subdued. He stood in front of me and shivered and bit his moustache.

"What's the matter?" I asked.

"I don't have any other students," he said. The classroom was so cold that clouds billowed from his mouth even there. But today barely a trace escaped him. I suddenly had the image of a fire burning very low inside him. I gave him all the money I had left.

"I hope you get another student," I said. I was shaken. I had been that man's only source of income. Now what was he going to do? I needed another layer of insulation.

The Swiss school, whose winter campus was in a postcard town called Zermatt, was for the upper-class problem-children of Chinese, Turkish, and German millionaires. It was called Lycée Jaccard, and there the haughtiness flowed naturally, unchecked by circumstances.

I had gone there at the suggestion of a friend of Van's who owned a private gambling club in London. He was a dangerous-looking man with a patch over one eye, and his son, a six-foot-seven-inch leviathan called Tiny, was the epitome of every bad dream of every schoolyard bully from every school I'd ever been to. I was convinced he'd followed me to Europe and now he was going to get me alone in the Alps and tear my arms and legs off and leave me to die on a glacier. This was the source of all the recommendations to this school. I wondered, are these people related to the people who recommended Harvard Military Academy?

My mother beamed. "Well, Neddy, won't it be fun to be up in the mountains with your new friend Tiny?" Tiny smiled and pretended to like me just long enough to get me on a train to Switzerland. Then, once we were en route, he grabbed me and yanked me into a compartment where I was certain he would hang me from my heels out the window until we got to a tunnel. Instead, there were a half a dozen other kids from the school in the compartment. Tiny pulled out his cigarettes and his bottle of brandy and we got drunk all the way to Zermatt. It suddenly made no difference whether Tiny liked me or not, this school looked like it was going to be OK after all.

I was further heartened to find, once I arrived there, that Lycée Jaccard, full of Europe and Asia's moneyed misfits, was really just a skiing club for spoiled brats. This was the school that invented time-out. It was also the Avis of Swiss academies.

Tracy, for years forced to either follow me to schools where I had already been accepted, or to end up at schools like Black Fox Military Academy which was an even worse version of Harvard, was finally sent to Le Rosey, a top-level Swiss school where he flourished. Compared to Jaccard, Rosey was the real thing. Although it was also a skiing club for spoiled brats, it had cachet and international recognition. While Tracy skied with the children of the shah, I skied with the children of the shah's secret police. While Tracy had tea with the sons of Irish gentry and ate with the future Aga Khan, I had gin and tonic with the sons of Chinese opium exporters, Malaysian white slavers, and German watch smugglers. It was great.

As everywhere, I had my enemies. Prime among these were an Iranian named Amir and his Turkish sidekick Nahim. They were like the bulldog and the little mutt in the Warner Brothers cartoon: "Hey, Amir, wanna chase some faggy American movie star's kid? Huh, Amir? Huh? Huh? Huh?"

"*Duh*—you know where it is, an American movie star's kid?"

"Yeah yeah yeah yeah." All of this took place in Iranian-accented French. Amir could actually speak English quite eloquently. His favorite expression, with which he often greeted me was, "Hey, Americaahn, I brack you fass." Stand in line, Amir.

Then there were the Molson brothers, sons of the Canadian beer manufacturer, whose idea of a good time was to wander the streets of Zermatt with hockey sticks, looking for penalty time. They used me as a puck once in a while, to point out to the students of the local spoiled girls' school, La Grande Verger, the proper stick-work on a short-handed goal.

There were four boys whom I got along with in the school—a

Chinese named Hof Lee, an Indonesian named Farid Noor, a German named Herbert Baumann, and a Greek from South Africa
named Nicholas Penesis. We were all more or less continuously
drunk. There were no laws governing drinking by minors in Switzerland, and there wasn't a single bartender who would refuse us a
drink. My youngest drinking partner was an eleven-year-old English
boy who was drunk virtually every day. He was a small, pink-cheeked
Saxon who drank like a hunter: gin, double shots with orange
soda—and he always threw up. He evoked in me a sense of responsibility. With great fanfare and chesty self-righteousness, I instructed
the bartender, a huge blond Italian-Swiss woman named Rita, to
serve him only singles.

When the school moved back down to Rolle for the spring term,
I waited in Zermatt for Van, who was coming to fetch me. When
he arrived, he came by himself. I found that in the mountains Van
was different from the way he was at home or even in London. He
was entirely relaxed. He seemed happiest now when he was away
from the family; for one thing the duties of husband and father,
something he had prized so much a few years earlier, had become
onerous to him. The happy family in the big house with the pretty,
able wife/mother and the smart, fluffy children; all that didn't have
the savor it must have had when he envied my father a similar setup.
It was no longer what Van wanted or needed in his life. Being away
from it he could ease up. And I think that while he truly loved us,
he could only take us in short bursts and then only one at a time.

Another thing that certainly helped Van's attitude was that he
was rarely, if ever, bothered in Zermatt. Few people seemed to recognize him, and if they did they didn't show it. And no one asked
him for his autograph, something that he detested.

We are in Coronado. We are sitting at a table in the hotel restaurant. I have a steak. It's all I ever order. Tracy, incredibly, has
liver. Schuyler has a slab of roast beef. It's her obsession. Once, in
the Stage Deli in New York, Schuyler, sitting with her governess,
eight years old and quite proper, looked over the entire menu then
asked the waiter if they had any roast prime rib of beef *au jus*. It
came out *Oh Jews*. "Do you have any prime rib of beef, Oh Jews?"
Oh Ye Jews, Ye Beefy Jews?

Two people rise from their table across the hotel dining room
and confer and giggle between themselves. Then they haul their
unfortunate child out of her chair and start heading our way.

"Christ," mutters Van. Van has an uncanny ability to spot autograph seekers through walls, around buildings, on adjacent floors.
There is something about the way they hold their heads, the way
they walk, sneaking looks at him as they come, then ducking their

heads toward one another, then moving forward again, eyes glistening, half smiling, self-conscious. He can tell by their clothes, their faces, their shoulders, everything shrieks to him: We want your autograph and don't you even think about getting away.

"Jesus Christ, Evie," he says. "Autograph seekers. Here." In the Hotel Del Coronado Beverly Hills Beverly Wilshire Plaza Pierre Trois Ours Hotel Du Cap for chrissake.

"This would never happen in Claridge's," I say, ass-kisser to the throne.

"Maybe they're just on their way out of the dining room," my mother offers, soothingly. Although this is not, strictly speaking, my mother's department, she feels responsible for the happiness and well-being of all those around her including kitchen staff, security personnel, children not yet born. Van is aware, however, that this is, in fact, his department and his alone.

They arrive, the hoi polloi, the great unwashed. Van's nightmare: Joe Blow and his regrettable family. They stop right in front of our table. We're all gnawing our food. Van pretends not to see them. I have also learned to do this. I have practiced for years the art of ignoring obvious things, especially people.

"Van? Can we have your autograph?" I can see Van react: Would they have called Sir Laurence Olivier *Larry*? Hell, no. The woman has been chosen to do the talking. She thrusts the child, nine, into Van's elbow, as an offering. Terrified, the little girl stands there hoping not to be eaten. We hold our breath. This could go either way. Van could be nice, or he could explode. Or he could do his middle-ground, controlled-furious sarcastic attitude. He opts for number Three.

"Oh, sure. Why not. My pleasure. I've got nothing better to do. We're only eating dinner," he says. Everyone shifts uncomfortably. "*Eughh*," Van adds in an aside to Schuyler. *Eughh, eughh, eughh.* He takes the menu they have brought over then waits for them to hand him a pen. No one seems to have brought a pen.

"No pen?" says Van, his eyebrows searching his hairline. No balls? No tits? No money no class no style no intelligence no art no life no existence? A pen is offered by a passing waiter. Van takes it. He signs the menu grudgingly, stabbing at the page, digging into the paper. On his face is a garish smile.

"We loved that movie, *Twenty-three Paces to Baker Street*, didn't we honey?" the woman says to her husband. She glances nervously at each of us. Will we help her? She doesn't like this any more than we do, she seems to say, but it just has to be done. *Eeeughhhh.*

"Yeah, we liked it," the man chokes out. He doesn't want to compliment this asshole.

"Yeah, yeah, wonderful, great, marvelous. . . ." Van says, glaring

at them through his smile, now more of a *sourire du mort*. The
husband is not entirely stupid. He senses Van's condescension. He
works forty hours a week so his family can spend four days in a
nice resort, goddamnit, and no fucking stuck-up movie star is going
to refuse his family this little bit of pleasure. He tries to recapture
his manhood, explaining that none of this was his idea. He smiles
grimly back at Van, the impenetrable Hollywood gargoyle. Spoiled
actor sonofabitch. Too good for us? I never liked your pictures anyway. It's only for my daughter wife aunt cousin nephew. If it was
up to me I wouldn't come near you. Can you believe that, Cynth, he
didn't have a pen!

In my own case I believe that what Van wanted was that I be
an adult. He felt more comfortable around me if I acted grown up
and didn't require too much of him in the way of guidance or parental support. Money he could provide and was always quite generous in doing so. But in exchange he wanted an intelligent, funny,
urbane companion in a son, so I learned to be an intelligent, funny,
urbane companion. By now I had so many disguises I was slipping
them on and off between scenes like an apprentice in a summer
stock theater: one for Van, one for Mom, one for Dad, one for
Grandpa, and a whole series of them for my teenaged peers.

In Zermatt the disguises slipped a little. No one bothered us. I
skied with Van every day, showed him the best ski slopes, ordered
dinner in German, with great flair. It was great to be with Van under
these conditions. Neither of us had to work at our respective roles
—stepfather, stepson. For a very brief time I felt like his friend. Van
was always a tremendous faker, pretending he was glad to see you
when he wasn't. But here he was genuine, unguarded, at ease.

We stayed there two more weeks until the *föhn*, a warm wind
from Italy, melted all the remaining snow. The streets became
muddy quagmires, the ski slopes rock piles. We stared out from the
balcony of our hotel. The village was beginning to go about its
transformation from fairyland to dairyland. Cows now owned the
streets. Cowbells clattered constantly. Steaming piles of cowshit,
Zermatt's chief new product, dappled the landscape like termite
mounds in Kenya. It was time to go.

Van and I went to Geneva and boarded a plane back to the
States. The plane stopped in Copenhagen, and I decided I'd like to
get off and spend some time looking around. Van gave me some
more money and his blessings. He left me in Denmark. I never saw
him that happy again. By the time I got back to Webb, Van had
become distant and withdrawn. I had no idea why, but the strain
was showing in his relationship with my mother. They were to stay
together another five years.

*   *   *

There is a crash from downstairs. I hear it. Muffled shouts, a scream. I lie in bed remembering similar sounds from years before. Fathers and mothers. Rats in the walls. But I'm older now, and I know what it is. This time it's stepfathers and mothers. I sit up in bed. I should do something. I should get up and go downstairs and save my mother. I should. But I don't.

Outside the streets are quiet. The palm trees rattle softly on Foothill Road. A car stops at the stop sign on Lomitas, then pulls away. Somewhere people are sleeping.

There's another shout. That's Van. Then a crash. Later I learn that he has thrown my mother over a table and onto the floor. Then he has thrown a chair at her. I silently vow to God and to myself that from now on I'll be the man in the house. I give myself a tearful pep talk. I'll be the man, I'll take care of my mother. From now on things will be different. I convince myself that I have done something good, even though I have not moved a muscle. I can save the world. But I'll do it from my bedroom tonight.

CHAPTER

I pick up a copy of the *Hollywood Citizen News*. On the front page there is a photograph of a man on the roof of a tiny one-story West Hollywood bungalow. He stands there silhouetted against the sky, his thin arms waving at the camera. His staring eyes are huge, amok. On his mouth is a strangulated grimace. Below him in the street the police stand uneasily. What's this nut gonna do? The caption reads: MAN THREATENS TO JUMP. HOLDS OFF COPS FOUR HOURS BEFORE SURRENDERING. I have to look twice. Yes. Yes. That's Uncle Sherry, all right. Hey, Mom. . . .

Sherry the beatnik. My father couldn't stand him. My stepfather pretended he didn't exist. Of course, my stepfather pretended my mother's whole family didn't exist. As for Mom, she loved him, but didn't know what to do with him. Tracy, Schuyler, and I adored him. His name was Sheridan Abbott Kimmel and he was my mother's younger brother.

The West Hollywood standoff was, in fact, not a suicide attempt, although he had a number of those. "I was hiding my stash," Sherry told me later. "I just bought five hundred bennies and I was trying to stash them when the goddamned cops saw me on the roof. I was hiding the pills behind some bricks in the chimney and they saw me. They got suspicious. I guess I look suspicious. Do I look suspicious, Edmond Keenan, nephew Neddy, oh nephew o' mine?" He clawed the air in front of his face and bugged his eyes out like a monster.

"Not to me." Who has roomed next door to Martians. No, sir.

"Well—I had to threaten I'd jump or they would have found the bennies. So instead of going to jail, they sent me to the V.A. for observation. I don't know what's worse, a cell full of pissed-off spades or a room full of guys that think they're Studebakers."

When Uncle Sherry was fifteen my grandmother had signed a piece of paper stating that he was seventeen. This allowed him to join the U.S. Marine Corps. He went to boot camp at Paris Island, Louisiana, and at sixteen he was flying missions in the South Pacific as a tail-gunner on a bomber. One day, somewhere in the Pacific, the air around this young gunner began to boil and turn red, and white, and black. Bodies billowed, rose, erupted, and showered softly back down on him in a grainy mist. Bits of skin and bone, woven suddenly into the khaki, rubber, and canvas splattered the sand and caught on his clothing and in his hair. These were the bodies of his friends.

He received a shrapnel wound from the exploding steel. The tiny piece of metal lodged in his brain and could not be removed. It floated there and waited. Now and then it shifted slightly, like the ground near a fault. These shifts, the doctors postulated, might be causing some of these mood swings of his, these "problems." They called it battle fatigue. Of course, they said, he might just have been crazy from the start.

Sherry was a cat, a cool cat. He was also one crazy mixed-up kid. Whenever he was around, my mother would be checking my eyes for dope. When the New Pharmacopeia came out in the fifties my mother was in the forefront of prescribed-for patients: Miltown to relax, Dexamyl to get skinny, Placidyl to rest, Darvon for menstrual pain, phenobarbital and chloral hydrate for that awful insomnia. The doctors were ecstatic. It was as if they no longer had to treat patients, just prescribe for them and go home early. The wait to tee up on the first hole at the Bel-Air Country Club was murder.

I learned which pills did what by listening and sampling. I didn't need Sherry to show me. My mother was convinced that since Sherry was on dope and I hung around with him, I was, too. Of course, she was right. Every time she walked out of the house Sherry and I dove into her medicine cabinet and all her drawers, including a false-seated hassock in the guest bathroom where she hid dozens of pill bottles. Then we picked the lock on the liquor cabinet and stole a bottle of vodka or bourbon. Sometimes we sat down and drank it right there while we discussed life on other planets, poetry, Buddhism, and black magic. Nonetheless, I had to deny it.

"Jeez, Mom, just because Sherry takes Benzedrine doesn't mean that I'm on dope. Jeez." I was wounded. I would cry and scream at my mother for accusing me of such things. My mother would ultimately back off. I had learned to intimidate her by using an intense and seasoned fury complete with tears, and I never relented until I had won. For a moment I actually believed it myself, even though the fact of the matter was that I was guilty as charged. The whole time I was screaming indignantly I was scheming on how to steal more pills.

There were periods when Sherry would shake off his drug habit, go dry, and then make a fresh start. He made lots of fresh starts. But he couldn't stay clean for more than a few months at a time. As a result, he was always at the end of a long sigh or an expletive from my father.

"Sherry ferblunget Abbott," he called him.

"Why don't you like Uncle Sherry, Dad?"

"Because he's a complete fuckup," said my father. "He's fer-blunget."

"Wasn't that the nickname Jimmy Backus gave you in summer stock?"

"All right, friend, simmer down." When Dad got really angry at me he called me friend.

Sherry wrote short stories—some of it pornographic science fiction in which small, naked, green women figured prominently—and poetry. He sometimes spent months in the desert near Palm Springs where he rode in Martian and Venusian space craft, searched for uranium, had sex with aliens, and ate peyote with the local Indians. What Sherry had really done and what he had only imagined he had done were often inseparable. It was easier to simply believe everything.

I remember picking him up at Synanon one weekend. He was on a pass. Chuck Diedrich, the monomaniac who ran Synanon, had recently decided that all recovering addicts there would shave their heads. "What's it like in there?" I asked as we drove off toward Beverly Hills.

"It's very weeeeird. Diedrich is very sicko. He's a Nazi. A Fuehrer. Hitler. And his little army of sycophant fags who do his bidding are also sicko creeps. Little fascist homosexual dyke faggot gnomes." He recounted tales of a rigorous, military mentality in the place. Cold showers, punishment, isolation. "It's the goddamned Marines all over again."

"Why are you staying there?"

He looked at me and bared his teeth. "I believe I'm beginning to make people nervous," he shrieked. "Especially Van Johnson and Keenan Wynn." Sherry had a wry attitude toward his sister's husbands. "How's my famous brother-in-law Van Johnson the movie star today? How *is* Laughing Boy?"

Sherry showed me, gave me, or told me about the following things: aliens, tarot cards, the cabala, flying saucers, uranium, Geiger counters, bennies, the blues, rhythm and blues, Louis Jordan records, the "Hungarian Suicide Song," a model engine for my train set, poetry, beatniks, Venice, a Purple Heart, an army jeep, a 1950 Plymouth, Henry Miller's *Rosy Crucifixion*, dirty pictures, Hoagy Carmichael.

What I did for Sherry was learn to treat him like the other adults in his life treated him. I learned to condescend to him. The last time I saw him I was twenty-two and far too old to be sucked into his Peter Pan crazy bullshit anymore. I had my own apartment. I was serious, grown-up, nobody's fool. I could no longer communicate with him.

Four years later, he was dead. He was forty years old. In the end he was out there. "Way out, nephew Neddy, way waaaay out." A schizophrenic alter ego of his, a demonic character he called Boris Bel or simply Baal, and another interior personality, the Egyptian god Horus, kept him awake night after night with their automatic writing, urging him to take more drugs.

My mother told me he was sitting in bed reading the newspaper when he died of a brain hemorrhage. From the little sliver of steel that caressed his frontal lobe with its thousand tiny burrs? From the drugs he had been given in the Veterans' Administration Hospital where he had been treated like a guinea pig? From three million bennies? From the Stelazine dextroamphetamine Percodan Codeine Millaryl Thorazine that Boris Bel told him to take? From conjuring Baal and Horus and Thoth? From the flak dreams, the floating black cotton behind his eyes that made him whimper and skitter in his sleep like a dog by a fire or hang in the air by his fingernails at the slightest noise? Sherry died from a lot of things. But mostly I think he died from exhaustion. It's wearying to live like that for forty years. It took a monumental effort to last that long, and finally it burned him up.

Sherry is standing in front of the open refrigerator. Delphine, the cook, a black leather thong of a woman from Nassau, "Nassau Bahamas," she always says, sits shelling peas and watching Sherry carefully. She knows him well. He stands and stares for several minutes at the food in the icebox. Delphine starts getting nervous.

"Sherry—what you doing? You letting all the cold air out the refrigerator. Shut that door." Sherry turns to her thoughtfully.

"Do you wonder sometimes," he asks, "if chicken is the tuna of the sky?"

Good-bye, beloved uncle. Crazy, man. Craaaaaazy.

In 1958, five weeks past my seventeenth birthday, I graduated from high school. My parents, in a convulsive twitch of relief mixed with an intriguing sense of proportion, gave me a brand-new Jaguar XK-150. Red with black leather seats. My father drove it out to the school that day. Slowly, so that the trees cast silvery ripples on the long shiny hood, he drove it down the narrow road past the dormitories. Everyone gaped. Jackie Hathaway punched my arm.

"Is *that* your new car?" he asked.

"Yeah," I said.

"Jesus." He stared. I thought, what's the big deal? He's a director's son. His parents had a lot more money than mine did. Where was *his* Jag?

I felt a strange mixture of excitement and self-consciousness.

And anxiety. Behind the wheel, my father's face was clenched like a fist. Don't scratch it, don't crash it, here's the goddamned Jaguar. Will this please the kid? Will this please his mother? Will this please the world? The Ed Wynn inside him was certainly not pleased. This was an exorbitant, ridiculous gift for a high school graduate to be getting. It reminded him, no doubt, of his own over-gifted growing-up in which he had been given, among other things, three speedboats and a Bugatti. What no one realized except, perhaps, my father, was that although I wanted the car very badly, as any kid would, part of me wished it would just disappear. The meter that monitored my particular conflict, that of wanting to be special while at the same time hoping to blend in with the crowd, was redlining on this one.

As with most things in my life, I could never absorb the results of my own cravings. Through the years this had become most apparent at Christmas, one of the single most gut-wrenching, stomach-turning times of all. Every Christmas, it seemed, Van the *Huffmeister* would get the ball rolling by blowing up and storming out. Once he had raced upstairs and slammed the requisite number of doors over something that pissed him off, something that had obviously been simmering in him all morning, but had been left unspoken, we would all guess fruitlessly at what it might be. Were we too loud? Did we get up too early? Was the tree not tall enough? It was impossible for us to know what was wrong, and Mom, her smile newly Turtle-waxed, would offer no clues. After that we tried to recapture the mythical Christmas moment.

The first thing we did was to pretend that Van hadn't really left at all. Quietly, by unspoken mutual assent, we pretended that some-how he was really still in the room with us, sitting nearby enjoying this Child's Christmas in Beverly Hills with the rest of us. We fash-ioned a kind of dummy of Van, a pleasant, cheerful guy, tolerant, patient, happy with Christmas, happy with Mom, happy with us. We had all known that guy, or a guy like that, not that long ago. So we propped him up in our memories while the real Van sat in bed upstairs behind his freshly slammed bedroom door fiercely watching television and eating marshmallow peanuts. Sometimes the bed-room wasn't far enough. If he was really pissed, he went into the back bedroom, also known as the Farley Granger room, because Farley had spent the night there once and ended up staying two weeks. From time to time Van would simply leave the house alto-gether and take a bungalow at the Beverly Hills Hotel. It didn't need to be Christmas for that. Any day was a good day for the Beverly Hills Hotel. I imagined him sitting in his bed in his bungalow with a box of chocolate-pecan turtles and marshmallow peanuts watching television while the world went up in flames.

Once we had fashioned that charade to suit us, we entered the next phase: getting tons of stuff because we were us. This brought me into contact with a strange and abiding dilemma: No matter how profuse the cascade of gifts beneath the enormous tree in the entry hall was, it was never enough. I would race from package to package, tearing off the paper in a kind of mindless frenzy, a gluttony it seemed, for the sound of tearing paper. I'd briefly engage the contents of the package, play with it ritually, then set it aside and tear into another one. Ten, twenty, thirty presents would not suffice. When the last one was opened I always experienced the same let-down, the same gnawing depression. Wasn't there just one more present to fling into the chasm? Something from an aunt in Florida, perhaps? A flannel shirt? A belt? Anything? One more sacrifice to throw King Kong, the Stuff Needer?

The car was like these presents. Even down to the anger my father showed, an echo of Van's. Was that it? Did our parents resent their children for their easy lives? Or did they resent themselves for providing us with those lives? I had been reminded often in my life that other children didn't have as much as I did. That I was lucky to have so much. It began to feel as if each thing was given with a little tag reading: undeserved and unearned. Of course I knew I hadn't earned it, but then, I had never earned anything. How did a person earn something? By getting good grades and getting accepted by an Ivy League school? I had been accepted at the University of Pennsylvania. I got a Jag. What would I have gotten had I been accepted at Harvard? A yacht? A private plane? And how did one get the money to pay for these things? I had no idea, and I wasn't about to start worrying about that detail now. My life was effortless, it seemed. All I had to do to pay for things was to live quietly with a perpetual little bonfire in my stomach, a fire that I had learned, through a variety of stratagems, to work around. And it had its compensations. I had made myself the center of attention by doing absolutely nothing.

Behind the Jag, in a new black Fleetwood, were Mom and Van, the latter extremely uncomfortable at the prospect of being out in the open, like an antelope who had wandered into the middle of a safari, fair game for heavy-breathing moms and dads. With them was my father's third wife, my stepmother Sharley. And behind them in his Rolls, Tyrone Power and his wife, Debbie. I had the market cornered that day: I had all the movie stars, and the best cars. I didn't know it, but at seventeen, I had peaked.

The only one missing at my graduation was Ed Wynn. I had wanted him to give the commencement address, but another class-mate's grandfather was chosen by the faculty instead. James Easton, the class brain, was the grandson of Will and Ariel Durant, and Will

Durant was to be the speaker. It would have been spectacular, I thought, if both grandfathers had addressed the graduates, a kind of Dueling Grandpas.

> **DURANT:** Ed, did you know that Marx was an inconsistent follower of Hegel?
>
> **WYNN:** No I didn't, Will, but I know that we got good Marx for our party the other night. In fact, I was told it was one Hegel of a good time.
>
> **DURANT:** You misunderstand, Ed. What I'm talking about is the concept of thesis, antithesis, and synthesis.
>
> **WYNN:** You don't say. Thesis something I gotta see.
>
> **DURANT:** What I'm trying to establish here, Ed, is that the struggle of socialism against capitalism is part of the historic rhythm in the concentration and dispersion of wealth.
>
> **WYNN:** Wealth. That reminds me of the Depression, Will. Things were cheaper then, remember? Even doctors were charging less. We got a nine-pound baby for eight bucks.
>
> **DURANT:** Well, that's what happens when less money chases more goods, Ed.
>
> **WYNN:** Soooo . . . that's why I had less money . . . and my wife had more goods.
>
> **DURANT:** Umm, figuratively speaking.
>
> **WYNN:** Oh, she had a great figure all right. And every guy on Broadway was chasing it. Hoo-hoo. Play that, Don.

The room was stifling. There was dust on everything. Ty Power sat in the chair by the battered desk and looked at me. "I'm proud of you," he said. "You're going to be a terrific writer, Neddy." He and I were sitting in my room at Webb after the ceremonies. He handed me a box. "You can take this to Penn with you when you go." I took more time than usual unwrapping it. It was a typewriter. An Olivetti portable. My name, Edmond Keenan Wynn, was engraved on the case.

"Wow, thanks, Ty," I said.

"Write me a letter on it once in a while, willya?" he asked. "I'd love to know how it goes back there. I know you'll do great at whatever you decide you want to be."

What I decided to be. I had never decided to be anything. Every-

thing in my life to that point had simply happened to me. It seemed
I had been naturally intelligent enough to absorb enough knowledge
to pass the College Boards and get into the University of Pennsylvania. Eventually, I knew in a foggy way, one went out and got
something called a career. But I had no idea what a career was or
how one went about securing one.

The man sitting on my chair in my room had a career. He was
a big star. I had never given the slightest thought to how he got
there. The same was true of my father and grandfather and stepfather. They all had careers. I assumed that you simply got one after
a certain amount of time, naturally, like getting older. The Popcorn
Theory. By the time I became aware of them, they were all very
famous, established men. I knew the stories of how they had become
actors, about summer stock, about the early days in movies. But in
my mind, I filtered out the struggle. After all, I had never seen it. I
knew nothing of process, only result. For me, desire equaled gratification, there was nothing between them. Therefore, I reasoned, it
would be much simpler for me. I was gifted, lucky, I knew people.
How could I have any trouble in the world? Actors acted. Writers
wrote. In fact, it seemed so natural and easy and proper than I would
just slide into the family business without trying. After all, my
mother had told me I was handsomer than Jimmy Stewart. What
else did I need to know?

"How tall are you, Ned."
"How tall do you want me to be?"
I'm talking to a casting director. I've made my first career move,
and a beauty it is. In order to learn about acting and being in the
movie business, I am to become a movie extra. The flaw in this idea
is on the level of getting a job as a popcorn vender at a ballpark in
preparation for becoming a pitcher. It's true you toss the bags to
the customers, but it's not quite on the order of a fastball down the
middle.

Being an extra was not a career springboard. It was more like
jumping off the side into an empty pool. But it was also the first
time I had ever really worked in the world and drawn a paycheck,
however haphazard, based upon hours worked at a particular scale.
At that time the pay was less than twenty dollars a day. But there
were always adjustments or "bumps" for doing little special things.
There was money for getting wet, money for being around fire or
explosions, money for being in a three-shot with the principal players, money for interacting with certain props, for wearing formal
clothes or costumes, for wearing body makeup, driving a car, riding
a skateboard. There were "silent bits," money for actually partici-
pating in a scene as part of the story, and then "bits" which involved

lines. The dream was to get a line. That was when you worked on your "A" card, your Screen Actors Guild Card. When you shifted jurisdictions, from Screen Extras Guild to Screen Actors Guild, it meant you were in the bucks.

I got a lot of lines tossed my way by friendly directors who knew or had worked with my father, stepfather, or grandfather. Someone usually saw my name on the call sheet, told the director, and he would make sure I got a line. When my father got a television series called *The Troubleshooters*, I worked on it. As an extra, of course. The director of most of the shows, Robert Altman, made sure I got lines. Whenever I worked a show with Bob I made good money. I was a regular out-of-focus shadow on a lot of shows Bob directed, mostly series, like *Combat*. For a few years I thought I was really working in the business. Basically, it was because of directors like Bob Altman looking out for me.

I worked one whole summer on *The Troubleshooters*. Dad was the star, of course, and his costar was Bob Mathias. Bob Mathias was famous for having come roaring out of the San Joaquin Valley in 1948 and again in 1952 to win the Decathlon championship in both the London and Helsinki Olympics.

"He's good, he's really surprising me with how good he really is, seriously. I'm actually quite amazed. He's really quite good." My father is trying to convince my grandfather that Bob Mathias can act. Grandpa shifts his cigar in his mouth. I chip in.

"Yeah. He really is. Bob Mathias is really good, Grandpa," I say. "You'd probably think he'd be no good, but actually, all things considered, why, he's really pretty . . . good. . . ." Grandpa is not convinced.

"Why didn't you get Lee Marvin to costar with you, Keenan?" he asks, his head starting to shake.

"Lee's gonna have his own series, Pop." Dad quickly goes behind the bar and pours himself a large vodka. "How about a drink, Pop? Bourbon and water?"

"It's a little early, isn't it, Keenan?" My throat is crying silently for the bourbon, but I don't want Grandpa to think I drink this early in the day. Also, it makes me feel slightly superior to Dad, which is a good, warm feeling.

"He's gonna be a huge star, Lee Marvin," continues Grandpa.

"He already is, Pop. I couldn't get Lee Marvin."

"You ride motorcycles with these guys, you get drunk with them. But when you need 'em to be in your series, they're gone. They got better things to do."

"Pop, I have probably one of the best directors around. Bob Altman. What do you want?"

"Bob Altman's a wonderful guy and I like him very much,

Keenan, but he's not a name director. Why not get Ralph Nelson?" Dad poured another vodka, dropped his jaw, clicked his tongue, and drank the whole glass in one gulp.

My grandfather knew who was who in television now that he had made a comeback. My father was kicking himself for ever having convinced him to take another shot. Ed Wynn's professional life, in decline throughout the early fifties, had suddenly resurfaced when José Ferrer and my father talked him into appearing in a small part in a movie Ferrer was directing called *The Great Man*. After that, Dad, who was doing a lot of live television, coached Grandpa through a part that was the turning point of his career, the part of the old trainer in Rod Serling's *Requiem for a Heavyweight*. Both Rod and the director, Ralph Nelson, wanted him out of the production. They were terrified he'd ruin it. Only Martin Manulis, the producer, stuck with the choice of Ed Wynn. It worked. He won an Emmy. Now he was giving Dad advice all over again.

"Ralph Nelson's a great director. Why not let me call Ralph for you, Keenan—or let Rod Serling rewrite it for you?"

"Thanks, Pop, but believe me, Bob Altman's a great director. The show's fine. Everything's fine."

"You're too easy, Keenan. Some guy is nice to you, and you think he's the greatest guy you ever met."

Grandpa was right about Bob Mathias. He was an incredibly nice guy, but basically he couldn't act scared in front of a firing squad. I knew he was bad, but I knew something else even more frightening: I was worse.

"Ned!" Bob Altman is giving me my line. "I want you to cut the engine on the cat, jump down, run across the road and yell up to Keenan, 'They found the kid!' OK?"

"OK, Bob," I say. I never really understood the concept of the show except that it seemed to be about guys who drove earth-moving equipment, leapt off the earth-moving equipment and climbed on motorcycles, rode motorcycles, leapt off the motorcycles, and went into mobile homes, studied surveys, drank coffee and sometimes got into fistfights in the mobile homes, leapt out of the mobile homes and got back onto the earth-moving equipment. In between, these guys ran off evil developers, saved wild animals, and found kids. It could have been called "The Good Contractors."

It was a nightmare for the sound man because of all the incessant engine noise. "How's that for sound!" Bob is yelling at the sound man. The sound man just nods and leans back in his chair and gazes at the sky. He can't hear a fucking thing. "All right," shouts Bob. "Let's roll it."

"Rrrrollling!" the A.D. is screaming. I sit in the caterpillar tractor, which is roaring at idle. I place an expression of grave concern on my face as I stare, hopefully like a hawk, off into the distance.

"Is sound rolling?" Bob shouts at the A.D.

"Sound! Are you rolling?" The sound man squints. "We're on a roollll!" The sound man grins.

"Speeeed!" he calls back gleefully.

"Action!" yells Bob. I don't hear him. I'm staring, hawklike, into the distance.

Bob has a dangerous heart condition, so he is trying to keep calm. He begins waving his arms at me. I've been told that Bob has a year to live. With luck, he won't lose more than a weekend on this shot. He starts jumping up and down, but I'm mesmerized now by the thrumming vibrations in the caterpillar engine, and I've about passed out from the fumes. My hawklike Indian stare isn't paying off. Finally, Bob catches my eye. He's flapping like a seagull and mouthing soundless obscenities. Gosh, he's not dying, is he? No. It's just "action."

I start to move, but I can't get out of the tractor seat. My ankle jams up in the half-dozen gear levers that fence in the cat's seat. I can't get off the tractor. I struggle for about ten seconds and finally free myself. It'll look good, I tell myself, it'll look . . . *real*. When I finally hit the ground I have forgotten something.

"Shut the goddamn tractor off!" yells the A.D. Shit.

"Cut!!!"

"Cut!!!"

"Cuuuuttttttt! Fucking shit."

"Let's run it with the tractor off, OK?" says Bob, smiling affably. Bob Altman is the nicest director in the business. He has to be. He's going to die any minute.

"I can shut it off, Bob," I say.

"Forget it. Easier if we just shoot it with the tractor off."

"OK," I say. We shoot this all afternoon. It takes half a day. Bob doesn't even bother to do a single on me when I'm supposed to tell Dad about the kid. If you don't get your single, it's not a good sign. I'll probably dub it later, in the studio.

"Too loud out here. Planes and stuff," Bob says. "You were fine, Ned. Just fine. We'll loop it. You were great." He smiles at me and gives me a big "O" with his finger and thumb. I smile. I was just fine. I don't ask him about my single.

The Troubleshooters was canceled, but I had made a dangerous and devastating discovery about extra work: I could screw around. I could make a small living and screw around. It was easy. There were few if any demands. I fell into the extra syndrome like a smooth stone. My life settled into a pattern that would hold for many years to come: Seek out the easy, pass on the difficult.

As an extra I only worked when I wanted to. We called in for work on a special number to one of several casting agencies. If there was work, I got a job, if not, I didn't. If there was no work, I went to the beach. Often, if there was work, I still went to the beach. I had rediscovered Will Rogers State Beach, five minutes from where I had grown up in the Santa Monica Canyon.

It was a classic Southern California beach, brown sand littered with broken glass and condoms, beer cans, bottle tops, and popsicle sticks. Across the Pacific Coast Highway, the sidewalks of the Canyon were sticky with Milky Ways and chewing gum; the booths at Roy's hamburger stand were slick with ketchup and french fry grease, and in the King Surf, later the Queen Surf in deference to the burgeoning gay clientele, the men's room was awash with piss and beer while the air reeked of barf and shuddered to the sounds of the Beach Boys and the screams of aging surf Nazis drunk on vodka tonics and Gallo wine. I couldn't think of a better place to spend the rest of my life.

I met a lot of people on the beach. I learned to smoke dope there in 1960. I used to see Uncle Sherry sometimes in the bars in the Canyon and get high with him. He gave me his jeep one summer when he took a sabbatical in Venice. I grew a goatee. I rode motorcycles with my father and Lee Marvin. And sometimes I worked as an extra. But not if the weather was good and the waves were hot.

I learned the drill quickly. You work just long enough to qualify for unemployment, then hustle over to Fifth and Broadway in Santa Monica to pick up your unemployment check. The unemployment maximum at the time was fifty-five dollars a week, and most extras qualified for that amount. The unemployment office became known as Club 55. If someone left the beach, he was usually going to Club 55 to collect his money. Then he'd come back to the beach and work on that tan. I lived on extra work and unemployment, sometimes working and collecting unemployment simultaneously, until they caught me. The sentence was suspension for a specified period and then reinstatement. While you were suspended you just worked a little more. It was a beautiful system.

For others, those who weren't afraid to spend the odd week in jail, there were less socially acceptable trades. Some were dealers, some were whores, others were thieves. Some, like me, continued to live at home and sponge off our exhausted parents like huge cuckoo babies that have outgrown the nest but can't leave it. With that kind of security I could continue with the pretense: Everything in my life was fine. College all winter, beach all summer. Eventually, in an effort to close the nanosecond of anxiety that sometimes appeared between desire and gratification, I dropped the college charade and made the beach my permanent waking abode.

The great thing about State Beach was that a person's professional status plus a dollar would buy him a cheeseburger and a chocolate malt. What counted wasn't what you did anywhere else, but what you were then and there, on the beach. This was before Free Speech, hippies, Transactional Analysis, recovery programs, Transcendental Meditation, the Beatles, Gay Lib, Womens' Lib, any Lib. Instead of "I'm OK, you're OK," it was more like, "We're OK, but who the fuck are you?"

A lot of actors hung out at State Beach only to find out that their status there was zip. Actors and celebrities tried for years to fit in with the hip crowd that camped around the "A" volleyball court at State Beach. These were the coolest of the cool. To be able to put your towel down among this group was the signal of acceptance into the absolutely hippest of societies. It pleased me to be accepted there when successful actors like Peter Lawford and Doug McClure could only hop eagerly around the edges. In fact, it was beach lore that Peter had bought a house on the beach and then gone and invited his brother-in-law, the President of the United States, down for a swim just to try and break into the group. For this egregious behavior Peter was labeled a kook.

There was a kind of subtle discrimination going on. If you had a career that worked, it meant that you worked, and if you worked, you didn't belong.

This world suited me. I wanted to feel superior to people who were succeeding in life, and in this perverse atmosphere of sybaritic surfoids and vitriolic volleybums the world was turned upside down. Success was failure, work was death.

On the beach, no one asked me about my parents. No one asked me what I was doing with my life. It was the Underachievers Bar and Grill and I had a permanent stool reserved. Being tan was a leg up. If you knew how to catch a wave and roll a joint, you knew enough. The feel of sun and salt water on my skin was reassurance that I was living right. Questions regarding my plans for the future, usually asked by my mother as I fled out the door every day, were met with a version of the fury I had developed over the dope issue. Don't ask me, goddamnit. Leave me alone. I had found, I thought, a way to ease the Greek fire, to keep it low and comfortable.

I was primed for a life of hanging out. I believed that I had mastered a great trick. I was still, in my mind, a prince of the town, a young duke whose invitation to the ball would always be good. Whenever I wanted to, I could take my life in hand and start that career up like my dad's Triumph. Everything was waiting for me. When I was ready, I'd just jump on, crank the kick-starter, and haul ass. I simply wasn't ready yet.

CHAPTER
9

In the next four years, I went to five different universities. What I learned in those five years following graduation from Webb was that, despite having the best education money could buy and dozens of bright, brilliant, successful role models, I had absolutely no idea what I was doing. I drifted from one college to another, one city to another, one country to another. I went to school with thousands of people who seemed to know exactly what they were doing and where they were headed. We went to classes together, played sports together, went to parties together, went on vacations together, got drunk together. They had majors and stuck to them. I had a different major every year. They graduated, I didn't. They drove off into their futures with jobs and wives and kids, smiling confidently, waving happily at an admiring world. I stood there with my mouth hanging open, fumbling for the keys while my parents allayed their anxiety with the bland assumption that tradition would assert itself and I would eventually become an actor. College was simply something for the résumé, something particularly cunning for an actor to have done. I wasn't any closer to becoming an actor, of course, but the Popcorn Effect was certain to take care of that. Results were guaranteed.

Every summer from the time I was sixteen, in between bouts of schooling, I hung out with my best friend Doug Tibbles, who lived in Westwood near the UCLA campus. We shot pool and snooker all morning at the bowling alley then went to State Beach and body-surfed all afternoon. Occasionally, we would venture out into the rich cultural landscape of L.A., which included the Griffith Park Observatory, the zoo, and the La Brea tar pits, a great place to drink beer and wax philosophic on the Pleistocene. When extra work was slow we spent our days usurping the territory of the local eight-year-olds by walking the neighborhood collecting pop bottles in a kid's wagon and turning them in for a few bucks at a local liquor store. With that money we could get a couple of double-cheese-burgers, a Pepsi, and go to the show at the Bruin. We did all this to the withering get-a-job stares of home owners standing in their driveways watching us trundle our wagon down the street. They didn't realize we were not only performing a service, we were researching life.

"Let 'em get their own goddamn wagon," Doug said.

125

"Fuckin-A rights," I said. "They're the ones with all these pop bottles stacked in their garages in the first place." Where would they be without a couple of enterprising self-starters like ourselves? Hip deep in empty pop bottles, that's where.

Doug was the son of George Tibbles, a television writer who had created a show called *Life With Elizabeth*, the world's first sitcom, starring Betty White, and later a very successful show called *My Three Sons*. But what we most admired George for was "The Woody Woodpecker Song," which he had cowritten and for which he had been nominated for an Academy Award. It was Doug who had come up with our life theme: Why don't we get paid just for being us? After all, we had punched in the day we were born, and we were always on the clock. Doug and I stuck like glue.

While at Webb I had always sought out the real guys in the public schools, and Doug, who went to Uni, was one of my finds. University High School was the coolest school on the Westside of L.A. While Venice High was tougher and had more car clubs, Uni was cooler. And the girls were cuter. So I began to hang around with Uni High people like Doug, Tim Newman, Alfred's son and Randy's cousin, Richard Lang, whose father was Walter Lang the director, Jim Mitchum, Robert's son, and a bunch of guys who personified everything I wanted to be. There was Dick Westbrook who taught me to double-clutch and downshift my Jag, and his sister, Carol, whom we called Sis, who taught me to make out, and Vickie Coe who looked like Mitzi Gaynor and who also taught me to make out. There was Sonny Daubenburger who graciously allowed me to watch him work on his Corvette in Joe Stanley's garage for hours on end, a rare privilege. There was Joe Stanley himself who invited me to sit in his parents' driveway in their house on Sunset Boulevard for more hours, a very cool place to sit and drink beer every night. Of course everyone was bored shitless, but no one ever admitted it. It was a kind of Zen exercise. We sat there until Joe's parents couldn't stand it anymore and screamed at us to get out. Then we drove to the Goody-Goody Drive-In in Santa Monica and continued to park for a few more hours.

At the Goody-Goody it was very cool if you lucked out and got to park next to Jack McGinity and his girlfriend Nancy Sinatra as they sat, the prince and princess, in her red Corvette. Jack had a watch, a Patek Phillipe or something, thin as a dime, that was inscribed "To Jack from Dad." Dad was Frank Sinatra. Big Frank, to us. It was beyond cool. It was almost beyond bitchen.

For variety one night, Pat O'Neal, who later changed his name to Ryan and became an actor, took me to a Flywheels party, the Flywheels being a local car club. I remember standing there, untouched through some kind of divine intervention, or more simply because Pat was standing next to me, in the middle of the biggest fistfight I had ever seen. I had a very healthy respect for violence ever since being cold-cocked by Debbie Daves in the second grade, and I wanted no part of anything that was being offered. There were dozens of red-faced white boys, screaming black hookers, ankle-deep beer, and bright, shocking blood. It occurred to me after an hour or so in which the violence seemed to ebb and flow around me like an endless brawl in a Western movie, that it was the whole point of the party. Pat nodded cheerfully. "We have 'em about once a week," he said. "Wanna join?"

Pat was the best pure fighter in the school, a trained boxer, and he reveled in what he called "punch-outs." There were some very scary guys around, mostly Irish guys like Pat, a rarity in Southern California. Two in particular I remember were Danny O'Mahoney and Eddie Sullivan. They were members of a vanishing breed, the tough white guy.

I'd never seen a real street fight until I watched these two guys in a couple of fights in the State Beach parking lot. It almost always worked the same way. They singled out someone who looked likely. I could never get the criteria straight. Maybe the guy buttoned his shirt wrong, or smoked the wrong brand of cigarette, or maybe his haircut pissed them off. There were lots of hidden crimes in high school, crimes you never knew you were committing until someone ran over you in his car.

Once chosen, they smiled and talked very calmly and insultingly to the victim until they were standing just to the side of him. Usually, he was another hardass himself, some very pissed-off guy who wanted to engage in preliminary chest shoving. Danny and Eddie weren't interested in that protocol. In a chilling explosion, one or the other would suddenly punch the guy from the blind side. They never squared off. They just hit. I realized then that there was no "fair chance." Guys who had been brought up using their fists didn't bother with taunts and tough posturing. They smiled and hit without warning. The fights never lasted long. I saw Sullivan break a guy's arm one night after getting a light for his cigarette. I always smiled very big when I talked to Eddie and Danny. And I kept them right in front of me. For some reason I got along OK with these guys. It was like a line in the Beach Boys' song, "Get Around": ". . . all the bad guys know us and they leave us alone . . ."

They knew me; I was a clown and a wimp, so they let me live.

In deep contrast there was college. I was the only one in that group I knew of who went East. After an initial flurry of registration

and attendance in my classes, I found that I could do pretty much
as I pleased in college, a disastrous discovery. I was a natural chameleon by this time and did not have difficulty fitting into the society
of students at the University of Pennsylvania, different though they
were from my friends at Uni. I pledged what I considered to be the
most socially irresponsible of the fraternities there, a toss-up between Beta Theta Pi, the Betas, and Delta Kappa Epsilon, the Dekes.
Two classmates from Webb, Franklyn Robbins, Joe Fidanque, and
I chose the Betas.

Being from Southern California, we were welcomed there as
examples of an alien culture. The Beta brothers were clearly enthralled with both our manner of dress, which consisted of levis,
T-shirts, and tennis shoes, and speech, which included the then-
unheard-of epithet "bitchen," unheard of east of the Rockies any-
how. The word *bitchen* was strictly a West Coast phenomenon at
that time, and it may have gotten us into the house. Bitchen babes,
bitchen game, bitchen day—the brothers loved to listen to us say
bitchen. It was kind of like me hearing the little Coronado/South
Bay girls using proto-Valspeak that summer. It was so—bitchen,
somehow.

I clearly remember staggering from the Beta house the day I
pledged over to the Dekes, a drink in my hand, to cry on the shoulders
of my Deke friends that I loved them, and that while they had a
better bar and a great jukebox that played "Sea Cruise" a hundred
and forty times a day, the Betas had a better location: They were
only half a block from Smokey Joe's Cafe, a bar and deli where a
whiskey sour cost fifty cents, came in a tumbler, and was the color
of dark Colombian coffee.

I often sat in the student cafeteria at seven-thirty in the morning
after a night at Smokey Joe's and four hours' sleep wondering why
I felt like dying. I had a hangover, even though it was the middle of
the week. I sat there smoking cigarette after cigarette, drinking coffee, and trying to study for a final in a class I hadn't even attended.
Even today I still have dreams about those finals. All I could think
of was, why do I feel so incredibly shitty? Does everyone feel like
this? By five in the afternoon I'd be in Smokey's looking for someone to drink with. Usually I could find a brother. The favorite
phrase at the Beta house was, "Are we gonna drink or are we gonna
talk about it?"

The real hard-core college drinkers, regardless of Greek affili-
ation, all belonged to a special drinking fraternity called the Jesters.
They wore lab coats so that when they puked they wouldn't wreck
their clothes. I yearned to wear the coat, to puke the good puke, to
be a Jester. They didn't allow freshmen into the Jesters, although
there was a grass-roots movement to change the rules in my behalf.

* * *

"Lessee . . . this says you're twenty-six? You're twenty-six? How can you be twenty-six?" The guy is an Irish-Italian with sparse hair, skin like cappicola, and a greasy apron. He is holding my driver's license in his hand and squinting at it with a flashlight.

"Korea," I say modestly.

"Korea?"

"Yeah. Panmunjom. Thirty-eighth Parallel—'52 through '53. Right after high school. Took me two years to unwind. Touch of battle fatigue. Stayed at the V. A. for a couple of years. By the time I got straightened out—well, let's just say it took me a little longer to make it to college than most other guys. But what the heck—I'm OK now. I'm here." I beam and shift my weight slightly to ease the pain in the old war wound.

"Edmond Keenan Wynn. Ed Wynn your grandfather?"

"Well," I lower my voice, "let's not make a big deal out of that. Yeah. But please, it's better if people don't—you understand." Tiny conspiratorial grimace here.

"Sure, sure. OK. Look, it's no skin off my nose. If the cops check, you showed me. But twenty-six. . . ." he shakes his head. Then he hands me back my license and a quadruple whiskey sour. I think about what the skin off his nose might be like in a sandwich and cancel my deli order.

Everyone in the place knows I'm Ed Wynn's grandson by now. I'm a kind of local celebrity. People like to meet me. One night a black doctor I know from nearby Jefferson Memorial Hospital introduces me to Johnny Mathis. I talk to them for a while. It's no big deal to me, and I don't think too much of it, but later one of my fraternity brothers comes over.

"Hey, that was Johnny Mathis."

"Yeah."

"OK, is he a fag?"

"Nah. No way."

"I thought he was a fag."

"Uh-uh. Just as straight as anyone." Unconsciously, I'm protecting people in the business. It's a show business thing. I think of him as "my people." Me and Johnny Mathis, bros.

I take my drink back to a booth. In the booth is a girl I've never seen before. She's sitting with a couple of friends and Peter Derks, my sponsor in the Beta house.

"Hi," she says and smiles at me. She's pretty, and she's older. I don't know how much older, but older. I've just turned eighteen, but she seems like an actual woman to me, different from the debs, the sorority girls, and the nurses from Jefferson Nursing School. She keeps talking to me, interested, gazing at me. I'm feeling a little superhuman anyway, Smokey Joe's whiskey sours being what they are, so of course I accept her interest. After all, I'm the same guy who had Elizabeth Taylor in the palm of his hand for eleven seconds one night, aren't I? We talk. I shout clever things. I feel admired. She tells me she works at the Wistar Institute near the university.

"What's that?" I ask, slipping a wedding ring on my finger. I've been carrying it in my pocket for exactly this kind of occasion. It's an idea of mine that has never worked, but that hasn't stopped me trying it.

"It's a research lab. We developed the Wistar rat. Do you know what the Wistar rat is?"

"No." I show the ring ostentatiously.

"It's a hybrid white rat. It's the rat everyone uses in experiments. We make them. Well—we developed them. It's a patented rat."

"Patented rat? You can't patent a rat." She smiles. I order another drink. She watches the ring. I play with it, then I pretend to try and hide it, as if suddenly I don't want her to see it.

"Are you married?" she finally asks me.

"Uh . . . geez, how did you . . . ? Oh well, yeah . . . but I don't live with her anymore. I want a divorce, but she's Catholic." I don't think of this as a lie, but really as more of a fiction, a little playlet, and for some reason I find this little fiction exciting. I even have a girl in mind as my fantasy wife, a girl I knew from Beverly Hills High School named Carolyn Trebilcock who wouldn't touch me with a ten-foot pole. I don't realize it, but this is what Stanislavsky's followers call The Method. Only if it's not on stage or on camera, it's called lying.

The girl looks at me in a way I don't interpret immediately. I'm feeling very high. Very good. "Would you like to see the Wistar Institute?" she asks, smiling.

"Well, sure . . ." I say. She looks at her girlfriend. Then she gets up. "Now?" I ask.

"Why not?" she asks. She grabs my hand. I feel a shock when she touches me. My stomach tingles. Her fingers slide right between mine. It's a very agreeable feeling. She's definitely older. No college girl has ever slipped her fingers right between mine in quite this expert way. I stuff my unfinished whiskey sour in my jacket and we leave Smokey Joe's.

We walk. I find that people walk everywhere in Philadelphia. Frank Robbins says that's why the East Coast chicks have such great legs. They walk. "Walking," Frank says. "Look at those pins. When's the last time you saw a girl in California walk?"

The girl takes me to a dark, unassuming building about ten minutes away. I am getting to that point where time is losing its edge. Maybe it was five minutes, maybe twenty. She has a key. She opens the door and we go inside.

Inside the Wistar Institute it's dark. She shushes me and we walk down a long corridor.

"Where are we going?" I ask.

"You'll see." The place smells of typewriters and formaldehyde, an interesting combination. "Do they embalm the secretaries each night after work?" I ask. She smiles in the dark. I know because I can hear her lips part. I'm aware of everything.

"No," she says, slapping me playfully. "No, they don't."

We enter a room at the end of the corridor and step inside. She turns on a light. It's a lab. There are row upon row of large jars on shelves. It takes a moment to realize that there are objects in those jars. At first I see only rats and rabbits, snakes, turtles. Then I see a dog. It floats in the liquid, its eyes like oysters, little wisps of tissue drifting like sea grass. Then I see the baby humans. Lots of them. Complete, whole babies at various embryonic and postembryonic stages. And parts of adult human beings as well, brains, hearts, etc.

"That's a dick!" I stare at a jar that contains something which looks more like a small gherkin. The thing that is most disturbing about this is that the penis is sliced in half lengthwise.

The girl stands next to me. "Isn't it interesting?" she asks. The thought comes: Am I in this building with an insane mass dick-slicer?

"Huh. . . ." I say. I can smell her hair now, mixed with the for-maldehyde. Testosterone knows no fear. There's another jar. In it is something that looks like a sea slug.

"She had cancer," the girl says. I look closer. "See the tumor?"

"Yeah." I don't really see anything. It's all gray, part of it flat against the glass like a child's nose in a toy-store window. "How did you know it was a her?" I ask. She laughs.

"Men don't have one of these," she says.

Back at her apartment I continue drinking. I'm now reaching the level of complete mental disengagement. I lie some more about my wife back in California. There are other people there, some are friends from the fraternity house, but I can't remember half their names. Everyone is grinning at me. I must be going over big. I go to the bathroom again and again. I no longer even close the door. In the bathroom I have a discussion with two other people about life, during which I cry and pull the toilet paper holder out of the wall. Finally, I come out and everyone is gone but the girl. She takes me into the bedroom and undoes my pants. She sits on the bed and pulls them down. I need another drink.

"No you don't," she says. She pushes me down on the mattress.

We start to kiss. I feel her pulling on me, turning me over, getting
me on top of her. She reaches down and draws me up inside her.
All the years of fumbling and wrestling, the contests of strength, the
weary muscles, the five-hour hard-ons, envying my Uni Hi friends
who have been screwing since they were twelve, are over. This is it.
The first time I have ever been inside a woman.

The feeling is better than I could have ever imagined. Drunk as
I am, the feeling overwhelms me. I teeter like a man on the edge of
a building. I feel as if I've been raised up on a platform tethered
only to the sensations of sex itself. I am clamped onto this woman
like a mollusk, my body is a steel beam curved in a U that enters
her and holds fast. The woman, I just dimly realize, is helpless. I
didn't envision this in my adolescence, the power and control. This
is different. Like a gyroscope, I'm spinning but steady. I look out
the window. There are lights out there, cars, an elevated train. Everything works. Outside and in here, it all runs smoothly. It's automatic.
Despite the booze, despite the absurd fiction, despite the bottles full
of dicks and vaginas and babies, this night was impossible to screw
up. For a moment, the Greek fire is still. I have no anxiety because
the future doesn't exist. This was going to happen no matter what
I did.

I have made it. I have gotten laid. More than that, I have gotten
laid in the fifties. Just under the wire, to be sure, but the fifties
nonetheless. In the ensuing years a veil of Rockwellian nostalgia is
drawn around this decade, when girls ostensibly all wore poodle
skirts over their winsome shanks and boys wore white buck shoes
which they kept firmly on the floor, and this is considered to have
been something of a feat. I rarely argue. Sex becomes my war story.
Later I find out her name is Betty and she's twenty-seven years old.

Outside the fraternities, in the world of debutantes and Main
Line society, things were a little more complicated. My mother had
laid the groundwork and there were people to sponsor me into that
rarefied blue-ribbon mob which provided all the free drinks on Friday nights and weekends at all the seemingly endless deb parties
that took place in Philadelphia. They held these parties so that their
daughters could be mauled by various young eligible males in the
playrooms and on the terraces of their tranquil homes, and so that
their liquor cabinets could be raided, their silver stolen, their carpets
ruined, and their bathrooms destroyed. It was evidently all worth it
to the gentle folk of Bryn Mawr, Saint David's, Malvern, and Valley
Forge, so long as the right young males were doing the mauling.
Imagine their dismay at finding an unpapered mutt rooting and
slavering among their quivering bitches. Unpapered insofar as they
were concerned, because my pedigree on Philadelphia's Main Line

was about as valuable socially as a doctor's report clearing me of having syphilis. What they saw was someone from Hollywood, the progeny of a, well, show business family.

This is where I began to discover the limits of my family and its influence. It wasn't so much that I was refused entry. On the contrary, I was welcomed. But there was a line over which I could not cross. A genteel barricade, like those loose little pieces of hemp strung between stakes to keep other law-abiding citizens from stepping on newly seeded lawns. You could easily march right through, but you didn't.

"Ned Wynn . . . are you related to Ed Wynn?"

"Yes, ma'am. He's my grandfather."

"Ahhhh—Carling, this is Ed Wynn's grandson."

"Who?"

"Ed Wynn."

"The Fire Chief?"

"Yeah, remember him?"

"Oh, yes—wasn't he from Philadelphia?"

"Yes, sir, he was."

"Wynn—Wynn—Irish?"

"Leopold, actually, ma'am." Silence. Very short one. "He got the Wynn from Edwin. Isaiah Edwin Leopold. Of course, he married an Irish girl, heh, heh. . . ." It's a mistake to explain, as usual.

"Ah. Clever. Very funny man, Ed Wynn. The Fire Chief. We loved him. Glued to the radio. A great comedian. Has a son, doesn't he? An actor?"

Extended modesty. "Yes. Keenan Wynn."

"Hmm. Can't place him. Well, enjoy yourself. Have a drink. There's food in the playroom." And if you touch my daughter's tits I'll cut your balls off.

I learned what my grandfather had learned years before among the same people. They would invite us to their parties, drink with us, eat with us. Be delighted, in fact, to do so. But when it came to the really important family affairs like marriages and christenings, confirmations and deaths, we weren't part of their crowd. It wasn't only a matter of Christians and Jews. At Hawthorne School I had never been invited to a single bar mitzvah by any of the Jewish children or their parents. I was raised a Christian, but other Christian classmates were always invited, and in Beverly Hills it had become something of an irrelevance anyway. It wasn't religion, it was a show business matter.

I was only accepted completely by the families of other show business people like Gene Kelly, Rosalind Russell, Dean Martin, Paul Francis Webster, Alfred Newman, Walter Lang, and Henry Hathaway. I hadn't understood this at the time, but it was becoming more clear. There was a certain gingerness in the acceptance of show business people. Perhaps it's because of the mercurial personalities of entertainers, their unpredictability. Unpredictable people are dangerous to make alliances with, at least not the important social and political alliances that govern so much of the upper-class society in places like Philadelphia's Main Line and, for that matter, Beverly Hills. On the other hand, I may have been a poor choice in guests, being as hysterical for attention as I was. I tired out my hosts.

My social sponsors were two rather wonderful exceptions to the rule, Tootie and Corty Wetherill. Tootie was a Widener, and Corty went to Princeton. They were beyond caring about who was what. Who was "U" and who was "non-U." Friends of my mother and stepfather's, they adored Van, finding him hugely amusing and the whole show business thing just too fun. They lived in Newtown Square near Paoli where they raised thoroughbreds. The place was called, miraculously, Happy Hill Farm.

Happy Hill Farm was straight out of Dylan Thomas by way of John Cheever. I spent my first snowy Christmas in their house back in 1952, and I had even climbed on one of the Saturn-eyed huge-nostriled horses they raised and rode it around the gentle hills and valleys there. I was friends with the groom and his family, who lived in a sturdy three-story farmhouse on the property, and I was allowed to stay with them one winter, like the wide-eyed David Copperfield at the seaside home of the fisherman Ham, mooning heartsick after the proud, table-setting daughters and running wild with the dusty, paternal sons.

When I came to Penn in 1958, Tootie and Corty opened their home to me and gave me one of their cars to drive, a Buick convertible with a prancing sterling silver horse as a hood ornament. Oddly, they never seemed worried about what might happen to their car or their house. It was the kind of complacency I had learned to count on from this echelon once they have determined you are OK.

Using Happy Hill Farm as a base of operations, my fraternity brothers and I ranged all over the countryside to parties everywhere, flying like a pack of Headless Horsemen down the dark and narrow country lanes in the dead of winter with the top down. We drank everyone's liquor, threw up in their bathrooms, stole money from the women's purses and silver from their cupboards, and generally behaved as young animals will behave.

It never ceased to amaze me, the extent to which this was tolerated. It may have been that far fewer of us were doing this than I thought. Like pesky bacteria, we weren't intrusive enough to do more than call out a few white corpuscles in the form of indulgent fathers and mothers who would give us black coffee, ask us to empty our pockets, clap us on the shoulder, recall their own college hi-jinks, and invite us back the following weekend.

My grandfather visited me that year. He came to New York to accept one of an endless array of testimonials he now collected on a regular basis. He stayed at the Algonquin.

"I always stay here," he said as he led me across the lobby. Everyone in the hotel watched us. Many came up and shook his hand. It was like old times for me, the eternal satellite to greatness. "This is my grandson Ned. He's in his first year at Penn." My grandfather was immensely proud to have his grandson in college, the first in the family to go. And to have me go to Penn, a vastly ancient institution even when he was a child, was a double blessing.

People shook my hand, then pumped more vigorously as Grandpa poured it on. I smiled. This was a familiar role, one I slipped into easily. Son, stepson, grandson. There were nuances, variations that I exercised in each instance. With Grandpa there was more decorousness, even a courtly deference. I was more willing to accept the attention in honor of both his antiquity and the veneration he was shown. With my father, on the other hand, we were both often drinking and hail-fellow-well-met, so the same rules did not always apply. With Van I was bright, clever, sarcastic, trying to appear as if Van and I were brothers, pals, members of a brilliant and classy team. It was tricky and exciting, a job I was good at.

I was particularly happy to see Grandpa in New York. It gave me a chance to come to the city, and it was a rare occasion for me to be alone with him.

He still smelled of talcum powder, but he had stopped smoking the cigars. Now he smoked cigarettes. "The doctor told me I had to quit the cigars," he said without irony. He almost never used irony, whereas I thrived on it. "That's the Round Table," he said, pointing to a table of no particular significance to me. "That's where Dorothy Parker sat. And Benchley. You know who Dorothy Parker was?"

"Sure." I had only the vaguest idea.

"Brilliant writer," he said. "Very funny." I always noticed that when comedy was being discussed, it was always done in a very serious manner, complete with furrowed brows and sepulchral tones. "Very funny," he said to me as if announcing someone's death. People were now gathered around him like monks around the monsignor. "Remember: Comedians are people who say funny things, comics are people who say things funny." So, was Dorothy Parker a comedian? "Dorothy Parker was a humorist." Oh. But she *was* funny, right? "Very," he said. They just dropped the bomb on Japan. "Very, very funny." A tidal wave just wiped out Honolulu.

Everyone nodded pleasantly. Some offered up respectful, serious chuckles. They were appeased, fulfilled. They'd seen Ed Wynn and heard him speak on the nature of comedy in the lobby of the Algonquin Hotel. Not five feet from the Round Table.

"What about clowns, Grandpa?" I'm overdoing it now, ingratiating myself with him. We're eating lunch, and I want to drink without being noticed. Grandpa, acutely aware of my father's immoderate nature, is touchy about booze and cautious about me. Will I turn out to be like his son? Or God forbid, his ex-wife? Any of his ex-wives?

The trick is to get a couple of bourbons into him. Although not an indulgent man, he can be gotten around. He is carefully giddy, expansive, never drunk. Waiter? Oh, please, waiter—hear your humble servant calling. Waiters hover when I'm with the patriarch, a decidedly good thing. I can simply nod and point ever so slightly to my glass while listening with fierce attention to my grandfather. A waiter responds to my minimalist pantomine with a fresh bourbon and soda. My heart cries thanks. I send him a soft glance. He probably thinks I'm a faggot.

Grandpa leans toward me and frowns. "Clowns do funny things while wearing silly clothes," he says. "Funny hats, or pants that don't fit or funny jackets and silly shoes." A FLOOD IN PAKISTAN KILLS THREE THOUSAND PEOPLE. "The funniest young comedian in show business today is Jerry Lewis. Now there's a true clown." FIFTY DEAD IN NEW JERSEY FIRE. "Funny face, funny voice, funny clothes. A very very funny guy." THREAT OF NUCLEAR WAR DRIVES MODERN TEENS TO SUICIDE. "Dean Martin is going nowhere without Jerry Lewis." Now *that's* funny.

There is a distillation of my life when I'm with my grandfather. He treats me with great love, even affection, something that I don't expect from him. But in this man, now past seventy, the unexpressed love is finding expression. He puts his arm in mine, and we walk through the lobby of the Algonquin Hotel. I like the feeling of proprietary kinship. I like the weight of my grandfather's arm on mine. New York is a great place to be with my grandfather.

We go to Jack Dempsey's Restaurant near Times Square. Dempsey is there. He spots my grandfather. "Ed!" he says, and comes across the room. "Hello, Champ," says Grandpa. I meet the Champ of Champs, the Manassa Mauler, Jack the Giant Killer. His enormous hands envelope mine in a handshake to remember. I am amazed at how soft they are. Watching my grandfather's face I realize it's the moments like these that people like Jack Dempsey and Ed Wynn come to love. This is the reward his career has brought him. The satisfaction for Grandpa comes in the greeting he gets from, to him, the greatest fighter who ever lived.

"I saw Jack knock out Firpo in 1923," Grandpa says to me. "You didn't give us a chance to sit down, Jack. Bang, the guy was through the ropes. Nearly knocked your grandmother over, Neddy, God's honest truth."

"Ya shoulda got there on time, Ed," Dempsey says, smiling. His face is enormous; up close it almost looks like a wooden sculpture. "Your grandpa never got to the fights on time," Dempsey says to me.

"You know I couldn't do that, Jack. See, Neddo, when you're a big Broadway star you can't get to the fights until at least the second round. With this guy, the fight was over in the second round." The two old champions laugh together. Sometimes, life is perfect.

I get the best of everything. It's the effortlessness of life with all three of these men, father, grandfather, stepfather, that affects me so strongly. I have developed an attitude about it that lives in my bones. Everything will happen, does happen, will always happen from now on. Nothing will be required from me beyond that which I was given at birth. It's an attitude which might be called blithe.

I left the University of Pennsylvania and transferred to the University of California at Berkeley. My decision was based entirely on the weather. Of course, the weather in Northern California was worse than it was in Philadelphia, but I never considered that. My mother had been in Europe with Van when I decided to change schools, and my father, not vastly up on this kind of thing, had agreed.

"Do me a favor, willya, kiddo, just go *somewhere*, that's all I ask," he said. "I'll never hear the end of it from Evie. I'm always in the middle, y'know, always in the middle."

I drove the Jag, my surfboard strapped to the top, straight up the San Joaquin Valley to San Francisco in less than seven hours, getting two speeding tickets in the process, one for going 110 miles an hour and engaging in a speed contest with a lowered Chevy near the town of Earlimart. The Chevy then passed me going 120 just outside Pixley. The California state highway patrolman, from Oildale and extremely bored, stopped us both.

The guy in the Chevy grinned. "This is the greatest ticket I ever got," he said. "One twenty. Fuck *me*."

"All these guys from around here want to race," the state highway patrolman told me. "They don't care about the tickets. They *like* to go to jail. They don't have anything else to do. You should be more careful. You got a life." He smiled and handed me my ticket.

The first thing I did when I got to Berkeley was to drive to the Beta Theta Pi house. Everywhere you go, they told me at Penn, the brothers will welcome you. You're a Beta no matter what. That's fraternity solidarity. Brothers in Pi, is how the Betas put it.

I cruised through Berkeley enjoying the sights, got two more speeding tickets from Berkeley cops interested in seeing my car, and finally I found the fraternity house. There was a group of guys standing in the lot watching me as I drove in and parked. Smiling broadly, I got out.

"Brothers!" I shouted.

"Who the fuck is this asshole," someone said.

"Get that fucking piece of shit car out of here."

"Are you a *surfer*? I think this guy's a *surfer* from *Southern California.*"

Someone threw a beer. It splattered near my feet. All of a sudden I felt like I was six years old again. They reminded me of all the children I grew up hating. They taunted me for having the Jaguar. For being a Hollywood kid, for being rich. Yet everyone of them was a banker's son or a doctor's son or a lawyer's son or a real estate tycoon's son. They came from places like Burlingame on something called the Peninsula. Everyone of them had an assured future. I found myself apologizing, trying to fit in once more with a group who had no use for me. But I still hadn't learned. I tried.

I hung around the house, showed up at the functions, ate in the dining hall, went surfing with them in Santa Cruz. I participated. I even changed cars. By this time I had gotten so many tickets in the Jag in and around the Bay Area that I had become something of a beacon to the police. I finally got busted for having a counterfeit driver's license. My license was suspended. I sold the Jag to my father and bought a Ford. It worked. I was less noticeable. All the cops really wanted was the punk in the Jag. But the brothers knew who I really was.

One day at a Friday afternoon sorority mixer I was put in charge of the music. So I took Ray Coniff off the record player and put on a record from my own collection. It was "Ray Charles Live at Newport." I put on a track called "Tell the Truth." It played for about sixty seconds before someone yelled, "Who put on the nigger music?" I was shocked. We were never allowed to say this word in our home. I thought it was a southern word anyway. Certainly not something someone would say in Berkeley, California.

"It's Ray Charles," I said. "He's great. It's not nigger music." I'd been listening to rhythm and blues since 1949 when Uncle Sherry played Louis Jordan records for me. I bought my first Ray Charles record in 1955. What the hell was nigger music? This was rock and roll, for chrissake.

"It's nigger music. Put Ray Coniff back on." I grinned like a field hand and complied. But from then on I began to affect a different attitude. Fitting in was becoming less important. It wasn't through any kind of righteous indignation or liberal compunction, but rather a simple question of taste.

Also there was the little matter of having been fingered, by a flouncing member of Delta Delta Delta sorority, who was also a fanatical Ray Coniff devotee, as the instigator of a regular peep show at her sorority house. It was true. I had inched open the communal bathroom window of the Tri-Delt House using an ingenious tool, a hanger attached to a long stick. This had taken days of care and planning to do. Then, for a few blissful weeks, we had sat there in the dark, several fraternity brothers, some housemates, and I, drinking beer and watching the Tri-Delt women towel off, one Delt at a time. Finally, we got busted.

According to an obscure section of The Rules, obviously from the same Manual I didn't get back in fifth grade, I was the only one directly inculpated by Missy Three-Delts, girlfriend and sex object of our fraternity president (also a Ray Conniff fan as well as the fraternity's unofficial Bert Kaempfert discographer), as the Main Peeper, a role I gladly accepted. I preferred being an originator of perverse activities to being devoid of any ideas at all.

The rest of them denied any knowledge of the whole thing. No one but me, evidently, had been watching. I expected kudos. Instead I was placed in the category of schoolyard molester and all-around sheep humper and shunned, like a bad Mennonite. I was just glad I hadn't put Thelonius Monk on the record player.

It was 1960, and I was beginning to noticing a strange phenomenon taking place on campus that spring. There were riots. They had something to do with the House Un-American Activities Committee. All along fraternity row angry, red-faced, shirtless white boys were throwing things at angry, grungy-looking, varicolored groups of students and nonstudents, who were throwing things back. The police were everywhere. These groups roared and surged up and down the streets from Strawberry Canyon to Sproul Hall.

It was indecipherable to me. I belonged to neither group in any case, unless they had an open bar, but I *looked* like a Beta: short hair, tan, gray sweatshirt with sleeves cut off at the elbows. Once, as I drove by another fraternity house on the Row, I saw Danny Guggenheim, a childhood friend from Beverly Hills and a scion of one of the richest families in America, waving at me. "Wynn, c'mon!" he yelled. He was holding a stick like a club in his hand. "We're gonna go get some beatniks!" Beatniks? Why? My uncle was a beatnik, for chrissake.

"Maybe some other time, Danny," I shouted back. "My good truncheon is in the shop!"

A couple of weeks later I called Betty. She quit her job at the

Wistar Institute and moved to San Francisco. She got a job and lived in an apartment in the city, and I ended up staying there most of the time. It was the first time I had had a woman available on a daily basis for sex. I treated it as I did everything—hysterically, ambivalently, as if, while I knew it was endlessly available, I was afraid at the same time it would be scooped up and taken away at any moment.

"Oh, Ned—can we rest awhile?"

"What's the matter?"

"I'm sore. . . ."

"Oh, geez, well, what if I make you a sandwich?" She watches in disbelief as I scoot through the tiny kitchen. Let's see—bread, cheese, tomatoes, bacon, fry the bacon . . . "Don't peek, you'll love this . . ." drain the bacon, slice the tomatoes, toast the bread, melt the cheese on the toast, layer the bacon, the tomato. "My specialty, ta-da. . . ."

"That's so sweet—but, I'm not hungry, really. . . ."

"Mmmm—just move your foot, OK?"

"Honey, I'm sore."

I'm sore too, but I'm not gonna let that stop me. Maybe this is how that guy's dick got into the Wistar Institute. So be it. "Try the sandwich, here, lemme just . . ."

"Ned, damnit, I'm sore!"

"OK, OK, is there any Vaseline left?"

"We used the last jar this morning."

"What if we try and work through the pain . . . ?"

Instead of going to classes, I spent the nights in North Beach trying to decide whether to see a new comic named Woody Allen at the Hungry I, or to sit in the jazz clubs and listen to Cannonball Adderly, the Montgomery Brothers, and the Jazz Crusaders. The jazz clubs were 90 percent black, and I found myself feeling more comfortable around black people. In my mind, even though I was white, that was OK. In fact, it was better. All I was was white; I didn't have to be anything else. I could accept judgment on that basis, and on the basis that I loved jazz, I felt I could fit in. I copied the attitudes of the black patrons, the way they listened, the way they drank, the way they nodded cooly or broke a careful grin in recognition of a nice riff. Occasionally, there was excitement. I saw a woman beat a man on the head with her high-heeled shoe as he sat on her boyfriend's chest and knocked his teeth out. This was life, I thought. This was real life.

The affair with Betty was rolling to a stop. The Christmas-present syndrome was beginning to kick in. I hadn't realized it, but it worked with people as well as stuff. Nonetheless, the more something looked like it was disintegrating, the more vociferously I tended to try and hold on to it. I invited her to spend spring break at home with me in Beverly Hills as a reaffirmation of love. Perhaps subconsciously I knew that the best way to get rid of a woman was to bring her home to Mother.

"My God, Ned she's too *old* for you! She must be thirty!" She was using the "Do you know what time it is?" voice.

"Chrissake Mom, she's only twenty-eight." And a slick piece of ass to boot, Ma.

"Well, get rid of her. I don't want her in this house." Get rid of her? Get *rid* of her? *Hmmmm.*

Betty stayed in Schuyler's room. Schuyler slept in the Farley Granger Room. Each morning at dawn I slipped down the hall and got into bed with her, into my sister's frilly little canopied bed with the fairy-tale figurines and the three-dozen miniature horses on the shelves, the Little Miss Muffett teeter-totter clock, the daybed laden with stuffed animals, the Elvis Presley pictures, all the paraphernalia of the thirteen-year-old. I got into this bed amid this welter of girl-hood fantasy and fucked my crone. Get rid of her? Well, can I get rid of her and still do this?

I had what I needed: permission from my mother to get out of this relationship. I didn't think of it as permission, really, but more as a mandate to do what I really wanted to do anyway. There was a subtle and important mental gyration going on here, a shifting of responsibility from me to my mother. Since childhood my mother had always been willing to accept responsibility for my emotions, so why should I change that now? It was convenient, and it took care of my feelings altogether.

I ended the relationship on the way to the airport. I simply told Betty I wasn't coming back to San Francisco with her. She started to protest. Weren't we going back together? When was I coming back? What about school? I pulled the car over, skidded to a halt on the shoulder, turned to Betty and slapped her. The dust from the skid rose around the windows as Betty started to cry.

"Goddamnit," I screamed. "Goddamned fucking bitch!" That was pretty much the extent of my side of things. She sat and wept, looking at me with eyes I can't forget. She had done absolutely nothing to deserve this. This was my system. I had discovered that anger helped me to do things that I didn't like doing. "Fucking bitch, leave me the fuck alone!" The adrenaline kept me in a state of isolation and aggression where I could continue with my plan regardless of its effect on her. This may be how criminals do their crimes:

flip out, become incensed at the victim, make them the heavy. It was a lot easier than confronting that little voice inside that wept for what I had become.

Satisfied that I had cowed her sufficiently, I pulled back on the road and took her to the airport. I put her on a plane. I saw her a few more times after I returned to Berkeley, but it was obvious it was over. Eventually, I assumed, she went back to Philadelphia. In any case, I never saw her again.

When the anger and self-righteousness subsided and the threat of remorse began to surface, I used my mother, as always, as my palliative.

"I want to transfer, Mom."

"That's a good idea, sweetheart. You transfer." Go anywhere, but get out of San Francisco where they have all those older women and those beatniks.

"*Hmmm*," said the dean looking at my grades. "Are you sure you're not taking this leave of absence just to avoid flunking out of school?"

"Oh, no, sir," I said. "There are problems at home." People always accepted the "problems at home" line from me. It wasn't hard to accept, show business families having the reputations they had, and I had learned to use it in a pinch. The problems were never specific. It was always imagined they had something to do with divorce and/or mental illness.

"These grades. D's. Do you even go to class, Mr. Wynn?"

"Well, that's the thing, see, I'm so distracted by all this *stuff*. . . ." It's important that I get a leave of absence. If I just leave I'll never get back in college, and I had already applied to the University of Southern California. Somewhere in the back of my mind some wisdom still functioned. "Anyway, Dean, I'm coming back next fall. After all this *stuff*."

He's not satisfied. He knows what I'm doing. He sighs. He's got a lot of things to deal with these days. Student riots, faculty protests. What's one screwed-up punk rich kid, more or less? "Very well, Mr. Wynn," he says reluctantly. "You are granted a leave of absence."

Grateful, sick of the whole place, I drove off the campus and back down the San Joaquin Valley. I was leaving not only a truncated college career, but a girl who had transplanted herself to another city to be with me. I just drove away, and all I felt was relief. All the way back to Los Angeles in the black two-door Ford, I didn't get a single ticket.

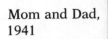

Mom and Dad,
1941

Eve Lynn Abbott,
ingenue

Evie and Baby Neddy, 1941

Heap Big Photo Session: Ned, Keenan, Tracy, 1946

The Harley, Mom's least favorite vehicle, Brentwood, 1944

Mom and Ty, 1938

The good old days:
Van (*left*) and Keenan
at Metro with starlet
Lina Romay

The really good old days: Van Johnson, Mickey Rooney, Peter Lawford, and Keenan Wynn, The Devon House in Holmby Hills, 1944

Keenan and Ed, Atlantic City, 1930

Ed Wynn, Ziegfeld
Follies, ca. 1914

Grandma Hilda

Luminaries of the legitimate stage: (*left to right*) DeWolfe Hopper,
Frank Keenan, Tyrone Power, Sr., Sarah Truex, Theo. Roberts,
William Farnum

"I never wanted to be
a real person."

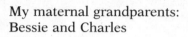
My maternal grandparents:
Bessie and Charles

With Tracy, Dad, and
Pledge on Chaparral in
Brentwood, 1947. Mom
was on her honeymoon
with Van.

The family, Brentwood, 1945

With Van at the Beverly Hills house, 1954

At the Hotel del Coronado with Van and Tracy, 1956 (Photo by Tommy Park)

Twisting the night away
with Lana Turner at my
twenty-first birthday.

Uncle Sherry

Beverly Hills: Maureen Reagan, me, Van, and Jane Wyman, 1954

With John Hillerman in summer stock, 1963 (Photo by Duncan Photographer)

(Courtesy of Orion Pictures Corporation)

The Beach Party era, 1964

Mother and Van meet the Queen of England, 1951. That's Burt Lancaster on the left and Dan Duryea on the right.

Two-fisted drinker
with Dad at the wrap
party for the remake
of *Stagecoach*.
Your basic photo
opportunity at 20th
Century-Fox

Another photo op.,
this one at Paramount:
with Jerry Lewis on
The Bellhop.

Captain Serenity,
India, 1969

The Big Time Writer/Actor on the set of *California Dreaming*, 1977

Unless otherwise noted, all photographs courtesy of the author's
private collection.

CHAPTER

10

A new version of the phony set-up summer job appeared when I was nineteen. Once more, my mother—in an effort to get me calibrated for something other than acute self-indulgence—got me into a summer-stock company as an apprentice. I had absolutely no desire whatever to do summer stock, and whatever an apprentice was, I wasn't interested. What was wrong with being an extra?

"An extra is not acting," she said. We were in the backyard. I was cleaning out the barbecue. My job was the barbecue. Van, once the head meat burner, had retired to the playroom where he loved to sit behind the bar, study his French Berlitz course, and drink scotch.

"*J'aime, tu aime, il, elle aime, nous aimons—nous-eh-mon—*remember that elide—*noo-zemon—*don't you love that—*voo-zemay—il-zem?*" French, what a concept.

"I had a line on *Combat* last year," I said, pronouncing combat *comb-bah. L'an dernier.* No elision there. "I worked with Don Rickles." It was cut, but never mind that. I got three hundred dollars for it. And working around professionals like Don, I mean, come *on.* What does she *want,* for chrissake?

My mother gazed at the sky. This woman, the wife of two movie stars, herself a radio and stage actress at one time, and an avid believer in the summer-stock system of theatrical training, was listening to her issue and doubting her own ears.

"I'm not talking about a line in *Combat.* I'm talking about you learning to be an actor. To be in a summer-stock theater. *I* did stock, *Van* did stock, *Keenan* did stock, *Ty* did stock, *Jimmy Stewart* did stock" —now she was invoking the gods—"*Orson Welles* did stock . . ."

"Orson Welles invented summer stock, didn't he? Or was he just the first to do it in modern dress?"

"That's funny, very funny, Ned. You should write that kind of thing down. You're much funnier than Ed Wynn, you know. Why don't you do comedy? You could do comedy. You could be a big star. Where's a pad and pencil? You should always keep a pad and a pencil with you. Carry it around with you. Your grandfather wrote down every joke he heard, he was always writing things down. You've got to get into the habit of writing these things down. They'll just disappear. You're brilliant, you know . . . and handsome, much

159

handsomer than Jimmy Stewart . . . you could do anything you want, if you'd just put your mind to it."

"I'd like to go to the beach. . . ."

"Monty Clift did stock, Gene Kelly did stock, Jimmy Backus did stock—we *all* did stock, and *you're* going to do stock. If it's good enough for Kit Cornell, it's good enough for you." Katharine Cornell was my mother's favorite actress and role model. She had been in summer stock with Cornell, as Mom called her, and Guthrie McClintic in Skowhegan, Maine. She had met my father there while she was still engaged to Ty Power.

"Why didn't you marry Ty, Mom?" I could usually get her going with that one. I had asked her this question about twice a year, when I really needed to sidetrack her.

"Because I knew he would never settle down with one person. He was too beautiful."

"Dad was just ugly enough?"

"Not ugly, certainly, but . . . well, less attractive."

"You mean safer?"

"I loved Keenan very much. I thought he was safer, yes." I was almost home free. She kind of went off into another world when discussing her relationship with Ty Power. Most people who had relationships with Ty reacted that way.

But today she had a new resolve. I was her latest project. "I've already written Anna Lee in La Jolla. You've been invited to audition." The lump in my throat expanded. Audition? My stomach clenched.

"You mean . . . try out?"

"We're going to La Jolla Saturday and you're going to audition for the La Jolla Playhouse summer theater." I just stood there in the backyard of the Beverly Hills house and listened to the day. Birds were tweeting, people were splashing in their pools, the *pock* of tennis balls drifted over the wall, and I was going to my certain death by humiliation in La Jolla. What about the beach? What about Doug and all my friends? Cruising? The Goody-Goody? Volleyball? Surfing?

"La Jolla?"

"Yes. You've been there. It's just north of San Diego." And Coronado. La Jolla was at the beach. Change in tactics here.

"John Wayne didn't do stock, Cary Grant didn't do stock, James Mason didn't do stock. . . ." I had to hold up my end, but this was in reality a little bit of the old Bre'r Rabbit trick. Don't throw me in that briar patch. La Jolla was, after all, one of the best beach towns in California, and bitchen chicks grew wild there, like dandelions.

"James Mason did RADA," she continued. My mother knew she could always use RADA, the Royal Academy of Dramatic Arts, when referring to any English actor, and not be wrong. The English did everything, took every course, studied incessantly, played in every regional playhouse, would walk miles barefoot in the snow just to stand on stage in some godforsaken rural backwater church nave and hold Richard III's crown on a pillow. Then they'd put it on their résumé and some groveling anglophiliac in New York would fall over in a swoon at their accent and declare them Actor of the Half-Millenium. A bunch of ass-kissing credential-freaks, the English.

"You could do RADA. We could send you to London. I'll write Michael Redgrave. Or should I write Larry Olivier?" Oh, fuck. Talk about far from the beach. I leaned my head against the side of the house and felt the cool plaster. Would I ever sleep till noon again?

"La Jolla's OK, actually. Certainly a lovely town. But unfortunately, I can't drive," I shrugged cheerfully. I'd had my driver's license suspended for the fourth time, this one was for six months.

"You can ride your bike. You'll live near the theater. They probably have a list of places for apprentices to stay. You can walk and ride anywhere in La Jolla." *Laissez les bons temps roulet.*

The La Jolla Playhouse, while not considered to be a truly serious summer theater, at least not in East Coast terms, was nonetheless a theater of some local repute. They ran plays for two weeks instead of the traditional one, using the apprentices as stagehands and minor players, and then brought in actors from Hollywood as "stars." Marie Windsor and Dick Crenna came to La Jolla that summer, as did old-timers like Lyle Talbot and James Craig, to play in hoary offerings such as *Dinner at Eight*—or more adventurous productions, adventurous for La Jolla, like William Inge's *Dark at the Top of the Stairs*.

If I thought I was going to be able to sneak through this summer exile quietly, I was wrong. There was no way my family was going to let the moment I first set foot on a stage go undetected. If anyone was going to get an inconspicuous entrance into the theater, it wasn't going to be me.

The first night I went on as Punky Givens, a character in *Dark at the Top of the Stairs*, I must have received thirty telegrams. My grandfather, and father, of course, Van, Mom, even Tracy and Sky, everyone in the family sent me one. And then there were at least a dozen from friends of the family: Gene Kelly, Peter Lawford, James Mason, Robert Wagner, Skip and Henry Hathaway, Rosalind Russell and Freddy Brisson, Ann Sothern, Ray and Mal Milland, Judy Garland, even one from Deborah Kerr and Tony Bartley, all the way from London.

"What? No telegram from Ike and Mamie?" Warren Berlinger grinned from the doorway of the dressing room.

"Yeah. I don't know how Mom missed them," I said.

"Break a leg," he said.

Theater people are protective of one another, and they are generous, but they also can spot a phony a mile away. Inside, I felt incredibly phony, and I was sure that everyone knew it. I didn't belong in this arena. I had no desire for this particular spotlight, afraid constantly that I would fail and be ridiculed. But at the same time I hated to be ignored. I was noisy and insistent, clamoring for recognition from everyone—friends, family, strangers. The problem with professional recognition, as opposed to recognition for being obtrusive and obnoxious, was that I hadn't earned it, and that always ate at me. I knew that I had never earned one tenth of the praise that had been lavished on me since childhood, and this theater thing was no different.

I got the role of Punky Givens by doing nothing more than standing around looking like him. I was typecast. Punky is an unconscious teenage jerkoff, a student from a military school and a friend of the young hero, played by an actor from New York named Warren Berlinger. Punky has no lines at all; all he does is shift from one foot to the other and grin stupidly, like an Irish setter. I had it down cold.

Punky is established on stage early. He walks in, looks around dimly, gropes his girlfriend, and then disappears into an unseen parlor. Hey, I can do that. There is a scenery change and he's offstage for a whole act. Then he comes onstage again. I could tuck in the shirt fifteen different ways. It's a nice, easy role for an underachiever. Basically, the role of Punky Givens is exactly what my mother was trying to wean me out of: Punky Givens was an extra.

To get all this attention for playing the role of a total nonentity was excruciating. More talented, harder-working actors were taking a backseat to all the noise surrounding their fellow player. One night Mom and Van came backstage. Another night, it was Dad and his wife, Sharley. And another night Ed Wynn came backstage causing a complete uproar. "Remember: Comedians are people who say funny things, comics are people who say things funny—clowns do funny things while wearing funny clothes." Grandpa was on a roll. Actors were hanging from the flies.

"Ed Wynn's talking about comedy." The press came backstage. There was a photo of my grandfather applying makeup to me as I sat at a mirror.

"Ned's the fourth generation in the theater," he said. Scribble scribble scribble. "Frank Keenan was his great-grandfather, Hilda Keenan was his grandmother, Ed Wynn is his grandfather, and Keenan Wynn is his father. Four generations of actors." Each name drove me deeper into my seat. Thanks, Gramps. Here he sits folks, a Punky Givens for all time.

"D'you think I'm ready to do Punky on Broadway, Grampa?" A startled look. Then he laughs.

"That's very funny, that's very funny—*hoo-hoo-hoo*, on Broadway, Punky Givens—write that down, you should write that down. I always wrote down every joke. Other kids were out with the girls, but I stayed home and wrote down jokes. Ask your mother." I will, I will.

Being in summer stock was exhausting. We worked all day as laborers, painters, and carpenters, and at night we either had a part in the play or we worked backstage with props and scenery. I had a girlfriend, Julie, a local La Jolla High School girl. Julie was seventeen and bright and shiny as a silver tea service. You could eat off Julie. We took to climbing into the scenery truck during the act when Punky was not onstage, and having sex. Then when I came back onstage, variously tumescent, the effect was even more realistic. It was like eighth-grade literature class all over again, only this time there was a paying audience. The Method strikes again.

I had an apartment one block from the theater and a hundred yards from one of the best surfing beaches in Southern California. Afternoons of dark nights, when there was no show, I went to the beach and surfed. Later, Julie would come to my apartment for an hour or so before she went home to her parents. Other nights I'd be in a local bar with the La Jolla/Pacific Beach surfing crowd. It was just like the Santa Monica Canyon. Sometimes, after leaving the bars at midnight or later, I'd hitchhike, drunk, the 120 miles back to Beverly Hills. This was before the 405 Freeway, and it often took three rides and four or five hours to get there. I'd break into the house, go to my room and sleep for three hours, get up, and have to call a friend to drive me back to La Jolla. Sometimes my mother never even knew I'd been home.

Three years later I would go through this whole drill again, in a creaky little "Z" stock company in North Conway, New Hampshire, the Eastern Slope Playhouse. This time my mother, ever more desperate as I was then three years older and even further mired in indolence and a kind of low-grade, torpid rebellion, went to the extent of sending me to Washington, D.C., to audition for Davey Marlin-Jones and Brian Clarke, the director and producer of the Eastern Slope Playhouse. I tried to stave off this latest effort at a remedial theater arts education by recounting once again how many people never did summer stock, only this time I used a different list.

"Danny Milland doesn't have to do stock, Bobby and Michael Walker don't have to do stock, Peter Fonda doesn't have to do stock,

Jackie Hathaway, Richard Lang, Tim Newman, and Terry Melcher don't have to do stock," I said. I was pushing it a little, but it felt so good when I whined that I never knew when to stop. Besides, Terry Melcher, Doris Day's son, was particularly galling to me. When he found out I was going to do stock, he never let up.

"Straw-hatting it this summer, Ned?" he grinned. "Hitting the old silo circuit there, are ya? Pancake number five and Albolene? We'll be thinking of you in Arrowhead. Too bad there won't be very many *girls* there or anything." Terry would be up in Lake Arrowhead at his mother's house with two other friends, Gregg Jakobson and Eddie Garner, all summer. They had a speedboat. There were rooms all over the place. I could see it all: drinking, water skiing, cadres of teenage wonder kittens like so many bikini-clad guerrillas slipping out of the woods and onto Terry's dock. But the Terry Melcher argument wasn't going to work. My mother had been on the phone with Doris.

"Doesn't Terry have a job at Columbia Records?" she asked, calmly. Shit.

"How long, exactly, do I have to be *in* Washington?"

It was vaporous in Washington, D.C., hot and muggy. I was truly dreadful in the audition which took place in a stuffy, un-air-conditioned hotel room. Obviously, my turn as Punky Givens, and later a waiter in *Dinner at Eight*, hadn't really honed my acting instrument. I read from some play or other I can no longer remember. Stiff, nervous, sick to my stomach, I quavered and cracked through this frightful afternoon. I could tell that the producer and director thought I stunk. But I also could see that they were going to hire me. Because I was Keenan Wynn's son. And because, I was fairly certain, my mother had made a financial contribution toward paying my "salary." It was the phoniest job yet, and it made me even sicker.

"That was . . . pretty interesting, Ned. We'd . . . really like to see you at Eastern Slope." Davey Marlin-Jones was curled up in a chair gnawing his shirtcuff. "Right, Davey?" Brian Clarke asked.

Davey just nodded bleakly and gazed out at the simmering heat. "*Mmm.* . . ." he said. Did these theater people have no shame?

For me, summer stock was another version of camp, a way of getting me out of everyone's hair. It was like a jail sentence. There was no continuity in my life. I was in a perpetual drift with no definable goal in sight. It seemed that if I hung around doing nothing one summer, the next summer I'd be sent to one of these camps. Only instead of making wallets and hiking, they made you act at these camps. And paint scenery. I wasn't addicted to the stage, I was addicted to pleasure. I wasn't addicted to acting, I was addicted to feeling good immediately. I was addicted to the result, not the process. The idea that you did such and such and it eventually led to something else was abstract to me. I couldn't see that what I was doing would lead me to a career in the theater. Besides, it was something I had never really decided I wanted to do anyway. I drifted through these experiences as I drifted through most of my life, on hold, waiting for the Popcorn Effect to blast me into the next phase.

The seriousness with which these people took their work in summer theater always eluded me. For one thing, the days were endless, the work was hard, the pay was a joke, and the experience was numbling. There were nights we literally played to four people in the audience, all of whom sat as far away from one another as possible, as if each of them thought the other was sick for being there.

I found that there were several people at the Eastern Slope Playhouse that I liked a lot. One was John Hillerman, an actor who had come there from off-Broadway. He was a funny, cynical, talented actor, and we spent many nights sitting up in our rooms drinking and running the world.

North Conway was near Conway, the town that Thornton Wilder used as his model for Grovers' Corners, the Ozzie and Harriet burg in his play *Our Town*. It was a true New England hamlet with a hotel, some clay tennis courts, a river and a theater. There were two places in the whole town to eat. There were three things they made that I could stomach, all of them containing either chicken or tuna. One of the places had a jukebox with "California Girls" and "Surfin' USA" by the Beach Boys on it. I'd sit in a booth and listen to the California surfing music and get maudlin over my hamburg, as they called a hamburger, and a pile of soft, slick, translucent french fries that looked like slices of raw abalone. Once I had become depressed enough, I'd go to the package store, as they called a liquor store, and buy a bottle of Jack Daniel's sour mash. I'd go back to my room and look in on John to see if he was up for it. He usually was.

We'd drink and bitch about the theater and about life, and once we were sufficiently drunk, we would go out into the square in front of the theater and begin shouting Emily's lines from *Our Town*. Emily speaks these lines in death with a new awareness of how much she really valued life, now that she was no longer living it. These lines were moving, emotional, the final heart-wrenching farewell to life. John and I, sick to death of the fatuous Emily, would begin screaming the dialogue from the play.

"Good-bye, Grovers' Corners . . ." John howled. Then I shouted,

"Good-bye, Grandma's butternut tree!" Then both of us screamed:

"Good-bye, Emily, you silly little *bitch*!"

Lights would go on in nearby homes. I once heard the sound

of a slamming door, then someone shouted, "Lew? Lew?" That was pretty much the extent of our entertainment in Grovers' Corners.

John Hillerman made me feel a part of things, as if I were really an actor, just like him. In fact, there was a moment, acting on stage with John, when I "got" it, a moment when I understood what my father and my grandfather and my stepfather, and people like John were all about. I was playing the role of Buddy Baker, referred to, in hushed tones, as "the Tony Bill role," in Neil Simon's *Come Blow Your Horn*. John was also in the play.

Neil Simon writes his comedies with such skill that, if you say the lines in the right places, you get laughs. For one week, playing in this comedy, I was an actor. John and I had our timing down spectacularly, and the play just rolled off our tongues. The first time I got a real, legitimate laugh, a laugh that came from the character itself, I lit up inside. A feeling of confidence and excitement over-whelmed me. At first I didn't know they were laughing at me—I thought it was a mistake.

John stood in front of me, his eyes gleaming. He knew what was happening. He also knew I had to get to the next line, and punched his dialogue just to jog me slightly. Without even thinking I went right ahead, flawlessly. More laughs. I was astonished. It was like being on a ride in an amusement park. I discovered that, as the play went along, I could continue to ride. Once the connection was made, the audience was tuned in, it was as if I were attached to them with invisible wires. Everything I did worked. I was conse-crated.

This, I imagined, is why actors act: the feeling. It's instantaneous and all-encompassing. You get a message that you're approved of completely. You own yourself and you own the stage, and the people are yours as well. I knew instinctively that I was getting laughs because I was doing it right. I was actually playing the role. For me, I got one week of that, eight performances.

Then, in the next production, I was given the part of the po-liceman in *Arsenic and Old Lace*, a part that Jack Carson had played in the film, and made into a small comic masterpiece. If there was ever the opportunity to make the leap, from watcher to player, this was it. But I had no insight, no real skill, and I floundered, I couldn't do it. I had no understanding of how to make it work. Neil Simon was easy: Diagrammatical staging and dialogue made his plays sure-fire. Other plays took more work, even farces like *Arsenic and Old Lace* required the construction, by the actor, of an attitude, a per-sonality that would drive the character. I found that with most other plays it was up to the actor to squeeze out of it what he could. That was really what acting was about, not just falling like a stone into a puddle of perfect laughs. I stumbled through the remainder of the plays at Eastern Slope in my usual position: John was an actor and I was still a camper.

I had an affair with another camper, a girl from Boston named Mara. Mara was sixteen. On hot, sweaty nights in North Conway, with the mosquitoes howling in our ears and the moths beating against the ceiling all night, we would roll in my tiny bunk until we both finally passed out. In the morning she would have to get up to build and paint flats for the next production. I was an actor now, not an apprentice, so I could sleep late, then go down for rehearsals at noon. This was an on-again off-again encounter that went on all summer.

There was another actor at North Conway named Reese, with whom I spent many drunken post-theater evenings. Reese had more or less the same problem I had: He was tormented most of the time by sexual desire. But he had a problem I didn't have.

"Do you think," Reese asked, "that North Conway, New Hampshire, is ready for a real Oklahoma faggot?" He smiled.

"Why don't you just *try* it with Karen?" I asked. Karen, an apprentice, had a crush on Reese. But Reese wasn't interested. He was horny, instead, for a local boy who was painting fences around the area that summer. Times and circumstances being what they were, this was a hopeless infatuation with no prospect of consummation.

"Ned, my dear boy, I'm not queer by choice, I'm queer because I'm queer."

"But she'd go to bed with you. And then you wouldn't be horny anymore." Solutions-R-Us.

"I've had women, Ned. They don't do it for me. Now, that devastating youth, *ahhh.* . . ." I had watched this boy that Reese craved, trying to see what it was he wanted. I couldn't see it, but Reese assured me it was there.

"His ass. Just look at his ass and pretend he's a girl." Well, he *did* have a nice ass.

"But that's dangerous. The people around here might not be so tolerant as they are in New York."

"Ned, Ned, Ned . . . I grew up in *Oklahoma*, son."

"Oh, yeah."

"We didn't even tell *ourselves* we were queer, never mind approaching a total stranger. I didn't actually know myself until the eleventh grade, for chrissake. I had no fucking idea. There was one other guy in my school. And when we found out what we were, we kept it real quiet. Can you imagine those good old boys? I mean, *everyone* got sucked off by the spring calves—farmers think nothing of fucking their stock. But fuck another *farmer*, boy. . . ." we hooted.

This was living. Talking about homosexuality with a real homo. Wide open, no holds barred. I was solemn. I was privileged. I was very worldly.

"I think it's fine that you're gay," I offered magnanimously. "I think there's lots of very fine gay people." It was apropos of absolutely nothing—I was just trying out my newfound office, in philistinic New Hampshire: Captain Candid, President of the Open-Minded Club. Reese looked at me and clenched his teeth.

"I detest the term *gay*. There is nothing gay about homosexuality."

"Why?" I ask her. I'm in Rome. It's eight months earlier, the fall of 1962. Tim Newman and I, on our way to Kitzbühel to ski, have stopped off first in London, then in Rome. My mother and I are standing in the lobby of the Excelsior Hotel on the Via Veneto. There is a huge press party going on.

Elizabeth Taylor and Eddie Fisher are giving a party for Kirk Douglas, a one-year anniversary of his movie, *Spartacus*, but the story is Elizabeth Taylor and Richard Burton who are costarring in *Cleopatra*. They have been spotted alone or together in eleven different places, and that special breed of Italian photographer known as the paparazzo is making his indelible mark on the face of journalism worldwide by grasping every conceivable opportunity to photograph this notorious couple.

A group of friends from home had come to Europe for a vacation, and we had all met up in Rome. Doug Tibbles, Jack McGinity, Ernie Heller, John Vincent, Gregg Jakobson, and I were holed up in one room in a local *pensione* not far from the Via Veneto. Richard Lang was also in Rome. He was working as the second assistant director on *Cleopatra*, and we had coerced him into getting us jobs as extras on The Movie.

"What about Van?"

We worked and took trips all over Italy, sometimes on trains, sometimes in a 1953 Fiat that my mother had bought for me in Florence. We raced motor scooters around the Circus Maximus like Ben Hur, climbed down into the Coliseum at night and drank wine with the bats and the ghosts of lions and Christians, or ran wild in the Roman nightclubs where Taylor and Burton and everyone who counted would be, having a whack at the *dolce vita*.

"What happened?"

"He doesn't want to be married anymore," my mother says. *Not married to you*, I think. She waves to someone. I look. It is Gina Lollobrigida with a dress that is slit up the back so far I nearly keel over trying to get a good shot.

"Why . . ." I mumble again. God, that Italian chick has a great ass. And tits that could share an apartment with Liz's. I wonder if I could meet her.

"He's got a place in London. He'll finish *The Music Man* and then, I guess . . ." she falters. They had been staying in England. Van was doing a very successful run of the *The Music Man* in London's West End. I had gone there for a few days to see him in the role. He was excellent as Professor Harold Hill, the epitome of the American spirit of sleazy enterprise, especially to the British audiences who were infatuated with him. He was still their Guy Named Joe.

I had been oblivious to problems at home. I had become used to the relationship between my mother and Van: over the years an increasing attitude on his part to put her down, to be short and curt with her, to be more sarcastic than usual to her, whom he referred to as "the mother of all living things." This increase wasn't apparent to me. It was subtle and gradual, and besides, I enjoyed it. It was funny. Van was always funny.

But more and more Van fled to the Farley Granger Room and shut the door. He was not around much. But actors are always on the fly. It never seemed significant.

I finally gave my mother some attention and realized that for one of the few times in her life, she was showing me the face of her own pain. She was telling me something vital. I tried to gather my wits. Van had left her. Why now? What was going on?

Then, as soon as I thought this, I realized that I didn't really want to know. My curiosity just evaporated. I felt as though it were inevitable that Van should leave her. I had never thought of this before, yet suddenly it was inevitable. I took comfort in the concept of inevitability. If things were inevitable, that meant I didn't have to wonder why they happened. I didn't have to imagine a cure, or a fault. My mother was just my mother. After all, hadn't she already fucked up one marriage, lost me one father? And now she had lost my other father.

For the past fourteen years, Van had done yeoman service in an effort to be a dad to two boys not his own, and a daughter, his only child. He had shown us a life of ease and comfort. My own father, who had remarried, was now involved with a new family, a wife, Sharley, and three daughters, Hilda, Wynnie, and Emily. While I saw him often when I was home, I rarely felt as though I were a part of this new life. They tried their best to include me, inviting me for dinner and parties and swimming and barbecues. There were hilarious nights of drinking and howling with my dad and his pals, especially Lee Marvin, whom I had grown to love almost as much as I loved Dad or Van. Lee was like Van before there was Van, and

Ty before that. A strong, charismatic male buddy/idol. Whatever they did I tried to be a part of it.

There were days back in the early fifties, out in the San Fernando Valley, when we rode motorcycles on the firebreaks in Encino and Tarzana. Later, when the housing developments were built over our spots, we moved out into the desert along with Bud Ekins and Steve McQueen, hauling the bikes on trailers to places like Pearblossom and Newhall. They were great days, full of dust and heat and noise. The August sun broiled me inside the leather jacket and the sweaty helmet, and the bike got so hot it was like riding a two-wheeled kitchen stove. We rode the river beds in the mornings until, as if by chance but always by design, we found that solitary roadside bar and fell into the cool darkness for hours of pool and shuffleboard and boilermakers before jumping on the bikes again so stoned that I, at least, could no longer ride. But it was cool because I got to be with Bud and Steve and Lee and Dad.

Still, for all the camaraderie and the kindness, I didn't feel truly comfortable with them. With Lee and Dad and Steve, I could never ride as well as them, I could never keep up. The fact was I was scared, and my fear kept me always hanging back. At home, my stepmother had an ambivalence toward me, never really sure if I was really OK or a threat. Sometimes we loved each other, other times, usually drunk, we fought, swearing and trading hang-ups on the telephone.

Now, here in Rome, with the paparazzi swirling around us chasing down the story of the century, life was once again heaving and reshaping itself, and I was, again, an observer, passive and immobile. Someone else was shaking the blanket and I was simply waiting for it to settle again. The fact was that while I hadn't felt comfortable with Dad's new family, I also was never really comfortable around Van or Mom or anyone. I was always more or less in a constant state of agitation, discomfort, and anxiety that only stopped when I had a drink or a girl.

So Van left her. Well . . .

"Screw him," I said to my mother. "He's an asshole." There, Mom, doesn't that make you feel better?

"He left me for the lead dancer," she said. Gina Lollobrigida had moved to a table, sat down, and crossed her legs. The dress rode high, like the flag of Italy. "The lead dancer in *The Music Man*." Probably got nice pins, this dancer. "Oh," I said, not really listening. "She English?"

"A man," she said. "A boy really. He's the lead boy dancer."

I almost missed that. My emotions fought for emergence. She's pissed. She can't face the fact that Van just got tired of her and left.

"I saw him once. Through a window in the theater. He was with another man, his dresser, that time. But he left with this dancer—this young boy."

"Well, OK." Don't care. Just don't care about this at all, and you'll be all right. What do you tell your mother when she says your stepfather left her for another man? "Fuck him, Mom." There, that ought to clear the air. It's an aberration. This isn't a good thing, this thing about Van. Let's accept and move on, whaddaya say, Ma?

"I never listened, you know. Laird Cregar told me. Laird told me years ago. And Henry Hathaway told me. I didn't listen. I thought it was just rumors." You thought you could change him. You thought you could change what you loved to suit you.

There had been several big rows over the years, and a few of the biggest had been in Europe: in Claridge's in London, in Gstaad and Vevey in Switzerland. I had never been present, and only knew about them later when Schuyler told me. Tracy had been in Gstaad during one incident when Van had hit Schuyler so hard she had slammed into a wall. No one talked about these things. They were never discussed. Van was very big and very frightening, and he was the star, the guy making the bucks, the guy with the career that we had to protect. I had never thought of the pressure that must have been on him, what it must have been like. He was an actor. Appearing to be what he was not was his job, after all.

I had stayed in Italy for several months. I was supposed to be studying something or other at the University of Florence. It was another bold experiment in education. All I knew was that, as with other remedial concepts, this one was also my mother's. My resentment and distance from her now grew. She couldn't run her own life, having driven away two men, but she was continuing to try to run mine.

I had an apartment on the Via dei Bardi on the banks of the Arno River. I became infatuated with the Renaissance and with the artists; Donatello, Michelangelo, Masaccio, Duccio, and Raphael. I spent my days wandering the streets of Florence, haunting the great galleries, the Uffizi, the Bargello, the cathedrals and palazzos of the ruling Florentine families, the Bardi and the Rucellai, now museums. At night I went to the few dim nightclubs in a city that was not known for its nightlife. There, in a suit and tie, I sat at a table by myself while a man rode around on a tiny bicycle juggling plastic rings, and a woman made dogs walk on their hind legs with parasols strapped to their heads. I watched the woman in her lipstick and powder and fishnet stockings. She was at least sixty. I yearned for her.

I wandered the streets mooning after the ungettable women or tracing the lines of the statues, the walls, the Baptistery doors with my fingers, touching what I imagined were the artist's own hands. All I felt was the bronze, cold as the winter sky.

Some nights I took a bottle of wine and sat out on the struts of one of the bridges and watched the muddy Arno pass beneath me. I couldn't get anything to turn over inside, to hook up. Around me was a city that contained the greatest concentration of genius and inspiration anywhere in the world, and I was untouched, unmoved. I wept at Donatello's tiny "David," and at Michelangelo's five sublime "Slaves." But immediately, I noticed myself crying and thought it exquisitely theatrical. Did the tourists wonder at this sensitive young man?

A month later I packed my bags, turned in the key to my apartment, and slouched toward Beverly Hills.

CHAPTER

11

When I finally returned to Beverly Hills in the spring, Tracy was safely away at Menlo College in Northern California, but Schuyler was there, trapped in this mansion with a constant stream of gays and Mom, who had apparently decided that the best medicine for heartbreak was homeopathic: If a snake bites you, get more snakes.

Henry Willson, an agent famous for naming actors Tab and Rock, had his stable of tan young men, eyes bright, nostrils flared, prancing through our house like a tiny herd of carousel ponies. These people were out of some homophobic nightmare. They sat around commiserating with my mother about Van and drinking her scotch by the gallon. In return for her feeding and watering them, they smiled and told her she was gorgeous, she didn't deserve such treatment, Van was a prick, etc. They swarmed my sister like aphids. One fatuous twit even changed his name to Schuyler then went whinnying down the hall to tell her of this great honor. Sky smiled politely and locked herself in her room for a week.

There was no respite. My mother seemed totally oblivious. Our house was like a popular nightspot going through its six-month heyday. There were parties all the time, a kind of flaming Transylvanian fiesta. The house was thronged with young boys and their priapic, ramp-sandaled old queens, screeching and twittering in the halls or lolling around the pool, limp and exhausted from changing their names.

I fled whenever I could to be with Dad and Lee riding bikes out in the desert or up the coastal canyons, or with my friends at the beach where I sometimes stayed in my car or slept in a sleeping bag on the sand. We traveled up and down the coast, north to Santa Barbara or the Ventura County Line, or south to Laguna, La Jolla, Little Corona, and San Diego. We body-surfed at Brook Street and the Wedge, played volleyball in Santa Barbara and Mission Bay, cooked on the beach, slept on the beach, drank wine and smoked weed on the beach. It seemed the most permanent home I had ever had.

I felt that I no longer had a real home anyway, may never have had one. It was beginning to dawn on me that I was a guest and had always been a guest, wherever I had lived, whether in a house with my mother and father or stepfather, or on the planet in general. For some reason, this pleased me. I felt a sense of righteous isolation from which I drew strength. I would be alone, face to the sea, sand

in my hair, fog in my head. I liked the indefinite grayness of the
ocean, mirrored by an indefinite grayness in my mind.

By now I had had my heart broken a couple of times, but I
couldn't draw an association with how I felt inside that summer
with how my mother felt. One girl, Suzi, had gone off with a volleyball hero in Laguna and I moped around from bar to bar during
the tournament, sick to my stomach and unable to eat. Yet my
mother's pain seemed remote to me, as if she had engineered her
own disasters, but mine were bestowed by fate and certainly felt
worse.

"We will always live in Beverly Hills," my mother had once told
me. It was part of the canon that included "You are handsomer than
Jimmy Stewart," and "People are watching us." It was one of the
things which I had implicitly believed long after I had given up on
Santa Claus.

Beverly Hills had been a wonderful city to grow up in. It was
crisscrossed with alleys for us to bicycle through and vacant lots
full of waist-high wild mustard in the spring. Every one of us knew
every inch of those alleys which, in the early fifties, were unpaved
and atomic with dust after a proper ten-foot full-brake brodie on
our favorite Schwinns. There were vacant lots for dirt-clod fights;
there was a Saturday morning Bugs Bunny cartoon matinee at the
Warners' Beverly Theater on Wilshire; there were drug stores with
comic-book racks and signs that said: THIS IS NOT A LIBRARY. There
were swimming pools, tennis courts, even a bridle path where people
still rode horses.

The neighborhood was impeccable. Our street was lined with
tall, graceful palm trees. Other streets were lined with maple, elm,
carob. Every house had a perfect lawn, a perfect wall, a perfect
driveway. Beverly Hills was symmetrical, safe. It smelled good. Fresh
asphalt in the streets, fresh paint on the houses, fresh wrought iron
on the fences; jasmine, tea roses, and honeysuckle lined the alleys,
tree branches heavy with avocados and lemons drooped from the
backyards across the walls and left their fruits in our pockets. The
whole place was amiable, benign. Once, when I was nineteen, I had
gotten on Joe Stanley's motorcycle, a huge Ariel Square-Four, and,
naked except for tennis shoes so I could shift, I had ridden at one
in the morning, up and down the streets at ninety miles an hour.
From Santa Monica Boulevard to Sunset Boulevard and back I rode.
Not one cop showed up. I never feared arrest, because I knew the
cops. I had already been picked up for being drunk in the streets at
least once, and all they had done was take me home. The cops were
our friends, our kind and indulgent uniformed uncles.

When you live your life in a place where you fear no interruption by any outside entity, a certain arrogance is inculcated into your personality. You get to where you brook no interference, refuse to allow for interruptions, and you are genuinely surprised when life actually does intervene in your otherwise seamless parade of pleasurable moments.

The fact was that time had been running out on the Beverly Hills life for a long time. One of the last gasps, although I hadn't known it, had taken place the previous spring. It had been my twenty-first birthday. If there was ever one last moment of promise that I was destined for great things, it was this birthday.

GUEST LIST   April 27, 1962

Henny and Jim Backus
Mitzi Gaynor and Jack Bean
Myrna Fahey and Richard Beymer
Frances and Edgar Bergen
Rosalind Russell and Freddy Brisson
Lita and Rory Calhoun
Cheryl and Steve Crane
Troy Donahue and date
Jeannie and Gene Kelly
Mr. and Mrs. Alan Ladd
Pat and Peter Lawford
Janet Leigh and date
Kathy and Marty Manulis
Jeanne and Dean Martin
Betty and Lee Marvin
Lana Turner and Fred May
Ray and Mal Milland
Martha Raye
Jill St. John and Lance Reventlow
Ann Sothern and Cesar Romero
Lovey and Everett Sloane
Carolyn Jones and Aaron Spelling
Maggie Brown and Jule Styne
Diane and Bobby Van
Henry Willson
Ed Wynn
Sharley and Keenan Wynn
Virginia Zanuck

There was another list containing fifty of my own friends. We had a tent in the backyard and a band. My father was the perfect host. He made the sacrifice of his life that night: He didn't have a single drink. Every few minutes I went up to him and congratulated him on this marvel of self-control. And smelled his breath. He was true to his word.

My grandfather was there. A few weeks earlier he had taken me to dinner. "I'll give you the twenty-five-hundred dollars or give it to your mother for the party," he said.

"Cash?" I asked.

"Cash?" His head began to shake. Dollar bills with wings flew from his wallet, and he actually patted his breast pocket. "Well, cash, no. I'll put it into a trust fund." Ah. The famous trust fund. How many occasions, throughout the years, had my grandfather regaled me with tales of the trust fund he had set up for each of his five grandchildren? They were for one hundred thousand dollars each. They would come to maturity and be disbursed in varying amounts at different times in our lives: when we were twenty-five, thirty, thirty-five, and forty. "That way," he said, "you won't just get it all and spend it when you're too young to know better." I was always very pleased and reassured at this idea, and, unconsciously, I applied the brakes. It was like a sign on an icy mountain road: MONEY AHEAD, SLOW PROGRESS.

Ed Wynn was a famous investor. People constantly proposed ventures to him. Once, in the twenties, someone had approached him with the idea of a kind of paper that you could see through. "What would anyone want," he asked, "with paper you could see through? It ruins the surprise." He passed on cellophane, opting instead for another man's invention of a tiny glass vial that held water and pinned neatly behind the lapel, to keep his boutonniere fresh. "Great idea," said Ed. "No one will have to go around with a wilted carnation in their lapel anymore."

So, I could add twenty-five hundred dollars to this trust fund, or I could have a huge birthday bash. I actually thought it over, instilling my grandfather with false hope. He leaned forward. "Gee, Gramps," I said.

"Twenty-five hundred bucks, kiddo," he reminded me. Yeah. In a trust fund. "The party is one night. It's over like that." Yeah. That's true. But I *love* parties.

"You're only twenty-one once, Grandpa." My wisdom overwhelmed us both. Grandpa just looked at me. Who was this child? Keenan's son, of course. The old man smiled slightly and nodded. So be it. It never dawned on me that I could have had ten great parties with that money.

The party was black-tie. I was the center of attention for a whole night. We twisted and did the pony. Like Boney Maroni. Did the monkey and the mashed potatoes. Do You Love Me . . . (Do You

Love Me?) Do You Love Me Now That I Can Dance? I threw knives into the cork-lined doors with Doug, a common entertainment of ours, and Cheryl Crane and I snuck into the garage and made out for half an hour in Mom's Cadillac. I think it was shortly after that Cheryl swore off men altogether. Some acts are just impossible to follow. We even threw out a crasher, dressed nicely in a tuxedo. Crashers in Beverly Hills work on it. This guy was one of the best.

"Look, I got all dressed up," he said. I handed him a drink.

"I know, but this is a private party," I said.

"But there's two hundred people here. And look at this tux, Champ. Twenty bucks to rent this tux."

"You're a pro. I can tell. And this is not to impugn your professional status. This will never leave the confines of this room. But you gotta go."

"Boogah," he said. He darted his hands out in a dramatic way, his fingers pointed in a personal mudra, standing sideways, as if he were on a board. I realized he had to be a surfer. "I'm such an artist, Boogah. Don't make me leave. It would be like—slicing up a Picasso, smashing a Michelangelo with a hammer. I mean, I made it here for fifteen minutes before you spotted me. I'm part of the *life*. Check the *tux*. Boogah!" In reality, I could have let him stay. But my ego was involved. It was him and me, warring over the party of life.

"I'm sorry, man, you gotta go." He shook his head.

"You're missing a great opportunity, Champ. I'm the top, the best. This party needs me." I nodded. This party only needs *me*, dude.

That following fall I went to Europe. It was the next spring, 1963, that the house was overrun with the carousel ponies, and my mother dyed her hair blond and started wearing orange lipstick. That summer I fled to New Hampshire and another season of summer stock. It was never our house again, if indeed it had ever been. It belonged to strangers.

The theater was in my blood, but in an altogether unexpected way. My whole life was becoming theater, yet I did not really like the theater itself. If I lived it, why be in it? Still, I had gotten that little taste from the laughs in the one play at Eastern Slope. I also enjoyed the absence of my parents in my life. There had been no big deal entrances backstage by glittering family members, no press except for the reviewer for the local paper, *The Reporter*, who wrote that John Hillerman and Ned Wynn, "share acting honors . . . both have a good sense of comedy." Maybe it was because I was so strongly influenced by John's enthusiasm for the theater. He convinced me that I should at least try to find acting work in New York, to see if I was cut out for it. I decided to go to New York after the stock company shut down.

Leaving Mara was difficult. Difficult because I had gone through all kinds of torture during the summer, being with her, breaking up, getting together again, breaking up, getting together. It was like a Lesley Gore record. At the end, we were suddenly, magically in love. We sat on the bunk in my stark little camper's room, scene of so many romantic mid-sex blackouts, while I waited for the bus that would take me back to New York. We held hands and hugged and cried for an hour, as campers are wont, recalling things that didn't happen the way we remembered, and feelings we never had. She promised to come and see me in New York. After all, she wanted to be an actress, and New York was where we all went to be actors.

I finally got on the bus. It pulled out, and I waved at Mara and the others who were out on the grass. It was too good an opportunity to miss. I opened my window and leaned out. "Good-bye, Grovers' Corners!" I shouted. "Good-bye, Grandma's butternut tree." Then everyone on the lawn shouted back,

"Good-bye, Emily . . . you silly little *bitch*!" I sat back down grinning. People on the bus looked at me. I gestured over my shoulder.

"Actors. . . ." I said, lamely. An old man turned around and nodded toward the bus driver.

"Be careful," he said.

"Why?" I asked, glancing down the aisle at the burly man behind the wheel.

"That's Lew." Then he turned back to his paper. Everyone on the bus was smiling. New Hampshire humor.

When I got to New York I looked up Tim Newman, who had an apartment. He was working for the J. Walter Thompson advertising agency at the time, and he and his two roommates offered me a bed for a couple of weeks. This stretched into a month, six weeks. I thought I was doing fine. Tim informed me otherwise. He sat down with me one day and told me that I was a Jekyll-and-Hyde character. A nice enough guy, if a little underpowered in the old job-hunting department, when I was sober. But that when I was drunk, I turned into this maniac who yelled and cried and beat on the walls. They had more or less had it with me. Would I please leave?

Incredible. Me, a Jekyll and Hyde. This from my pal, my skiing buddy, my friend from high school. How could he call me on the kind of behavior I thought we all shared? Didn't he drink, too? Didn't he get drunk as well as me? What was it that made him think he could bust me on something like that? Just because he graduated from college, got a job, became self-supporting, entered the main-

stream, where did he get off telling me I couldn't handle my liquor?
I was a liquor-handler from way back. I'd stopped throwing up when
I drank, I never got mush-mouthed, I was a controlled drinker.
Sometimes I burst into tears at parties. OK. I overshot the mark.
Well . . . if Tim couldn't handle it, if he was so *sensitive*, I'd move.

Deeply misunderstood, I left. I found an apartment and a roommate on West Eighty-sixth Street, a walk-up with a bathroom down
the hall which we shared with two Puerto Rican families who always
seemed to start the day off by throwing some appliances down the
stairs. Then the kids' lunch boxes. Then the kids. It was better than
a cup of coffee.

My mother had a friend in New York named Buffy Cobb. Buffy
was the daughter of Irvin S. Cobb, a writer and humorist of an
earlier era. She had produced a show that was running on Broadway,
a Shaw revival which had won a Tony. I had known Buffy since
childhood, and I threw myself on her mercy. She took me to readings
for another play she was casting. I sat at the door with a list and
checked the actors off as they came through. That was the extent
of my job. For this I got lunch.

I even went on some auditions myself, quaking in the wings,
my stomach on fire, trying to learn my sides, to understand the
words, to understand what I was even doing there. Other actors,
real New York actors of the kind revered by my father and mother,
wandered around outside practicing their breathing, chattering excitedly with each other about directors and producers, the names
of Joe Papp and David Merrick flying from their lips like little spit-
balls of rank. I hated every one of them.

I was totally out of place. I had no more connection with these
people than I had with anyone else in New York except for Buffy
and Buffy's obnoxious boyfriend, an aging roué named Alan, who
wandered drunkenly around her flat mumbling about how he had
regularly "serviced" this Famous Broadway Musical Star when she
was doing a smash hit show, and had continued to do so over the
years whenever she was in New York.

I had never heard the term "serviced" before when referring to
humans. At Happy Hill Farm I'd heard the word from a gentle, quiet
little man I met one weekend. This man was with a stunning model
who looked as if she had stepped straight off the pages of *Vogue*,
which she had. They were both extremely quiet, pensive people. I
found out this handsome, somber fellow was Prince Aly Khan and
the woman was Bettina, his girlfriend. Whenever he spoke, it was
with ineffable woe. "I have a nice stud, Cortie. He could service that
mare for you. A gift, of course. A gift." He looked like he was going
to cry. Horse people, I assumed, talked about servicing the way my
grandfather talked about comedy.

Now here was this Alan character talking about servicing Famous Broadway Musical Star, making it sound as if she were not only a horse, but a horse with money. I thought of Famous Broadway Musical Star's body, which at forty was still spectacular and not at all horsey, and wondered if I could get that job. How exactly had Alan gotten this servicing gig? Did a lot of Broadway stars require servicing? Were only soggy, middle-aged drunks up for those jobs? Could a callow twenty-two-year-old do it, too? I was broke, and I was horny. This would solve my problems. I could become a stud.

"Hey, Alan. What's Famous Broadway Musical Star's number?" I was at Buffy's flat on Sutton Place, a beautiful address overlooking the East River. She invited me at least once a week for dinner. There, one night in seven, I could pretend I was still a princeling, a familiar of crystal and porcelain, of Châteauneuf du Pape and Château Margaux, able to converse with women in slit gowns and men in black tie. I fell back upon my upbringing with ease. It never occurred to me that this moment in New York was anything other than that: a strange, uncomfortable, but transient moment, an adventure in a special section of my own personal playground called Realityland.

"What do you want her number for?" Alan was suspicious immediately.

"I want to service her."

"Punk. You have no style." He went into the kitchen where Buffy was preparing a salad.

"I'm young. I have hard, firm flesh. It stays hard and firm for hours. Days sometimes. It even hurts. It's like a crowbar. Blue-steel." I followed him in.

"Buffy! Tell Ned to leave. He's upsetting me." Alan was weaving. He became mush-mouthed and petulant around nine.

"Oh, Alan, can it," said Buffy. Then she grinned at me. "Isn't Alan an incredible asshole?"

In desperation, hoping to be rid of me, Alan sent me to see a friend of his at ABC Television where I got a job as a page at sixty-five dollars a week, ten more than at the Eastern Slope Playhouse.

A page was merely another version of an extra, only at one-tenth the wage. The man who supervised the pages at ABC was a former military officer who actually made us stand at attention every morning and inspected us, then sent us out on the streets of New York City dressed in black pants, black ties, white shirts, and little red jackets with ABC on the pockets. This was very close to a capital offense, in my opinion. Why not simply put a little sign on the back of every uniform: KILL THIS PERSON. HE'S TOO MUCH OF A DICKWIPE TO LIVE.

Every day I stood on various street corners of Manhattan and handed out tickets to *Girl Talk* with Virginia Graham, *The Jimmy Dean Show* with the pre-sausage magnate singing cowboy songs, and *The Price Is Right* with Bill Cullen. I was cursed, smacked, spat upon, and constantly ridiculed for my costume. I had to stick. This was the only job I could get until the stud thing got going.

The point for us as pages was to fill the studio theaters, one of which was on Fiftieth Street, with people—any people we could find. So we had a large contingent of drunk and/or crazy street people whom we would round up, load into buses, and take to the theaters. These people were generally quite well behaved, feeling honored for the moment and clutching their tickets as if they were passports. There was the occasional throwing up in the aisles, of course, and screaming matches, fighting, and a certain amount of intellectual intercourse with kindly, sympathetic doorknobs and elegant, swagged theater curtains. But for the most part we had good, enthusiastic audiences.

I had a strange fascination with the New York street folk, known in the early sixties simply as bums. I knew that all that stood between me and being one of them was a name and a family. I had no more understanding of how to run my life successfully than they had. In fact, I felt that, since they could make it on the street, they were that much more capable than I was. They had something I lacked: raw nerve.

I watched a man only a couple of years older than I run all the way across Broadway at Times Square and grab an apple core from a trash can, an apple core I had just tossed there. He wolfed it down and stared at me. We stood there for a moment staring at one another. I could have sworn I was looking at myself. The recognition caused a chill. Then he loped across the street again and took up his station near the Nedick's stand. Every day I came to the same spot and watched him. Then one day he just disappeared. I was depressed when he no longer showed up.

There were traveling punch-outs on Broadway. Once or twice a week someone would run by me and someone else would be chasing him. One guy got hit by almost every passer-by along the whole length of the Avenue. He was pummeled by a dozen people between Forty-second and Fiftieth Streets. People, seeing him get punched, stepped up and punched him as well. I got a strange feeling inside watching this: I wanted to punch the guy, too. The mob excited me. As long as we were in agreement as to who was the target, and as long as the target wasn't me, it was OK. Back in my mind I always felt that *I* was the weird guy. To take the heat off me, I was always relieved to find someone weirder, some poor bastard who had been found out. It was Bob Roos out there running. It was Howie Rosenberg, another poor kid we'd terrorized at Webb, punishing him for the felony of blatant uncoolness until he finally ran away. Now, on the streets of New York, where could anyone run away to? Where could they hide? This was it, this was Judgment Day. When I asked someone what the man had done, the guy shrugged. "Musta done somethin'," he grinned, blood on his skinned knuckles. New York humor.

It turned out the man had attacked a woman and tried to steal her purse down around Thirty-ninth Street, and had run the gauntlet from there. Relieved that there was a real crime available for my conscience to nest in, I smiled. Musta done somethin'. I swaggered around Times Square handing out *Girl Talk* tickets and regaling the lingering mob with tales of the street.

Some nights I went to plays. Ionesco was very big among the hip actors at all the auditions. I wandered into a small off-off-Broadway house where I saw *The Typist* and *The Tiger*, to get some culture, something to discuss with the spitballing actors—and passed out in my seat. I visited John Hillerman in his tiny bin on Avenue B, the filthiest, funkiest place I had ever been. I thought, *this* is an actor. This is what it takes to get along in the world. Nerve. Without my parents I felt I would have died in the streets of New York. But John was cheerful.

"Fucking pig sty, isn't it?" he grinned.

"How do you stand it?" I asked him as we picked our way down the urine-soaked corridor to the street.

"I don't breathe in," he said.

I had all the bland inner assurances of any mindless rich kid. Even when I would walk across town and up to the West Eighties, not chic in 1963, even then I never thought for a moment that any of this had anything to do with me. The real me was a Prince. Princes have these kinds of adventures before their true destinies materialize at last to sweep them up and into the arms of their radiant futures.

Other nights, before my radiant future took hold, I either sat in my apartment eating TV dinners and staring out at the backs of the other buildings, or I went to the Village to find some sex or some form of companionship, things I never found there or anywhere else in New York. I did find someone who would sell me some marijuana, and so I got stoned by myself and wandered the streets of the Village, dropping into bars, drinking, and continuing to wander.

Some nights, with the idea of hearing some jazz, I would wander into a subway, get on the A train, lie down, pass out, and wake up in Harlem. I didn't need to go to Harlem to listen to jazz, of course. There were some of the best jazz clubs in the world right where I was—the Half Note, the Five Spot—I even wandered into Birdland from time to time just to watch Pee Wee Marquette announce the latest trumpet sensation since Clifford Brown, hoping to catch the next Bird, the next Miles Davis.

But I went to Harlem because all princes should see all of the kingdom. And because I wanted to be accepted, to hang around black people, to be cool. I had no idea of what I must have looked like. Floating along 125th Street like a little scrap of Kleenex, wandering into Small's Paradise, (yo, Wilt!), walking up to the bar, ordering a drink, watching the bartender hesitate and finally serve me with a bad look. He must think I'm cool. Didn't these people just love me? Didn't they just see this jazz groover who knew (and sang, loudly) all the famous solos by heart? This white guy who broke all the barriers? Wasn't I the cultural astronaut?

"Hey, man, what are you doing up here?" A scientific-looking colored guy sits down next to me at the bar.

"Listening to jazz," I say.

"Do you realize what's going on?" he asks.

"I'm just trying to enjoy myself," I say.

"You shouldn't be here," he says. I look at him. He's a little older than I am, maybe twenty-five. He wears glasses, dresses preppy, collegiate, hence, the scientific look.

"Why not?" I ask.

"In case you haven't noticed, this is Harlem," he says.

"Nobody minds . . ."

"They mind. They think you're a cop." I'm shocked.

"I'm not a cop. I'm just listening to music." The guy shakes his head.

"Let me help you get outa here," he says. "Pay for the drink and leave a two-dollar tip."

"Two doll! . . ."

"Leave a two-dollar tip." He looks at me as he gets off his stool. He's very serious. I leave a two-dollar tip. We exit to Broadway. He walks me to the 125th Street station, gets on the train with me, and we ride back down to Manhattan.

He is a graduate student at Columbia, and we spend most of the rest of the night sitting on the steps of the apartment talking about "life." I'll be his friend forever, as I always am with people when I'm drunk. He finally leaves. I never see the guy again.

When I woke up that afternoon, Mara was there. Finally, a piece of ass.

"Neddy," she says, as I push up her skirt and tear at her underwear, "please . . . wait . . ." I can't. I haven't been laid in two months. We have sex. I come immediately. She simply holds me. I finally look at her. She's crying.

"What's the matter?" I sit on the edge of the bed and light a cigarette.

"Neddy—I'm pregnant." My vision needles down to a tiny pinpoint of light. All I can see are the scratches in the linoleum floor. I suck on the cigarette like it's made of oxygen. My throat won't open up. Are you sure are you sure are you sure. . . .

"Are you sure?"

"Yes," she says, her eyes frightened. It's mine? Are you sure are you sure are you sure. . . .

"It's yours. I haven't been with anyone else." I didn't have to ask. I wasn't an asshole. I look better. I feel better. No reason. I feel great. But I'm crying.

We wandered around New York talking, holding hands, weeping, laughing. Me, twenty-two, broke, useless, frightened, and this girl, sixteen, from Boston, pregnant, terrified. Her parents have the solution: Why don't we two great kids get married?

The warm breeze of reason accompanied me to the shuttle from New York to Boston a month later. I would be brave, I would be responsible, I would be all those things I was taught. I'll be honest, straightforward, courageous, upstanding, dependable, reliable, honorable, and true. These are a few of my favorite things.

The old woman wanders through the house like something from Madame Tussaud's. "Don't say anything, Neddy. It would kill her. She doesn't know I'm pregnant." I look at Mara. She looks like she swallowed an antelope. The woman doesn't know her granddaughter is pregnant? "She doesn't see very well." No shit.

The entire weekend is a tense, anxious farce. Mara's parents are nice, upstanding suburban Catholics who will simply not allow their daughter to get an abortion. Abortion is out. Ball's in your court young man.

"Well, Ned, what will you do with your life." Fuck. Oh, Jesus.

"Well, I'm going to be studying acting," I say. Out of my mind. I'm completely out of my mind.

"That's nice," says Mara's mother. "He's going to study acting, Mother," she says to the old lady who supposedly can't see the pregnant girl and would evidently keel over dead as a doornail if she could.

"Do you think she knows we're in the room?" I whisper to Mara.

"Do you think you can make a living acting, Ned?" Mara's father asks me. I couldn't make a living if I fell into a vat of thousand-dollar bills.

"*Um* . . ." Quick, quick, what's the line? "Well . . ." Come on, the guy says can you make a living acting, Ned, and you answer . . . I'm up. I need someone to cue me.

"Ned's a terrific actor, Daddy," Mara offers. Thank God for her theatrical training.

"Well, that may be, but can he make a living at it?" Everyone stares at me, even the grandmother. I just don't have an answer.

"I don't know, sir," I finally say.

"Well, at least he's honest about it, dear." Yes, but honesty is not what's needed here. Lies. We need lies.

"I think I can, I mean, I'm going to give it my best shot." I already gave Mara my best shot and look where that got us. Everyone looks reassured. I just hope I live long enough to get on the god-damned plane out of here.

The last day Mara and I walk by a reservoir and hold hands and talk about the future. I have learned to hate the future and at the same time to live in it constantly. She is adamant about the abortion. Her parents are completely confident that somehow I'll marry her. I know I can't. Mara knows it, too.

"Don't worry about me, Neddy. I'll be all right. I'll have the baby and you can be with us or not. My parents will get over it." I'm so grateful to Mara for letting me off the hook, I nearly promise I'll marry her after all.

I am disturbed by this feeling: anguish and relief together. Checking the real reasons: I find that I'm scared to get married and to have a kid. Natural reaction, I think. But the other reason is that I am constantly aware of the deeply embedded commands of the family: We are being watched, don't embarrass us. And worst of all: Is this girl *worthy*?

If Mara had been any one of the rich girls I had grown up or gone to school with, a Strawbridge, a Doheny, or a Firestone, my mother would be ecstatic, offering to make the arrangements with the Bel-Air Hotel for the wedding. It would be *their* parents who would be doing the objecting. But I knew that a little Irish-Catholic girl from a middle-class suburban family in Boston was not going to fill the bill at home. All this was made on the grand assumption that fed continuously into my already warped sense of self: I was special; was *she* special enough for me?

Ever since I had first started to date girls, I had always had this governor in the back of my mind. This was implanted by my mother who had never approved of a single girl I liked.

"Why don't you go out with Casey Doheny?" she asked. The Dohenys were one of Los Angeles's most prominent families. I knew several of the kids including Larry and Casey, a very sweet girl.

"She's Guy Webster's girlfriend, Mom."

"Well, they're not *married*, are they? And what about Lindy Firestone? She had a big crush on you in dancing school. Why don't you ever call Lindy Firestone?"

"Lindy Firestone does not know of my existence on the planet,
Mom." What is it with you these days? Tires tires tires, morning
noon and night.

"Oh, that's ridiculous. You shouldn't hide your light under a
bushel." You oughta see me at parties, Mom.

Of course, whatever their origins, I was all too ready to use
these handy concepts to distance myself further from accountability
and obligation. My internal setup was primed for flight. Remorse
was nonexistent. I heard what I wanted to hear. A little guilt might
have been healthy, but guilt was preempted by another imprimatur:
If she ain't rich, haul ass.

Mara's father drove me to the airport. On the way he talked
about what a decision we had to make, that he would leave it up to
us. I could tell by his tone that he was confident we'd "do the right
thing." In the backseat Mara and I sat and looked at each other. She
knew she'd never see me again. All I could think about was that
freedom was just minutes away. I nodded and answered unconsciously. Yes, yes, anything, yes . . . I'll definitely think it over carefully, yes I care for Mara, yes, yes, yes . . . I was in New York in two
hours, and two weeks later I was back in California.

I approach the front door. From the street I can see there is a
chain on it. A sign has been tacked up. In essence it says that by
order of the sheriff the house has been condemned in order to satisfy
a federal lien. I stare at the sign and then finger the chain. It rattles
against the door. It is ludicrous. Humorous. Come on, chains?

"They took the Palm Springs house, too," my mother told me.
"They took both houses. They left me a car. That's all. And I'm still
liable with Van for a quarter of a million dollars." This is a joke,
right? I mean how theatrical can we get with chains on the doors?
Let's just call someone.

"Can't you call someone?" I asked. "Calling someone" is always
the first move. These someones were usually Ray Stark, Greg Bautzer, or Lew Wasserman. But these men were, for the first time I
could remember, unable to help us. This was the U.S. Government
we were in trouble with this time. I was shocked. For the first time
in my life I watched my mother simply shrug and shake her head.
Something was different.

"It's all that goddamned Jerry Rosenthal's fault." People in the
movie industry often turn their entire financial lives over to a group
of professionals called business managers. These men do everything
from then on: They even make out the checks to the Arrowhead
Water people. All you have to do is sign them. After opening the
monthly packet of checks, it becomes a habit to sign everything.

After all, the business manager is a pro, he's got a handle on it, it's all taken care of. Jerry Rosenthal was our business manager.

I had never realized, or even thought much about it, but our whole existence was very shaky from the day I was born. My parents never knew what was actually going on with their money or their property. The Jerry Rosenthal hustle that sunk our ship was simply part of the pattern of some artists in Hollywood who don't have a single idea as to "how it all works." There is a certain arrogance about having a lack of knowledge where financial matters are concerned. My father was almost proud of the fact that he didn't know how to write a check, only how to sign one.

In our case, through some very complex oil lease schemes, Rosenthal had maneuvered Van into a shelter that was supposed to decrease his tax bill. It was completely bogus. Rosenthal had made investments that lined his pockets and put Van into a tax-delinquent situation of which neither Van nor my mother was aware until it was too late. We were liable in full. On the downside of his career, Van had no way to pay this bill. So the government took the property.

It was years before anyone caught up with Rosenthal. Doris Day sued him and won a twenty-three-million-dollar judgment against him. My mother fumed for years about Jerry Rosenthal, and Van's lawyer, Jerry Lipsky. She blamed all our problems on these two men. As with anything, it was a shared responsibility. Ethics in the film business have never been anyone's first order of the day. It seemed like you either had to learn it all yourself, an impossible task, or you just took your chances. And then there was greed. How can we keep all our money from the government? A tax shelter? Great. Why pay the government when you can find some way around it? Never mind if you don't completely understand the complexities of the scheme. Even Jerry was a little foggy on that. I could see it was futile. There was no redress. The fact of the matter was, we were fucked. Something was different, all right. The someones could no longer help us.

My mother had moved into a house on Sunset Boulevard in Brentwood that was owned by Ella Logan, a former Broadway star. It was a charming house with a pool and a guest house which was made up for me to stay in. This was the first in a series of houses my mother was to move in and out of over the next ten years. Her friends, the people whom she had known for twenty years, some of her closest friends like Rosalind Russell, suddenly didn't know her. They didn't return her phone calls. She was no longer invited to their parties. Something was different, all right, Van was gone. Many avenues, both personal and financial, closed and remained that way. In a matter of a few months, a great wind had blown through our lives and slammed all the doors. The real friends, among them Jim and Henny Backus, Betty Grable, and George Hamilton's mother, Ann, remained. But the others dissolved like gossamer, such is the nature of Hollywood friendships.

I spent the next two years living in various apartments in and around West Los Angeles. I spent part of the time opening and closing safety-deposit boxes for my mother, who had become obsessed with hiding what valuables she had left. She was positive that the government was going to come in one day and take her rings and her bracelets and the rest of her jewelry. So I kept shifting them all over town until I started to get confused about where I had put things. I had keys to safety deposit boxes and no idea as to which ones they opened nor what might be inside. Finally, I took everything out and returned it to my mother. It was obvious that I was going to have to leave. I simply had nothing to offer her, and it was time to go.

I was still making a living doing extra-work. Occasionally, I was able to get a few days acting here and there on movies and TV shows like *Stoney Burke* with Jack Lord. I worked with Jerry Lewis in a couple of movies of his like *The Bellhop*. Some of these things, Jerry's pictures and Disney films like *Son of Flubber*, turned out to be three-generations-of-Wynns deals. Three-generations-of-Wynns deals were pictures that had both my father and grandfather in them. So for a few thousand bucks, they'd throw in the third generation, me.

My father had introduced me to Bill Asher, a director who worked for Samuel Z. Arkoff, whose American International Pictures had just made a surprising little hit called *Bikini Beach*. Starring Frankie Avalon and Annette Funicello, it was a mindless bubble of idiotic antics with motorcycle gangs, girls in bikinis, men in gorilla suits, and my father as the bad guy who wanted to take all the fun away. The formula was a hit. More pictures were planned. I was hired to play one of the eternal skateboarding background pals of Frankie. It was easy to see my career was in ascendance.

CHAPTER
12

"Boogah." The voice comes from behind me. "Are you the Star? Are you the Name?" I turn around. It's the crasher from my party two years earlier. He tips his head to one side and shoots out his fingers, gesturing like a stage hypnotist. "Are you the Man, are you the One?" He grins and shifts his feet. He has a habit of sticking his tongue out and pressing it between his lips while he poses. He never seems to keep his head in one place, tipping it to one side then the other, looking sideways, standing sideways, arms bent at the elbows or out, casting spells, hands carving the air in front of him, one foot always forward.

"I'm just one of the beach boys," I say.

"I like the music, Boogah, but I don't see the piano."

"No, I'm just being one of the beach people on this movie," I say. Ah. He nods as if I have revealed something uncommon.

"It's true then? We're beach people?" He looks around. "Are these all . . . beach people?"

We're standing on the drag strip at the Pomona County Fairgrounds. It's a rough, sandy, gritty, oily piece of ground. The sun is beating down. The smog is deep and infinitely carcinogenic. We're all in shorts, tennis shoes, Hawaiian-style shirts. We clutch our skateboards, the instruments of our profession, in our hands. Around us people are trying to make a movie: grips, electricians, sound and camera, props, production coordinators, assistant directors, the director, and the actors—Don Rickles, Harvey Lembeck, Frankie Avalon, John Ashley, occasionally Keenan Wynn, and even more occasionally, Annette Funicello, who keeps herself in her trailer, above the fray.

"She's really very kind," says my father of the elusive Annette. "She has actually spoken to me."

"It's that Mouseketeer training," says the crasher. "It stays with you."

We were making one of the "Beach Party" movies. The first one, which I missed, was called simply, eloquently, *Beach Party*. This was followed by *Bikini Beach*, *Beach Blanket Bingo*, *How to Stuff a Wild Bikini* (my personal favorite), and something called *Ski Party*, which I also missed. It was possible, in 1964, to make a living off these films. All it required was no pride, a low overhead, and a total lack of ambition. I qualified on all fronts.

Another beach-movie regular named Michael Nader and I lived in the same apartment building. Each morning, a dozen fresh joints rolled and stashed in my bag, we'd head out for either the studio for interiors, the beach, or someplace like the drag strip where the non-sand action sequences would be filmed.

Few people, if any, understood these sequences which often involved a man in a monkey suit, a motorcycle gang, bald-headed rock bands, dragsters, Frankie playing his own cousin with an English accent and a wig, and Annette, wondering when they were going to get married. The constant was Annette wondering when they were going to get married. This was the *idée fixe*. If Frankie didn't come around quickly enough, which he never did, then Annette would deliberately misunderstand some innocent but seemingly compromising situation in which Frankie would have been discovered in the arms of a twisting rock-and-roll virtuoso with a great ass and fringe on her clothes, or a butch-leather maiden on a motorcycle—and stalk prettily off, presumably to her hut.

Everyone lived in some kind of hut in the Beach Party movies.

"Just like all real beach people," said the crasher. We were in a bus going to location. We always sat in the back and got high so that by eight o'clock we were ready for the day. The crasher turned and offered me a grapefruit. He seemed to possess an endless supply of grapefruit which he peeled and ate virtually all day long.

"What's your name?" I asked him. Mike was astounded.

"You don't know Mickey Dora?" he asked.

"No," I said.

"This is Mickey Dora, fool." I looked at the crasher, who grinned and did a spectacular series of finger-slashing mudras in the air. "The greatest surfer in the world."

"The Champ remembers me."

"Yeah. We threw him out of my birthday party."

"A disaster. A blow to the rep. I recovered in time to crash the Las Madrinas Debutante Ball at the Bel-Air Bay Club. *Mucho* rich poosay, Boogah."

There was a group of about ten regulars on those films, including Mickey Dora, Mike Nader, and Eddie Garner whose grandfather, H. B. Warner, had played Jesus Christ in the silent version of *King of Kings*, thereby, according to Hollywood Absolute Rule 36, ruining his career.

"If you play Christ," my father/stepfather/grandfather said, "that's it. It's a career killer. You can't follow Christ in the movie business."

None of us, including Eddie, had this problem. We showed up, skateboarded, played volleyball, pretended to play instruments, and said, "Awww, c'mon, we're not doing anything" a lot in the background in response to someone's assertion that we were noisy, disruptive youths interfering with very important stuff—another *motif* in the films.

Mickey Dora was considered the premier surfer in the known universe at the time. He had a particularly fluid style, cutting and carving like an artist with a block of liquid stone. He was twenty years ahead of his time. He hated to hear about other surfers.

"I'm the best," he said. "The rest are primitives. They've nothing. They ruin the waves. Cavemen on logs. I won't share a wave with a Cro-Magnon." Then he'd go back to the *Times* business section. He always sat at the beach reading the stock quotations.

"Do you own stocks?"

"Of course I own stocks. I like to see what the capitalists are up to."

"Are you a communist?"

"I'm a wave rider. A Maoist-socialist wave rider. Death to all surfing and nonsurfing capitalist polluters of the waves! Boogah!" Then he'd offer me a grapefruit.

For all his talk, Mickey was very money-oriented, worrying constantly about it. Were they screwing with us? Were they getting footage of him surfing without proper compensation?

"I live on the waves, they are my home. They have to pay me for that. Exploiters and robber barons, all of them, making their fortunes off the labor of sweating surfers. I want that overtime. Think of what it costs me just in wax alone. Compensation, Boogah. For the board, for the radical baggies, custom-sewn for the Champ, for the T-shirts, the tennies, many pairs of tennies. They must pay. Surfers rule. Vals go home." Vals were people from the San Fernando Valley. They were not welcome on Mickey's waves or Mickey's beaches. There was a certain parochialism here. "Let them get their own beaches. Let them go to Florida to surf. Euthanase them, put them out of their misery. If God had wanted them to surf, he'd have put waves in Northridge."

"Do you believe in God?"

"Does he believe in me?" Have a grapefruit.

There were at least a dozen pretty girls on every show. I was in love with every one of them, particularly Sallye Sachse, a girl with a perfect body, a perfect face, and a husband. She had a friend, Linda, identically beautiful, and also married. Mary, Patty, Stephanie, Candy. All perfect, all utterly uninterested in me.

There were other surfers too, like Johnny Fain, a brilliant small-wave rider, who also worked on these films, as well as other "children of the famous" like Meredith and Jody McCrae, Joel McCrae's children. Jody was a barely conscious individual, a young giant whose repertoire of jokes consisted mainly of walking up behind people, grabbing their ear, twisting it, and then standing there with their ear gripped in his hand. He was a good deal bigger than I so it was not unusual to see me being towed around by Jody like a third-grader on the playground. Meredith simply shrugged and looked pretty. "Yes. I know. Jody's, well, funny that way." Hilarious, Mer.

"How can I get him to stop?"

"Well, you can't really. He's just too big." She smiled. How many years had he towed her around by her ear? I wondered. Is that why she's always smiling?

There were also, amazingly, beauty contest winners, generally from the South. Some agent would see that Sam Arkoff was about to cast another Beach Party movie and send his contest winner-client over. The next day Miss Georgia or Miss Alabama would be on the set covered with body makeup, wondering why she was there. These beauty contest women were total non sequiturs. They bore absolutely no resemblance to the California beach girls the movie was showcasing. They would stand or sit stiffly, their makeup, hair, and demeanor in total contrast to the hang-loose aura given off by the regular female beach cast. They seemed continually uncomfortable and bored until Someone Important came on the set, then they underwent the most incredible transformation. Their faces split open in these world-yampfing smiles and they started cooing in dulcet tones, oohing and aahing over everything the Important Person was saying. As soon as the Important Person left the set, they calmed down and returned to their chairs, where they occupied themselves keeping their bathing suits smooth.

From time to time extras were hired for the party scenes, in which there would be a lot of dancing. One particular dancer who sometimes worked on the Beach Party movies was a girl named Teri Garr. She had great legs. Naturally, I was a goner. I followed her everywhere offering my expertise.

"I've been in a lot of these Beach Party movies," I said. "I can introduce you to lots of people."

"I'm all atwitter," she said.

"Teri, why do you toy with me?"

"Because you're a toy. A boy and a toy. It's fun. Let's wrestle." Things were never too clear with Teri. She had a way of making a serious face and then saying something unexpected. "Do you think," serious face, "that the world of cinema," she asked, pronouncing it *see-nay-mah*, "is *really* ready for Tippi Hedren?" *Hmmmmm.* "I mean, does Alfred Hitchcock need a checkup?"

Teri was a Hollywood dance extra, not a beach girl. She looked around the set one day. We were all in pajamas for some reason. Perhaps a movie slipped in there, one called "Pajama Party." It's possible. She looked at the beach girls in their shortie nightgowns and turned to me. "Are they perky enough? The beach girls? Do they exude the proper amount of perk?"

The Beach Party movies were eclectic. They threw everything into the pot. Sam Arkoff had a magic touch. It didn't seem to matter that the films made no sense: Don Rickles doing his putdown act in one scene, Little Stevie Wonder playing the harmonica in another. If it was out there, Sam seemed to say, let's put it in the movie. The movies did phenomenal business. I wouldn't be surprised if someday they study the films of Samuel Z. Arkoff. At least in France.

I also found a place, briefly, in the Jerry Lewis stock company. By 1964 Jerry was producing and directing all his own films and like a lot of moviemakers, he liked finding a group of people—actors and crafts people—and using them as much as possible. My grandfather had declared Jerry Lewis the greatest young clown of the day, putting him in the same category as Red Skelton, another favorite of his. The feeling was mutual. Jerry had hired my grandfather for *Cinderfella*, in which Ed played the fairy godfather—and Jerry was going to give me a small part in *The Bellhop*.

I was towed down to Paramount for the hundredth photo opportunity of my life, all of them having virtually nothing whatever to do with me beyond the continued, and somewhat sadistic by this time, exhibition of me as this ongoing nonentity member of a high-profile show business family. Ed Wynn, Keenan Wynn, Jerry Lewis, and the tall geek. I never understood, even then, what the hell was expected. I knew I was supposed to stand there with these men once more, smile, and pretend to be a part of whatever it was they were, but the fact of the matter was I had no feeling of connection with them at all.

"OK, Ned, When you hear me hang up the phone, count one-two, then knock. OK?" We're on the set. Jerry is directing me. I'm to come to a door and knock. It's easy. Then I'll say a line. That will be in another setup. For now, it's knock, he opens the door, we cut.

"OK, Jerry." It's eleven-thirty in the morning. We have gotten in exactly one shot since seven. Jerry has changed clothes five times. Literally. He claims to be allergic to dry-cleaning fluid and so he owns twenty-five of everything. Twenty-five pairs of white duck pants, twenty-five pairs of white Sy Devore golf shirts, twenty-five pairs of Sperry topsiders. He changes clothes about every forty minutes, right down to the new white tennis shoes. Between setups he scoots into his dressing room, changes clothes, and bounces out, pressed, clean, immaculate. Same identical clothes, all brand-new.

If there is no scene change, he calls a break and does it anyway. I think there is something vaguely unhealthy about it, but then I'm used to eccentricities. In a way, it's as if a poor kid, guilty at his good fortune, is now trying to get rid of all the money he's suddenly immersed in. But Jerry is so good at making money he can't spend it fast enough. Guilt doesn't work for him.

Once, in Las Vegas a year later, he invited me to stand next to him at the crap table for luck while he proceeded to bet twenty thousand dollars on a roll of the dice. He won, of course. "Last week, I lost," he laughed. He gave me five hundred dollars in chips. Eddie Garner and I were in Vegas on a weekend bender. We'd already been stopped and searched at the airport. I had a lid of marijuana in my bag. They searched the bag and impossibly, they missed the marijuana. I was low on funds at the time and five hundred dollars was a nice piece of change for me. With the money and the dope, I could have a good time.

"Go ahead, Ned, have fun." A hooker would be fun. Five hundred dollars and some grass would buy the attentions of a great-looking hooker for the whole weekend. Never mind that I had never in my life bought the services of a hooker. In fact, I had only recently become aware that some of the incredible-looking women around the casino were prostitutes. Money would get these women. Dope would get a discount. I wanted to pocket this money. Jerry watched me expectantly.

"I always bet the come," offered Jerry. My thoughts exactly, Jer.

I suddenly found that I had a drink in my hand. And then another. I was with a high roller, and I had some money. Beautiful women seemed to materialize at my shoulder.

Vegas gave me the exact feeling I was always chasing, the feeling I had first felt that night in Coronado. Taking those pictures with Jerry and Dad and Grandpa didn't do it, being on the set and saying lines on camera didn't do it, having my own dressing room with my name on it, also courtesy of Jerry Lewis, didn't do it, but this feeling of power and wealth standing here at the crap table at the Sands in Las Vegas with three bourbons in my brain, did. I bet the money. I lost. Jerry slapped me on the back. "Easy come, easy go," he said. "Say hello to your grandfather." He walked away. So did all the hookers, the waitresses, all the women who were smiling at me three seconds earlier. They left on a parade of four-inch heels and black stockings. The feeling drained right out like sand. I had to find Eddie. He had to lend me some money. Then another voice.

"Hey, Ned Wynn, don't you say hello to your friends?" I turned around and found Frank Sinatra standing ten feet away. He grinned.

Yes, Virginia, there really is a Vegas. I had seen Frank in the casino, but I hadn't dared walk up to him. He knew me not only from my family, but from a song that I had written with my friend Larry Marks. Frank had actually recorded this song, and I had gone to the session.

He remembered. He bought me a drink. I ordered a Jack Daniel's. I'd been practicing for years to be Frank's drinking buddy. This was it, this was my tryout. You never know when fate is going to tap you on the shoulder. . . . "Say hello to Van, willya?" Frank said. Yeah, but Frank . . . Smiling, he and his entourage disappeared into another group of gladhanders.

Later that night, nearly broke, I wandered the strip. I went to the lounge of one of the hotels. Frances Faye, the outrageous cabaret performer, was singing there. I walked in. It was three in the morning. I had enough for one last drink. Then I spotted one more person, one more family friend. At a table, looking wasted and almost unrecognizable, was Judy Garland. She looked at me vaguely. I introduced myself. She seemed shocked. She invited me to sit down. She was with her manager, who looked tired and bleak. Judy was in a deep state of depression, but she managed a smile. This was the woman who used to come to my room and talk to me in the middle of the night. The woman who used to dance and sing at our parties.

"What'll you have, Neddy?" she asked.

"Bourbon," I said. I suddenly didn't want to have anything anymore. The waiter got the drink. We listened to Frances Faye sing her famous renditions of Cole Porter. We barely spoke. When the set was over, Judy turned to me.

"I'm supposed to go to bed now," she said. "Say hello to Van. Do you see him?" I nodded. I never saw him anymore, but I nodded. "Give my love to Evie." She walked out. The feeling of power I had earlier in the evening was long gone. I went back to the Sands.

Eddie had two girls in the room. "My treat," he said. Everyone got high. This was 1964, and not a lot of people came to Vegas with drugs then, unless they were in the band. The girl with me was being turned out. I was her first. She might have been seventeen. She was my first hooker, red-haired, freckled. She was adorable, but it didn't work. I told Eddie I was just too high, which by then was true. But what I really wanted was a girl, a regular girl. Someone who was there because she knew and liked me. Not a friend of my parents, not a hired hand. I was relieved when the whores left.

"I can't hear you hanging up the phone, Jerry," I say. "Do you have a louder phone?" This cracks Jerry and the whole crew up. The laugh makes me feel good. Jerry sticks his head through the door.

"I'll do the funny material," he says, then he disappears again. Being on the other side of the door I am blocked from view, so I can't see when Jerry hangs up the phone, which is my cue. We work out a signal. I will watch the A.D., who will watch Jerry from another vantage point.

"Action," shouts Jerry. I knock. Oh, shit. "Ned, why—cut, god-damnit! Why did you knock? Let's go again right away." Sorry, Jerry.

"Have you hung up yet, Jerry?" I crack the crew up again. Jerry opens the door and sticks his head out.

"Hey—what is this, comedy tryouts? Come on, for real." He shuts the door.

For me, the fun is in the banter, not the work. I don't really like it when the camera is actually rolling, when the audience is in its seats. I like it on the fly. I like things to roll on their own. When it settles down, when they open the mike, I get nervous. My father calls this being a "living-room comedian." I'm a living-room co-median. Trouble is, they don't pay scale in the living room.

We did the shot, I said my line. Jerry kept me on the show a week. Around that time, I also worked with my father on the remake of *Stagecoach*, and there were more Beach Party pictures. I never got used to any of it. But things were changing. I had no idea what I was going to do, but it seemed less and less like it would be acting.

The year before, while still in New York, two things had happened. John F. Kennedy had been shot, and I heard the Beatles. The Kennedy assassination happened while I was doing page duty at the ABC news division. I saw the news come across the Teletype machine. I was shocked, excited, and scared. I was so scared I actually went to church every day for two weeks and prayed.

Praying was not new to me. I generally prayed when I was frightened or in pain. I had tried it back in military school sitting on the toilet with a stomach ache, and I had tried it once when my first heartbreak had occurred.

A girl I had fallen in love with at nineteen had dumped me. The pain was both unexpected and much worse than I had imagined it could be. It was my first encounter with the real-life diet. I lost about ten pounds. I couldn't eat or sleep. This went on for three months. Finally, sick to death of the feelings I was having, exhausted from trying to imagine her back in my bed, tired of weeping over her toothbrush in the bathroom, and totally whipped by the daily aching, I actually had gone down on my knees in the driveway of our house and prayed one night.

I prayed differently that night than I had before. Instead of asking that God bring this girl back to me, I prayed to be rid of my need for her. Instead of making deals, I was acknowledging defeat. Within days, this prayer was answered. I woke up one morning feeling the greatest feeling ever: indifference. I was free inside, free of the maddening obsession.

Praying for Kennedy was new also. I sensed that I was merely acting out a little melodrama for myself and others, walking solemnly into church, getting on my knees, tears glistening in my eyes. I even attracted the attention of the priest, who came and talked to me one morning. He was so genuine and kind that I felt phony and quit going.

The Beatles were something else altogether. The Beatles simply made me feel good. Their music satisfied me in a way that only Ray Charles and Chuck Berry had ever done before.

Early on they had had their effect socially as well. On one of the Beach Party pictures, the director of photography was an Academy Award–winning cinematographer named Floyd Crosby. One day his son, David, came on the set. David had just started a rock band with some friends, and he was excited about his new group. He had begun to grow his hair a little bit, and it looked like the Beatles' cut of the day, just a tad over the collar. Very neat, really. An English schoolboy haircut.

Some of the actors in the movie motorcycle gang put him down for copying the Beatles. "Why don't you guys do something original?" one of the actors yelled at David. Something original like being in a gang of movie pseudo-toughs called the Rats and the Mice in black leather jackets, perhaps? I saw David's face fall. He'd been there to see his father and to meet the people on the show. He was excited and happy. Instead, he'd gotten shit from some asshole actor about his hair. Within a year and a half David Crosby, Jim McGuinn and the Byrds would be one of the biggest rock acts to come out of Los Angeles, and that actor would still be bitching about how his agent never returned his calls.

Over the years, one of my best friends had been Terry Melcher. His mother, Doris Day, and his father, Marty Melcher, had been friends with Van and my mother for a long time. Terry and I had certain things in common, attitudes and experiences that made us able to communicate quickly and easily. Terry wasn't always comfortable with people, which suited me just fine. We understood that aspect in each other.

Terry happened to be the producer of the Byrds' records. He also produced Paul Revere and the Raiders. He had introduced me to Lou Adler, another record producer, who invited us to go with him to Palm Springs one weekend. He wanted us to meet the leader of a group he had just signed. The group was called The Mamas and the Papas, and Lou, who had an uncanny ear for commercial sounds, predicted they'd be a smash. The leader was a song writer named John Phillips. John was writing an album, and they were going to the Springs to lay back and give John the opportunity to work on some songs.

I'd never been around anyone quite like John Phillips before. One of his specialties was getting everyone high, then playing music, certainly one of the most seductive combinations in his repertoire. He was a master at pill doling. He knew more about psychophar-macopoeia than most Nobel chemists. After he had engineered the proper chemical aperitif, and we had washed it down with bourbon, we sat around in the living room listening to him play and sing. I was totally convinced I was hearing the best stuff I'd ever heard.

We stayed up all night drinking Crown Royal and smoking weed while John played song after song. An array of pill bottles stood nearby like little sentries, always on duty. Tired? Take an Escatrol. Fading? Try a little Ritalin. Nerves jangling? Open wide, here comes the Valium Doriden Percodan Placidyl choo choo. It felt just like home.

I was enthralled. I even learned some of his songs and sang along with him. This was heady stuff. That night with John and Terry and Lou was pivotal to me. There was another world of cre-ative people who were easier to be with, and more in tune with me than the people I had always known in the movie business. I wanted to be with them. I was a guest here, and a guest at home. This was more fun.

My father was friendly at the time with Ricardo and Georgiana Montalban, and through him I had met and gotten a crush on their daughter, Laura. Laura was stunningly beautiful. Having two par-ents from the deep end of the gene pool, this was not surprising. The fact that she also liked *me* was what was surprising. We went on rides together, she riding behind me on a motorcycle I had bor-rowed from my dad, her arms around my waist. We rode through Griffith Park, to the beach, everywhere, spent hours with each other, never getting bored. It was a warm, romantic friendship full of excited conversation and ardent kissing. Laura was what was known as a nice girl. A Catholic and a virgin. I was not a nice boy, and I wasn't getting any nicer.

When Terry called me and asked if I'd like to rent a room in a house he was leasing, I was ready. Terry already had one other roommate, Mark Lindsay, the lead singer in Paul Revere and the Raiders. A word or two about Mark. He never left the house, in the year I lived there, without being in full makeup and costume. He spent at least an hour or two in front of his mirror every single morning making up.

"You doing a concert, Mark?"

"Uh-uh. Going shopping."

"In makeup?"

"I can't let my fans down."

"Yeah, Mark, but foundation? Eyeliner? Lipstick?"

"I like to look my best. What if I run into a chick and she wants to, y'know, come home with me?" Then he'd put on his Paul Revere and the Raiders boots and his Paul Revere and the Raiders shirt and Paul Revere and the Raiders vest. Come on, Mark, 'fess up— it's really an interview, a TV show, some big deal public event, right?

"Where ya going, Mark?"

"To Federated Electronics. There's a sale."

The maid's room, behind the kitchen, was unoccupied. For a very low rent, I got this room and the run of a beautiful house in Beverly Hills overlooking the whole of Los Angeles. I moved into the house, which was up a street in Benedict Canyon called Cielo Drive. It was at the end of a cul-de-sac, the last house on the street.

I had been introduced to cocaine by Cass Elliot, the lead female singer with The Mamas and the Papas. An enormous woman of appetites yet unfathomed, Cass had literally chased me around a house at a party John had taken me to one night. She had cornered me and actually spooned coke into my nose. Caught like a rabbit in the glare of Cass's eyeballs, I wrinkled and twitched and snorted and lit up like a little light bulb. Cass, you dog. I was in.

All this led to a situation that made my relationship with Laura Montalban change course. How was I going to deal with this, Terry asked me, this nice girl whose parents were friends with both *our* parents? How was Laura, the nicest girl in the known universe, going to fit into our hip and special society of nosers and acid heads? Did I plan to have Laura over? If so, was everyone else going to have to go into other rooms to do dope? That wasn't the way we did it on Cielo Drive. We were cruising. We had The Mamas and the Papas over, the Lovin' Spoonful, the Byrds, the Beach Boys. Shit, Donovan even showed up. I mean, we were too cool for that kind of shit.

Catholic, virgin, nice girl. Inside, I never measured up to these things. I was trying to measure up as a drunk and an addict, for chrissake. I had enough on my mind. When the day finally came that Laura decided it was time she took things that one forbidden step further, and I was the one she was going to take it with, I freaked right out. In the back of my mind another little Catholic girl in Boston was weeping on the phone. She was telling me she had had the baby. It was beautiful, Neddy, looks just like you. I'll send you her picture. I'm calling her Laurie Ann. I'm putting her up for adoption. Don't worry. We'll be fine. I love you and so does Laurie Ann and we hope you get all the things you want in life.

I was never a stranger to opportunity, only an expert at avoiding it. I stopped seeing Laura. Abruptly, without explanation, without a phone call. In the old days I had had my mother do these things for me. Now, when unpleasant situations faced me, I simply avoided them, turned them aside, deflected them. How else did anyone get ready for rock and roll? A few years later, one of Laura's cousins cornered me in a club in Beverly Hills and raked me over the coals for my treatment of her. There was nothing I could say. My explanation no longer worked for me either.

Terry, though immersed in the music business, still had his social life positioned firmly in the movie colony. His girlfriend around that time had been Candy Bergen, then Claudia Martin, Dean Martin's eldest daughter. During the Martin phase, I, in true guest tradition, took the opportunity to ingratiate myself with the Martin family. Dean and Jeanne Martin's house, a showcase just above Sunset Boulevard, was our headquarters.

I was instantly at home in the Martin house. There were half a dozen children, young Beverly Hills cygnets like Terry and me, and the place was the perfect surrogate for the Foothill Road home that now lay, shackled and manacled, six blocks away. That house had been, in the fifties, the best house for hanging out in Beverly Hills. My mother had always welcomed my friends there, eminently generous, endlessly cheerful, notably tolerant. She had done her time as High Hostess and was now living in semiretirement in a much smaller house on Coldwater Canyon. John and Michelle Phillips had not yet bought their Bel-Air mansion, an old, elegant home once owned by Jeanette MacDonald, which would prove to be yet another grand pad for play. It was the Martins' turn to carry the ball for a while, and Jeanne Martin, Dean's wife, became the new High Hostess.

In truth, she had already been that for a long time, but we brought in the new wave, the new era. We brought drugs. We would go out in the backyard by the pool, smoke some weed, then return to the living room glassy-eyed and friendly, licking our lips and tossing back screwdrivers and vodka-tonics by the hour. The Martins' living room, a huge marble-and-wood playground with a great sunken bar, became the center for us. It was exactly like my old home had been. Jeanne was a gracious and unflagging hostess who loved her kids and their friends. There was almost no line between being friends with Dino and Claudia and Deanna and Ricci, and being friends with Jeanne and her pals.

For some reason I fell into the mold I felt most appropriate, House Clown. It was the role I had perfected in school. It was the role I had learned through the years kept me out of trouble, as it was the court jester who usually kept his head when the heads of those about him rolled. I knew the kings and queens, and I knew the boundaries, instinctively. For playing by the rules I was allowed unlimited access to the bar, my number-one priority, and I was always included in the fun, the parties, the trips to the private clubs like the Daisy and the Factory, the cruises to Catalina on chartered yachts, etc., along with whatever women might find me attractive. If it involved free drinks, I was there. If there were girls, it was even better.

This instinct of mine was probably due at least in some part to a crushing lack of self-confidence. Whether I inherited this or learned it, I don't know. But it was always in my nature to accept the bits from the table in exchange for witty repartee and never outright ask for anything. That would be gauche and punishable by banishment. I had thought that you didn't use these connections for networking. If you were broke, you didn't mention that. If you needed money, you never tried putting the touch on anyone. If you needed a job, you didn't ask for one. You didn't talk business. You played tennis and you socialized. It was genteel, pleasant, unforced. It was also slightly schizophrenic. There were lots of successful people around, and they all seemed to be doing all right, playing by these rules. My attitude was that as long as I was hanging out with these people, I must be doing all right, too.

Richard Zanuck, whom I had known off and on most of my life, had given me a job at Twentieth Century Fox reading and analyzing material in the story department. This was Easy Job Number Two, right after extra-work. So I was paying my bills. But I wasn't going anywhere. While I thought I was doing what I saw others doing, somehow I was missing the connection. While it was true everyone else was playing, they were also engaged in successful careers. Terry and Lou were number-one record producers, and Lou had already built up and sold off one company and was now in a deal with Herb Alpert at A&M, and had a new record company of his own called Ode. John Phillips was a master songwriter and vocal arranger with a career in high orbit. My old friend Doug Tibbles had become a successful television writer, Richard Lang was a director, Jackie Hathaway was a real estate tycoon. I was living by appearances only. That in itself was a job.

It was as if, in some unconscious childhood prayer, in a moment of terror, I had asked God not to make me an adult, not to make me a father, not to make me be responsible, and He had said, OK, Ned, it'll be kind of hard, but we can do that; you'll have to learn to ingratiate yourself with the people in power, take what they give you, hang by your fingernails, have absolutely no self-esteem, and never know peace. But, hell, son, if it's what you want. . . .

It figured that *that* would be the prayer He answered. Say *one* thing, *one* time. . . .

CHAPTER

13

Rock was less sure of itself in the sixties than it is now; movie stars were old money, rock stars the *arrivistes*. My name, my family's name, had currency in this new society. People in rock and roll were still awed by the mystique of movies and movie stars, and I found I was accorded a place at the table of the new Medicis. I was a curiosity, a novelty, and I was always introduced by my full ambassadorial title: "This is Ned Wynn, Keenan Wynn's son, Ed Wynn's grandson. His stepfather's Van Johnson." While people didn't exactly go to their knees, they did react.

"Wow, man. Heavy. Want a hit?"

For the first time, I was consciously using the name as a passport, my ticket to ride. I could never maintain anything like the kind of life I needed to live on the money I made. It was possible, however, to live the life-style of the rich and famous without being either one, if I was willing to trade on my origins. Displaced and impoverished European royalty did it all the time. Why not displaced and impoverished Hollywood royalty?

"I need you guys to do me a favor." It was John Phillips. He was on the phone. "Will you and Terry meet me in fifteen minutes? I need you to go with me to Laurel Canyon."

"Sure, John," I said. Wow. John needed us to help him. "Hey, Terry, we gotta meet John and go up to Laurel Canyon."

"Sure," said Terry. "Why?"

"Why?" I asked.

"Gotta get Polly's things," John said nonchalantly.

"Help John get Polly's things," I relayed to Terry.

"Great," said Terry.

Polly. Polly was a pretty young woman whom John was keeping company with. He and Michelle were split, and Michelle was now hanging around with Gene Clark from the Byrds. Polly was a maximum of eighteen years old, fresh, quiet, thin, taken to wearing short flimsy shifts with nothing underneath. She had stayed at our house for a week once while John and The Mamas and the Papas were on the road, and we had treated her as if she were Marion Davies. Hungry, Polly? Thirsty, Polly? Can I get you another towel? Is the pool warm enough for you? Terry and I would look at each other as Polly wandered by, her neoprene ass quivering under the cotton dress, tight as a tom-tom. But neither of us ever touched her. She was John's chick. This was high romance. Now John was going to fetch her stuff from where she lived in Laurel Canyon. We were the Three Musketeers.

"Why do you need me and Terry just to get Polly's stuff?" I wondered aloud. I mean the average weight of Polly's daily wardrobe was seven grams. How much could there be? We were in John's car winding our way up one of the myriad goat tracks that pass for streets in Hollywood's Laurel Canyon. Haight-Ashbury may have been Mecca, but we had Laurel Canyon. Houses hung on hillsides like scattered children's blocks. Hippies dragged their leather-fringed and Indian-beaded asses up and down these streets like wandering Himalayan mendicants. Finding an address in this maze was always an adventure. It was not uncommon for me to get lost even when I was going somewhere I'd been to a dozen previous times. But John knew right where we were going.

"I just need you in case Ramblin' Jack gets upset." Hold on. One moment, please.

"Ramblin' Jack?"

"Ramblin' Jack Elliott. He's a folk singer."

"Oh, yeah. But why would Ramblin' Jack Elliott get upset if we're gonna get Polly's stuff?"

"Well," John smiled at me, "Polly's his wife." Terry and I looked at each other. "I don't expect any trouble," John said. "But you never know with Ramblin' Jack."

"You don't?" I asked.

"Just *what* exactly don't you know with Ramblin' Jack Elliott, John?" asked Terry.

"Whether his gun is really loaded or whether he's just trying to scare you."

Ramblin' Jack lived in a ramshackle house on a narrow road, exactly like everyone else's house in Laurel Canyon. When we got there, Ramblin' Jack was standing outside. John got out of the car. Terry and I got out of the car. Ramblin' Jack said nothing. John went straight into the house while Jack stood there, silently, watching us. I grinned like a Labrador.

"Hi, Ramblin'," I said. Terry elbowed me in the ribs. Ramblin' Jack glowered at us. Do folk singers really carry guns? I thought about another favorite folk singer of mine, Phil Ochs, who seemed to be a pretty pissed-off guy. At least he was pissed at the government and the cops, like everyone with an ounce of sense in the sixties was. I hoped Ramblin' Jack was a love-and-peace kind of guy, too. Like old Phil Ochs.

"Boy that LBJ sure is an asshole, isn't he?" I mused. Terry closed his eyes and breathed out. Ramblin' Jack began pacing. I looked for a telltale bulge, his folk singer's heater, poking out of his vest pocket. There didn't seem to be one. At least he was small. I thought, boy, glad this isn't Barry McGuire, who was built like a linebacker, and eminently pissed-off. If you're gonna steal a folk singer's wife, pick a small folk singer.

It turned out Ramblin' Jack Elliott wasn't willing to turn to violence over this woman. He simply stood there in pain and said nothing the whole time. He even nodded once at John as John came back out with a suitcase full of Polly's stuff. I went from being afraid to feeling bad about what I was doing. This was none of my business, and this poor bastard was watching another guy rip off his old lady. I suddenly felt like a bully.

On the way back down the hill we lit a joint. "John, next time, just make sure you don't start something with Merle Haggard's wife, OK?" I asked. John laughed. What the hell? It was romantic. John obviously loved Polly and was willing to risk his friends' lives to secure his relationship in the face of the fire-breathing Ramblin' Jack Elliott, terror of Laurel Canyon and the twelve-string guitar. You had to take these kinds of risks for true love.

In a month Polly was a memory. John was back with Michelle, and they had bought a house together. So the thing with Polly, it wasn't true love. But my job was more or less clearly outlined by now. I was the pal with nothing to do except hang out with the superstar. Terry, while he had gone on the jaunt, was really only along for the ride. As a working record producer, he was in another category. I, on the other hand, was always available, and for that, I was always welcome, and the drinks were on John.

"Grandpa's dying." The voice on the phone was Dad's. "You better come over and say good-bye."

Ed Wynn was seventy-nine. He had been living for some years now in an apartment building at the corner of Beverly Glen and Wilshire in an area between Beverly Hills and Westwood known as Little Holmby. I often saw him driving his 1957 Ford Fairlane in those years along Wilshire or Sunset Boulevard. Both hands on the wheel, head erect, sitting straight, eyes on the road. Gone were the long Cadillacs and portholed Buicks he loved so much. So were the houses, the grandiose monstrosities he had occupied over the years. He had begun the process of minimalization sometime in his sixties, and he had succeeded in compressing the package, ultimately cutting off the unessentials until a honed, neat, defined human being was all that was left. He seemed harmonious, perfect. No further improvements were possible.

In his seventies he had become the Grand Old Man of American comedy. He was geared to the testimonial. He was expert at receiving awards, accepting kudos. He had successfully bridged the gap from stage and radio into movies and television, from clown to dramatic actor. His career was preserved as a wonder of perseverance and accomplishment. It was the final phase, and no one was ever more adept at it.

I wonder if I have ever known a more graceful man than Ed Wynn. Massively egocentric, ponderous, and pedantic, nonetheless, in him all the beauty of fame and fortune had become quintessential. The ugliness of it, the helpless, clamorous excess, had been stripped away. He was like polished wood. He shone in the attention of others, glowed till you could see the grain. He patiently, genially recounted his tales of greatness, spoke of his associations, recalled his life in the spotlight, but he was never rude, never unkind, never arrogant. Like wood, he was smooth to the touch. His greeting to us all, son, grandson, granddaughter, was "Hello, darling." He still smelled of talcum powder and tobacco. He was extremely gentle and kind. He wore silk foulards and carried a small leather purse. He drank bourbon and never got drunk. He would go on telling his stories and having his spotlight, it seemed, for a thousand years.

The old man is sitting on the couch. It's June. Outside it's sunny, pleasant. Life is clamoring around us, taking our attention. The old man is watching the Dodgers play the Pirates on television. It might be the Phillies. He is very wan. The tumor in his neck has grown and prevents him now from speaking, though he can, just barely, whisper. Tracy and I have come to say good-bye. Dad is also in the room with us, as is a private nurse. Grandpa, thin and limp as a doll, has been sitting there each day now, watching the Dodgers. He loves baseball. He has always been a sports fan. The last time I had been with him at a sporting event had been at the first Clay/ Liston fight, a closed-circuit showing. That evening, proud to be with my grandfather, we had walked together from the restaurant the half block to the sublime Wiltern Theater, a building straight from the heart of the Emerald City of Oz. There we would watch the clash of the new Goliaths, Cassius Clay, a tall, agile young fighter with a terrifying left jab and flying feet, and Sonny Liston, a glowering monster with at least four ripples on the back of his neck, a man who had destroyed the immense, muscular Cleveland "Big Cat" Williams in two rounds, Zora Folley in three. It was as close to the Dempsey/Firpo days as a young man could get, and every bit as theatrical.

"Who ya got, Ed? Who d'ya like?" The crowd in the rich, ornate lobby was swirling, noisy, and excited. It was a mixed crowd, a lot of fight people, and a lot of people anxious for the glamour of a major sporting event.

"I like this kid, this Clay. He's fast."

"Yeah, but Liston hits like a train. Like the Super Chief. Or should I say, The Fire Chief." Everyone laughed at the reference to the Texaco days.

"Mr. Wynn, oh, my, we loved you on the radio way back in the thirties. We just loved your show . . . that's The Fire Chief, dear, remember?" Of course they remembered. No one forgets The Fire Chief.

"Thank you. Where are you from?"

"We're from Chicago."

"Who do you like in this fight?"

"Oh, they both seem like nice men to me." My grandfather's high-pitched laugh rose above the crowd.

"They both seem like nice men," he said to me, giggling. "Funny, that's very funny."

Clay upset the monster that night. We discussed it for days. Now, mostly alone and silent, he watched the Dodgers.

"What's the score, Grandpa?" we asked. He held up his fingers. Two to one. I wondered, how long do we have to stay? Do we have to sit around with him now? What's the procedure? He's dying, but I'm not. And anyway, he's not dead yet, is he? How am I supposed to act?

The old feeling of separation and fear was pushing me again. Get out of here. I had learned never to look at people if their faces were sad. I didn't want to know about their pain. It was as if pain was catching, and if I saw it, I'd get it. Now I saw the face of a dying man and rejected it instantly.

"Pop," said Dad, "we're going." Great. Let's get out of here. Grandpa nodded slightly. It was an extreme effort. The fact was he was so tired he didn't even want us to stay. Once out the door I breathed again. I nearly ran down the hall to the elevator. I leaned on the button and grinned at Tracy. Back out into the open, into the swirl of life. There was sunshine to feel, and breezes to smell. There was life to be lived.

I was making love to a friend named Pam one morning, three days later, when the phone rang. It was my stepmother. Ed Wynn was dead.

At the funeral, at Forest Lawn Cemetery in Glendale, the coffin was set out for viewing. The casket was closed. I was stoned, having smoked half a joint while wandering out among the graves. I stood and listened to the buzzing in my ears which turned out to be voices. A man was inviting us to pay our respects. Red Skelton, Milton Berle, Jerry Lewis, Shecky Greene. I watched as Louis Quinn, a comedian mostly famous for wearing a loud sport coat on 77 Sunset Strip, walked up to the casket and stood there. He stood there a long time with his head cocked as if he were listening to something. Then he came back and squeezed my shoulder. Then he spoke with great reverence and solemnity. "He was there," Louis said. "He talked to me. He told me, 'Louis, where I am is fine.' " I stared at Louis, but my mouth was dry and my throat was locked tight. How do you answer that? Did he leave a number where he could be reached, Louis? After Louis moved on, my dad leaned over to me.

"He spoke to me, too, kiddo," Dad said. "The night before he died." I turned slightly to my father. "He motioned me down near his lips and whispered to me."

"What did he say?" I asked.

"He said, 'No Jessel.' "

Ed Wynn's death passed through me like water. I'd known him all my life, and at twenty-five I'd learned how not to react. I was stoned at his funeral and I was stoned a few months later at a memorial held in his name. I was there with Pam, and we were both completely gone. Bart Lytton, the financier, was waxing eloquent about Ed Wynn's contributions to America. His speech began to enter the political arena and his voice began to rise and quaver with righteous indignation. It was something about welfare and hand-outs, and it seemed that he was using the occasion as an opportunity to run for office of one kind or another.

This struck a nerve in a lot of people there, but in none more strongly than Bob Altman, who sprang from his seat and started haranguing Lytton, chastising him for using the occasion to forward his own right-wing agenda. I was in heaven. It was clear now that lines had been drawn in our culture. Nothing more crystalized this confrontation than Bart Lytton and Robert Altman, toe to toe on the dance floor. Grandpa would have approved of Bob's position, not because Grandpa was left wing, which he definitely was not, but because Bob wanted the evening to be about Ed Wynn, not about politics, and Ed Wynn was Grandpa's favorite subject. Mine too, of course. After all, here comes the money.

"Here you are, Ned. I want you to know what an honor it was to be able to be involved in your grandfather's estate." The business manager smiled as he presented me with what I assumed was my first check. It was for twenty-five hundred dollars. "Of course it was originally five thousand, Ned, but we had to take out taxes and of course you had borrowed a thousand a few years ago. . . ." He cleared his throat as I stared at the check.

"So, do I get these every month? Every week? Or how does it work?"

"No, that's, uh, that's it."

"Twenty-five hundred dollars? What about the trust fund?"

"There is no trust fund, Ned."

"But Grandpa was a millionaire." And Papa was a rollin' stone. The man just shook his head.

"No. Not really, Ned. Not anymore. When he died he was not a millionaire." He began shuffling papers on his desk.

"But he had more money than this. He told me. He promised all his grandchildren . . ."

"Ned. This is really not my business. You should ask your father and stepmother."

"What have they got to do with it?"

He shrugged. "You should talk to them. Maybe they know something about . . ." he just trailed off. The phone rang. He answered it, smiling apologetically to me.

I walked outside onto Santa Monica Boulevard with the check in my hand. I stared at the new buildings going up in a place called Century City, all new glass and steel. Bart Lytton territory. Bart Lytton. Now there was a guy who knew what to do with money. Of course, he wasn't a real funny guy, no funny hats, no funny shoes, no eleven-foot pole for people you wouldn't touch with a ten-foot pole, but you had to give the guy his due about money. Ed Wynn, on the other hand . . .

I recalled an afternoon at my father's house. Grandpa had been there. Dressed as always in his foulard and carrying his purse, he had been on the way out as I was coming in. My father and stepmother stood with him in the driveway. They all seemed flushed, happy, as if they'd just had a day of sailing, or an invigorating round of golf.

"Neddo," my grandfather said. "I've just made an arrangement with your father and Sharley."

"Hey, kiddo," my father said. "Grandpa has just helped us out tremendously. You know how pressed we've been financially. . . ." It was my father's eternal cry. Crying poor. I just nodded dully, as I did about most things those days. Uh-huh. Yeah. Of course I had no idea why my father, who worked constantly, was well paid, and seemed never to be without, was always in financial straits. I just accepted it. "Well, Grandpa has given us enough to pay off all this debt—and have something left."

"Great, Dad," I said, genuinely pleased.

"Three hundred thousand dollars. Free and clear. Taxes already paid on it," my grandfather said, beaming at me. "I figured, why wait? Why spread it out over years? Your father and Sharley need it now, I have it, so I gave it to them." I smiled. How nice. Hell, if Dad and Sharle needed it, I'm just glad Grandpa had it to give.

"Terrific," I said. I didn't get it completely, the significance of it. He had given Dad his legacy early, I thought, that's all. It was a lot of money in 1964. But, hell. Grandpa was rich.

"Not really, Ned," the business manager had said. "He didn't have the money that he once had." That three hundred thousand dollars turned out to be the bulk of his estate. He had given my father essentially all the money he had been holding for his grandchildren.

Now this meant that there were no trust funds, no more money coming from beneficent forebears. I had twenty-five hundred dollars to do with what I wanted. That was simple enough; I promptly drank it. In a month of playing the big shot in clubs and restaurants, it was gone. The truth was, had I been given the trust fund, I would have speedily used up whatever stipend I got each year in about a month. It would have been fun. A challenge. How long would it have taken me to drink up a trust fund? A year? A decade? A lifetime? It took my dad about ten years to drink up three of them.

The sixties settled down on me like a virus, a delirium of amnesty and irresponsibility. There was a falling away of rule, of order, of restriction. Every impulse I'd ever had as a child, and refused to let go of growing up, was now embedded in something called the counterculture. The sixties were tailor-made for someone like me who never knew how to do "the businessman trip" in the first place.

Colors, balls of pastel colors, burst around my head like tiny clouds of chalk. Each flower in the garden has a dozen shimmering traces hovering in the space between us. I think: Hello, roses, and the roses nod. I say: Hello, trees, the trees bow to me. Everything is connected by infinitely fine threads of consciousness, webs of energy that move the birds and the leaves and the sun in concert, the ineluctable modality of the visible. The fingers of odor reach me and peel my nostrils back like the skin on a banana, welcoming the cosmic music of scent. Dear roses, dear life. What the ground gives forth rises into me through my feet, now muddy blobs growing downward, the green frog moss darkens the corners of my eyes, the roots of the trees dip into my pockets looking for sugar cubes. I'm a child of the forest. Once again I'm at the fairy pond. My beribboned shirt from New Mexico plays with the breeze, my Jimi Hendrix haircut ruffles lightly at my neck, the soft Navaho moccasins are growing cool as the damp soaks into them. My feet are wet. God's feet are wet. It's all One. My feet are God's feet. I—am—God.

"Jesus Christ," says a voice. I smile benevolently. Of course. I've been recognized. It does happen. I turn. My father stands in the driveway looking at me. I smile generously at him, my eyes soft as a kitten. It's Easter, after all. I am risen.

"Yes?" I say, kindly. I should bless this man, the man whose seed gave me life.

"Sharley, this you gotta see. Sharley!" he shouts. My stepmother walks out onto the porch.

"Keenan, what are you shouting at?"

"Look. I take one look at Ned here with the hair and the beads and the fay shirt and the Sheriff of Nottingham brogans and say, 'Jesus Christ,' and he says, 'Yes?' I love it. I say, 'Jesus Christ.' He says, '*Yes?*'" My father starts to laugh insanely. He's drunk. It's Easter Sunday. He's smashed on Jim Beam, and I'm blown to the four winds on a thousand micrograms of Owsley purple.

I look over at him, his red face crumpled with bourbon, and inwardly, I condemn. I'm a gentle creature now, a member of the new generation, the generation that has done away with war and strife, the generation that has abandoned all falsehood and pretense and bourbon and soda, the generation that has dared to challenge the material world and to seek the God within. This poor creature, my father, drunk in the middle of the day, is a man starving for spiritual release. He's a creature of the darkness, a pitiful human caught in the boundaries of a false reality. I know, here with the scent of roses playing a rondo on my olfactory receptors, what the reality is. I know, as a second odor plays an obbligato on my sensitive cilia ... that reality is ... I wrinkle my nose. This second odor is somewhat obstreperous. I sniff several times. Roses, yet not roses. Maybe very old roses. Very, very old roses. . . .

"Ned," Sharley says to me. "You're standing in dog shit." Ah. I turn to Sharley.

"An organic soil amendment," I say. "A natural substance." I step gingerly away from the reedy brown mass and start wiping my feet, skating on the grass.

"Jesus Christ got dog shit on his feet?" My father is now leaning against the garage and sobbing. I am not to be ruffled. To them it's dog shit. But I know its universal, cosmic significance. It's the remnant of an energy exchange. It's part of the perfection of life. The dog eats, the dog gives back. The earth takes in and the earth gives back. It's perfect. This grass is a waste of space. We should plant corn. We should turn this place into an agricultural free zone, let the Goddess take charge.

On the other hand, it also smells incredibly bad, this cosmic moment. Wait. How can it be bad? I'm only perceiving that it smells bad because of years of overlays of false concepts. Years? Millennia. It doesn't smell bad, it only smells—like itself. It smells this way because, because ... wait ... because the Cosmic Intelligence is signaling us with this odor to tell us that something organic is disintegrating, rotting, changing—it is of course the perfect odor for such a process. Yes. Perfect. The smell cannot be improved upon. Nonetheless, it stinks to heaven. In fact, it smells so awful that it's possible soon I will be adding a little cosmic energy exchange of my own. I will barf.

"Jesus Christ . . . got . . . dog doodie . . . on his . . . chukkas?" My father is on his knees. He's really overdoing it now. I am maintaining my poise as only a man in touch with his inner godhead can. I continue to skate around the lawn until all the shit is off my shoes. I do not throw up. This was the new person, the new man, the peaceful, the tolerant. And I owed it all to LSD.

Acid was a revelation. It had transfigured me. I saw myself as a new person. I had become thoroughly sick of myself as I had been. I was tired of hearing my own weary litanies. At twenty-five my life was vaporous, meaningless. A joke. I had no career, no romance, no money, no place to live. Something had to change, but I had no idea about what or how I wanted it to change.

Acid was a continuation of the same process I had always indulged in. After all, when I was fifteen, alcohol had saved me. At fifteen I took a drink and became someone new, someone more confident, funnier, cleverer, handsomer, and braver. Marijuana had always left me with mixed feelings. I was often paranoid while high on marijuana. In fact, I usually retreated to wine while high on grass. Wine settled me down, gave me back my familiar world. Acid was the logical successor to alcohol. Acid promised change without work, my principal prerequisite. Like the Beatles song, I only wanted to turn off my mind, relax, and float downstream.

Part of the problem was that the same fear I had since childhood, that growing up would hurt, had never left me. If there are things in life that we are supposed to grow out of, I had never grown out of this one. Consequently, it was not a large stretch to imagine that I would be staying with my mother again. This was one of my MOs. I would strike out boldly on my own for a while, maybe a year. Then that experiment would sour for one reason or another, usually money or a woman, and I would straggle back to my mother's house, wherever she might be living.

After the divorce from Van, my mother began a series of moves. The latest one had placed her and my sister in Coldwater Canyon, one of the two main passes that connect Beverly Hills with the Valley. It was a sparse tract house, a dream for most, but modest by my mother's standards. There were no servants here except for Stella, a maid who came in once or twice a week. This was far different from the years when we had four live-in domestics: a maid, a cook, a butler, and a governess and several part-time employees including a seamstress, a laundress, as well as a full-time secretary who helped her organize and execute her social calendar.

Now, my mother had no social calendar. She gave no parties. The bathhouse gang was gone. They had scattered to the winds when the money began running out, and the scotch ceased to flow. From time to time loyal old friends like Jim and Henny Backus invited her out to dinner at the Bistro where for a few hours she could revel in the old life. She was still Mrs. Van Johnson, the former wife of the former star, and as such was still greeted in places like Chasen's, the Bistro, and La Scala with a lot of bowing and rubbing of hands.

Van himself had by now sunk into a kind of Leading Man Oblivion called the dinner-theater circuit. While certainly lucrative, it was nonetheless far removed from the glamour of movies and even from the dull wink of television. During all this time, I had only seen Van twice. Once, two years earlier, he had come to L.A. to play in a touring company of *The Music Man*. He was still Van then, still my stepfather, loving and friendly to me, fun to be with. But there was a slow disintegration taking place in our relationship that I just hadn't noticed before.

The show was at the Coconut Grove. Van got me a seat at a ringside table. He was great as always; to me he was the quintessential Professor Harold Hill, larger than life, an amiable, ambling giant, the man who could span the universe in three strides and sweep me up in his arms those eons ago. No wonder they bought band uniforms from him.

I had an evening with him, supper after the show. We talked about everything except Mom and Schuyler. Why he left, the breakup of our home, all that, was not mentioned. It was as if he were on the road, and we just met up and chatted, had a couple of drinks, a bite to eat, and that was that. I went backstage. Van introduced me, as always, as his stepson. I ended up taking a girl from the chorus home. To me, that was how I measured my success. A free dinner and a piece of ass, and I was in the Hall of Fame.

Several years later, when my sister went into the hospital briefly, I saw Van there on one of his last visits to his daughter. I had been into the hippie counterculture for about a year by then, and when Van saw me he giggled. "Look at the beatnik," he said. We all giggled nervously. I looked at Schuyler as if to say, did you hear that? *Beatnik!* But she was so flustered, so excited to see her father again, she was beside herself, oblivious to whatever else was going on.

I realized then that she worshipped him. He was the whole universe to her, and he had simply, drastically, removed himself from her without an explanation. He had made no provisions for her to visit or see him. Whenever the inclination struck him, which was rarely, he would call her or see her for a few minutes. That was it. Schuyler might wait for a year or more before he called or wrote. Her own calls and letters to him went unanswered. Her perplexity and confusion was painful to see. My father had taken over in part, acting as the dad as best he could. But it was not what she wanted. She wanted her father back.

By then, Van had changed a lot. He seemed powdered up, rouged, florid, and soft. The old combination of good looks, size, and presence, was now an overstatement, a gauche and stagey misrepresentation of the man I had always known. His attitude was stiff, almost silly. He didn't know what to say to his daughter anymore, or to me. It was as if he had stumbled into the wrong room. Not long after that, he ceased to have any communication with Schuyler whatsoever. Baffled, Schuyler hid this enormous pain with food, anger, and finally an attitude of furious indifference. It was one of the cruelest turns of her life, if not the cruelest.

But if it was inexplicable to her, and to everyone who knew her and Van, I understood it implicitly. I had the same kind of fear and terror of emotional attachment, of giving love, and worse, of receiving it, that Van had. I would have run too, earlier and faster than he had. My solution had been never even to start a family in the first place, so fearful was I of having to show up daily for anyone or anything.

What my mother did to keep from agonizing over her own Paradise Lost was to storm angrily and briefly about Van, and how she had been screwed in the divorce, and then, calmed down from her outburst, she would bustle. She bustled a lot in the kitchen. She bustled in the garage, in the living room, in the bedrooms. While she bustled, Schuyler and I would sit around the house and smoke weed and laugh till the tears came. The sixties were upon us all, and the terror about drugged children was only just beginning.

Mom had always handled booze with food and vacation plans. She handled dope with Glade. Whenever Mom would enter the living room, she'd come in behind a hissing can of Glade. It was the difference in her state of life that she could no longer afford the expensive solutions. Enablers like her are nothing if not resourceful. Like marijuana, Glade was cheap and readily available. Fight fire with fire, or fight drugs with air freshener. Confronting the situation was never the issue. I had no desire for my mother to confront anything; denial was our stock in trade. Glade provided us with a solution we all could tolerate. We lived on Glade.

"Oh—it's so stuffy in here!" Spray spray spray. Schuyler and I are sitting right in front of her on the couch smoking dope plain as day. "Isn't it awfully stuffy in here?" Spray spray. "How can you two sit around in this stuffy room? Why don't you go out in to the backyard and get some fresh air? Do you want to start the barbecue, Neddy? I have some nice steaks." Spraaaaaaaaayyyy. . . .

The backyard was dirt and weeds, unplanted as yet. As it turned out, it would never be planted. So Sky and I would walk out into the hummocks of mud and gravel, I'd start the barbecue, and we'd stand there in the evening with the barbecue sending up three-foot-high pillars of fire—and we'd howl into the darkening hills.

My mother dealt with the drug era as if it had never happened. For me, it had happened a long time ago when I was twelve and stealing her drugs from her bathroom cabinet and getting high with Uncle Sherry. I was slotted for a visit to the netherworld; all it took was a few years of empty, wasted life wherein three vodkas and a whole bottle of wine would leave me depressed and wondering what was wrong.

"Hi, Mr. Webster, is Roger home?" I was standing at the front door to brothers Guy and Roger Webster's home on Crescent Drive in Beverly Hills. I had just finished dinner at my mother's, followed by my inevitable bottle of wine, and I was feeling nothing but the familiar. I was bored and depressed.

"He's in his room, Ned," Paul said with a sigh. Then, hopefully, he said, "I have a new first edition." He opened his locked bookcase. He took out a delicate, leather-bound volume and showed it to me. It was Sir Francis Bacon. Or maybe it was Samuel Johnson. Or Mark Twain. He looked at me, and I thought I could see it in his eyes: Does anyone give a shit? "Roger's in his room," he said again and put the book carefully back on the shelf.

"That's a great first edition, Mr. Webster," I offered.

"Upstairs," he said kindly. "In his room." Paul was very fond of Guy, whom he saw as the achiever, the son with something on the ball. His idea of Roger, however, was different. Roger perplexed him. Roger was the strange one in the family, the oddball. Roger was often withdrawn and sullen around his parents and given to fits of anger, after which he would slam up to his room and lock the door. Getting into Roger's room was a lot like getting into the castle of a very pissed-off medieval baron as he nailed the door shut. Literally. With six-penny nails.

"Hey, Roger, it's me. It's Ned!" I banged on the door. After a few moments I heard the bumping of a clawhammer against the door frame, and then the screech of nails as they were pulled out of the wood. The door swung open, and Roger yanked me into the room. He then slammed the door and nailed it shut again.

Roger and Juju, a friend of Roger's from Chouinard Art School, were stoned. I knew that, but I didn't know on what. They took one look at me and Juju reached into a bag around his neck and pulled out a pill. He handed it to me.

"What is it?" I asked.

"LSD," said Juju. He looked at me and a slow smile formed on his lips. "Acid." My heart started beating. I'd heard of this stuff. It was 1966, and people were taking LSD. But I had never known anyone who had taken it before, and I was a little scared. Still, placing a pill in my hand was a powerful act. I was used to taking pills. I loved taking pills. I knew inside that this was a moment I had sought. My life was coming down around me and I couldn't find an exit from myself anymore. This pill was foreordained. I swallowed it.

"When does this stuff start working?" I'm complaining to Roger, who is lying on his back staring at the ceiling. It's been thirty minutes and nothing is happening. Juju is wandering aimlessly around the room stopping every once in a while to examine something. He holds up a marble.

"Hey, Ned—look at this." I walk over to him and look at the marble.

"Yeah. Big deal. It's a marble."

"Let's go out to the pool house," Roger says.

We walk downstairs and out into the backyard. As we walk across the lawn to the pool house I realized that I'm feeling quite good. It's really very beautiful here in the Websters' backyard. The pool is extraordinarily beautiful. In fact, I've never seen a swimming pool quite like it.

"Rog, you know, this is very beautiful back here. This pool is really very beautiful." Roger nods pleasantly.

"How do you feel?" he asks.

"Fine. Nothing special. Just, you know, regular. Are you sure this is really LSD? Juju, is this really LSD?"

Juju nods. "One thousand micrograms," he says. "That's the dose." Ah. Well. If this is all it does. . . . As I walk I run my hands across my torso, feel my ribs. Feel each rib. Each single rib. My fingers slip between the ribs. Fingers and ribs. Me. I flow from my ribs, I flow from my fingers. I can see that. I can see the ribs and the fingers. Funny, I never noticed that before, how I flow in a circle like that from my ribs to my fingers all a part of one interconnected. . . I look into Juju's face. He is talking, but I can't hear the words. Juju Pang is Chinese; now, as I look into his face, I am looking at the oldest man on earth, prehistoric man, the progenitor of the human race. The face broadens and flattens, the jaw juts forward. I am looking into the face of Peking Man. Then the face splits into several faces, each one a stage in the development of man. They flow from one to another in rapid succession. I witness the evolution of the species in the face of one man standing there by the extraordinary swimming pool, the Pool of Life, the water that laughs at the sky.

A shaft of light from the pool springs up and into my eyes, exploding like a pane of fiery glass. Deep within this light I see a tongue of flame. It laughs. I know that this tongue of flame is a disguise. It is very simply God. My chest fills with love. The flame retreats as I move toward it. I spin around and the whole universe tilts and spins with me. I am sucked into the sky like a piece of paper in a tornado. I fly above the world. I fly over Beverly Hills and gaze down at my mother's house two miles away. Suddenly my mother and sister come out and stand in the driveway. They gaze up and see their wonderful brother/son flying over them. They reach for me. Dear Mother and Dear Sister . . . I reach down to pull them up with me into the sky, but they cannot come. They are tied to the earth. I am overwhelmed with sadness. I begin to cry. Then I see that I too am tethered with cords that come out of my eyes and fingers and toes. If I can let go of these cords, if I can just let go. . . .

"Roger? Guy? . . ." the singsong voice paralyzes me. It's Gloria Webster, Roger's mother. I suddenly grow fearful and I fall from heaven. The light around me darkens.

"Roger," I say. "Don't let her come out here, please, don't let her come out here. I'm fucked, I'm completely fucked." I'm sobbing now.

"Don't worry, go out to the pool house . . ." he says, then he turns back toward the main house. "I'm out here, Mom!" Holy Christ . . . is *this* what this stuff does?

In the pool house, once I realize that Roger has intercepted his mother and that she won't come out, I feel better. Juju picks up a portable radio, turns it on, and hands it to me. I hold it out in front of me. A group called the Turtles are singing something. About the sun—the sun is shining like a red rubber ball. I begin to feel better again. Of course. The sun *is* exactly like a red rubber ball. I've never noticed that before. How absolutely wonderful the Turtles are. How simple and dear. A red rubber ball. It's unbearable. I love the sun, I love its red rubber ballness. The tinkling sound of the music on the tiny portable streams from the speaker in little lashes of silver. I can touch the sound. I put my fingers into the silver notes as they sprinkle the air about me. My mouth is open, I'm totally taken away, agape. The whole world, the universe, is alive with movement and love. Everything is part of the whole, and the whole is in me, contained in me. How can I do anything but love the world?

"Let's go for a ride," Roger said. He was back.

"When does this stuff wear off?" I asked. I was exhausted. Roger and Juju just smiled. Not soon, I gathered.

"Let's go in my car," Roger said. We walked out into the front yard. I glanced up the street. A police car was turning the corner. Instantly I was frozen with terror. There were black waves billowing off the car and flowing toward me, down the street.

"Shit, Roger, the cops."

"Don't worry about it. They're not coming here."

"But there's like black waves . . ."

"It's just the negativity coming from them. It's a negative trip, man. Cops." I flashed on my Uncle Sherry. Did he see this stuff all the time? No wonder he was so paranoid.

We got into Roger's car and drove, it seemed, all over L.A. from Hollywood to Venice. From time to time Roger or Juju would see someone they knew and we'd stop and get out. I was tripping, every other thing I saw was *wow*. There's a McDonald's. *"Wow . . ."* There's a Colonel Sanders'. *"Wow . . ."* There's a bus stop with people on the bench. *"Wow . . ."* There's a guy in a suit. *"Wow . . ."*

We went all night. I saw people I didn't know existed. Freaks. They were suddenly visible, as if a layer of culture had been pulled back like a blanket to reveal a wriggling mass of dope-smoking, acid-dropping, grublike children, determined to be butterflies, to undermine the existing order by grinning beatifically at everyone and getting heavily into handicrafts.

"This is a God's eye," the girl says. I am lying on the dirt, on scraps of paper and crushed cups and popsicle sticks. We are in a small vacant lot somewhere in Venice. It's around noon the next day. We've been up all night. For some reason, lying on a pile of refuse doesn't bother me. On the vacant lot there are some hippies, strangers to me, yet people I now recognize as my brothers and sisters. They have set up a stand and are selling multicolored bits of loosely woven yarn on sticks. Certainly a business I could get into. The girl has handed me one of her products, and I gaze at the pattern of yarn and once again I travel up into the sky searching for the tongue of flame. Of course. A God's eye. How did she know?

"He just took his first acid trip," Roger says.

"Wow . . ." the girl says. She must have grokked it.

She is wearing a long skirt and a leather buckskin vest and boots. She is almost pretty. She reaches over and puts her hand directly on my peter. She kneads it as if it were the neck of a cat. I open my eyes and gaze up at this creature.

"Who are you?" I ask.

"Linda," she says. "But my real name is Caroline."

"What do you mean your real name?"

"The name my teacher gave me. Bapak, he's my teacher. I sent my name to him and he sent back Caroline. He's in Indonesia and he's just the most incredible man. He knows what your real name is."

"Can I get a real name from Bapak, too?"

"First you have to spend some time in the Latihan." This was getting complicated. On the other hand, it didn't feel half bad.

"What's the Latihan?"

"It's where we go in Subbud." I am not following this, but as long as she kneads, I listen. "It's a room."

"What do you do in that room?"

"We do anything we want. It's a kind of energy thing. It's real spiritual." So far, this spirituality thing was right up my alley.

"Listen, Caroline, maybe you and I can get together. Can I call you?" She rears back and looks at me like I fell off a commuter train.

"*Wow*," she said. "Call me?" She removes her hand from my pecker. I had a lot to learn about spirituality.

CHAPTER

14

I had become a believer in the possibility of societal regeneration through the administration of psychedelics. In fact, in order to promulgate better understanding at home, I had turned my father on to marijuana.

The justification here was his drinking, which was becoming a problem of monumental proportions. He worked constantly, made more money than ever, lived in bigger and bigger houses, and drank himself into oblivion on a more or less daily basis. More than once I was up at six in the morning sitting with him in his kitchen watching him pour a shot of vodka into his coffee.

"Gotta get the old engine started, boy," he'd say as he stirred the mixture. I deplored the practice, feeling very superior that all I had rolling in my head at six A.M. was *Cannabis sativa*. It was not relevant that I had been up all night taking pills, smoking dope, and drinking wine. The important thing was I didn't get up in the morning and pour vodka into my coffee.

This difference was crucial to me—the minor discrepancies of no importance. I brushed aside the fact that every single day when I got up, I rolled a joint from the bowl of loose marijuana I kept by my bed. I didn't brush my teeth without a couple of tokes. And wine, which I always drank, didn't count. In the sixties, if it was necessary to cloud the issue to prove a point, the issue was duly clouded.

"Don't just puff it, Dad, hold it in." My father sat there with the smoke in his lungs like a twelve-year-old kid with his first cigarette. He shuddered and coughed. All the smoke billowed out.

We were sitting in my car in his driveway getting stoned. "I can't hold it in. I can't do it."

"Dad, just be patient. Now you just take a drag, just a little one, not too much, you're taking too much. You always take too much."

"I'm not taking too much, I'm just not a smoker. I tried this, y'know, in the thirties with some spade musicians in New York. Couldn't do it then, either." He took another drag and spit it out. This precipitated a coughing fit. His eyes were watering.

"C'mon, Dad, this is the dawning of the age of Aquarius, for chrissake."

"I know it's the dawning of the age of Aquarius. Can I please go in now?"

"What do you have to do inside?"
"I need a drink."

By now I was no longer living with Terry Melcher on Cielo Drive, but had moved into Beverly Glen, one canyon east. I was renting a house on a dead-end side street called Beverly Glen Place.

I raised organic vegetables in the backyard, eschewing all chemical agents, including fertilizers. The plants muddled through, but as they were grown organically, I never got to eat any of them. I grew them, but the bugs basically owned the farm. Finally I made a deal with the white flies, the tomato hornworms, and the thrips —they got three quarters of the goods, I got the rest. It took five doses of acid and a lot of lying down in the furrows between rows of broccoli inwardly communicating with the order lepidoptera to do it, but it paid off. I got three zucchinis, a cup and a half of peas, and sixteen leaves of lettuce. Being a living exemplar of the sixties was a full-time job.

I had bought the full sixties parcel by now. My attempts to free my father from his bondage of old ideas and old practices had failed, and somewhere at this juncture I formed the opinion that my parents weren't "real people."

I found myself drifting naturally away from the movie business and the people I had known in it. I felt easier in the presence of song writers, musicians, and singers. I preferred their avant-garde attitudes, their freer society, their looser women, and their high-class dope.

It seemed everyone was a songwriter. It was hip to write songs. I had written a song some years earlier which had been recorded by Frank Sinatra. Now, with the explosion of music in the late sixties, I wanted to try to do it again. I still had my job at Fox, but I needed to find a place in this new world.

John Phillips and Lou Adler encouraged me, first as a writer, later as a singer. I spent most of my time either at my own house in Beverly Glen or at John and Michelle's Bel-Air mansion where we often sat up all night singing and playing. The Mamas and the Papas were one of the biggest acts in rock and roll at the time, and John had built a recording studio in his house complete with a then state-of-the-art eight-track system. Between Lou and John and Michelle, there were a lot of parties, and it was not unusual to see stars of rock like Jimi Hendrix, Judy Collins, John Lennon, Mama Cass, Brian Jones, Barry McGuire, Stephen Stills, and Cher, songwriters like Jimmy Webb, and movie personalities like Roman Polanski and Sharon Tate, Marlon Brando, Peter Lawford, and Steve McQueen, all at the same party. Lou and John had set out to consciously recreate the glamour of the early Hollywood days. Lou had picked up a new girlfriend, Tina Sinatra, to add some ambience, and Annie Marshall, the daughter of English actor Herbert Marshall, and an old friend of mine, had also become part of this circle. It was as if I had slid from my childhood in my parents' star-embossed living room right into the next version, just as glamorous, just as exciting, and infinitely more hip.

I had added a smug antifilm attitude to my repertoire, and now I felt superior to anyone in my parents' business. I thought they were Johnnies-come-lately. If I saw Rod Steiger or Steve McQueen loosening up at a party, I looked down on them for trying to be cool. I was merciless. I acted as if it were my turf and they were intruding. Why didn't they stay at Chasen's where they belonged? A case in point was McQueen. We were at a huge party at the Phillips's when Steve saw me from across the room. His face lit up. He was happy to see someone he knew. Steve was naturally shy anyway, and he was more comfortable around his motorcycle pals like Bud Ekins, Lee Marvin, and my father than with all this flash. He came over and shook my hand, cracking a relieved grin. Then he said, "How's Keenan?" I squinted at him with a deliberate vacancy, like, "Who the fuck is Keenan Wynn?"

"How should I know? I never see the asshole." Steve just stood there in shock.

"Oh, uh-huh, that's cool," he mumbled, and walked away. I felt as if I had scored some kind of victory in that exchange. I had shown my credentials as a member of my g-g-g-g-generation.

I was tired of the litany of family ties. I didn't want to be identified with them, but perversely, I needed to be; I had no identity of my own. My whole social life revolved around my fulfilling this status as the child of Hollywood. Why else, I reasoned, would anyone want me around? So I hated them even more because I couldn't free myself from their influences and still have the necessary cachet. Worse, down deep, I didn't want to. Without them my coin was brass.

I was still good friends with Terry Melcher, and I spent a lot of time visiting him at the house on Cielo Drive, which he was still renting. I saw Peter Fonda there one evening for the first time since we were teenagers. He had not yet released his movie *Easy Rider*, but he was already thinking about things I had never considered.

Peter was dressed in a stylish gray suit. Peter's immaculate cool was his trademark. Everyone else was funked out in their latest hippie accoutrements, but Peter was bucking the trend, something he could do beautifully. He reached into his pocket and pulled out a couple of joints and gave me one. "You have to be able to write your own ticket, Ned," he said. We lit the dope and smoked. "You have to shake 'em up, show 'em something they think they haven't seen before, even if they have." I nodded, but did not comprehend. I was by now so far behind my compatriots that I had no idea of what writing one's own ticket would provide. Write the ticket to do what? Weren't we already doing that? How did Peter get so goddamn mature, anyway? Besides, it sounded suspiciously businesslike to me—something Lou Adler might say.

We smoked and sat out in the yard overlooking Los Angeles. Brian Wilson was also there along with his brother Dennis. I had met Brian and Mike Love and Dennis Wilson through Terry some years earlier. They were Southern California guys from somewhere like Torrance or Inglewood, and we always loved hearing them because they were the only singers in America carefully enunciating the hard "r." They sang like South Bay surf rowdies spoke: The word "there," for instance, was pronounced in its entirety, "thairrrr." I also liked the way they said *now*: ". . . like she told her old man, naaaaaaowwww . . ." It was like hearing a West Los Angeles gas station attendant and his buddies with their rags and their grease guns suddenly burst into song standing under the lube rack. Before them Jan and Arnie had sung this way, then Jan and Dean, and the tradition of Southern California middle-class white-boy street/beach music had been born. They called it the Southern California sound, and Brian was its Mozart.

Over the years Brian's descent into a kind of mental white-water wipeout became a part of the lore of rock, almost mythical in proportion. He had become more and more a recluse. I had visited his house with Peter a few months earlier in Bel-Air—just a few blocks down the hill from the Phillips's. Signals of Brian's mental state were apparent through a cursory examination of the beautiful sunken dining room. It was filled with sand. A classic French parquet floor under at least a ton and a half of sand. "If I can't take Bel-Air to the beach," he told me, "then I'll bring the beach to Bel-Air."

We sat on the bluff at the edge of the property and watched the lights come on in the city. Brian suddenly looked over at Peter and me. He was dressed like a farmer in bib overalls. He seemed about to burst.

"Isn't this . . . cool?" Brian said, waving his hand across the assorted group of rockers and rollers on the bluff. Peter and I nodded vigorously.

"Yeah . . ."

"Yeah, Brian. Really cool." Brian grinned. Someone came over and spoke to him.

"Well," he said abruptly, "I better get going." Without another word Brian stood up and followed the other person to his car and left. Peter turned to me.

"Probably expecting another delivery of sand," he said.

Terry was producing a new group called the Gentle Soul. Rick Stanley and Pam Polland were the singer/songwriters, and I began to hang out with them in a house that Terry and Columbia records rented for them off Laurel Canyon in Hollywood—a typically faded twenties Gothic manor house frequented by hippies and musicians.

Riley Wildflower, the bassist of the group, and I often took LSD at my own house in the Glen to start the evening. My house: I had painted the floor black and the walls yellow; I had a dozen cats scratching and puking in every room; I had taken all my grandfather's foulards and ascots and hung them with thumb tacks from the ceiling, so that when I walked through the house, they brushed against my face like branches and leaves in a forest of silken trees. Riley and I would pace the floor, trying to see each other through the scarves, waiting anxiously for Willie, a Methedrine addict from Alabama who weighed maybe one hundred and five pounds, to bring us some acid. I wore rings on all my fingers, and I would stick birthday candles on each of these rings. Once Willie arrived, we'd drop the acid, hang around until things got really weird, then I would light the candles on the rings.

With my hands "on fire," loaded out of our minds, we'd all jump in my VW and hurtle along Mulholland Drive like little cosmic bugs on a wire, flames leaping from my fingers, our brains sizzling with hallucinations, the road pouring out of the hood of the car just in time for us to ride on it, the vibes from the San Fernando Valley going wong-wong-wongONG as we braved the highway of light. This was our "safe" route into Hollywood. We were always holding so much dope that we lived in a constant state of paranoia and took elaborate precautions to stay out of sight of the police. We figured, flaming fingers aside, we'd never be noticed.

At the Gentle Soul House there was always a loaded bunch careening from wall to wall, with Rick almost always at its center. Rick was a serious pursuer of the elusive state of cosmic consciousness, and he had taken just enough acid to discover that in another life he had been St. Francis of Assisi. This was apparent because of his clear and obvious ability to converse with animals.

"Look—see—the squirrel knows who I am." We are standing in Rick's room one afternoon, on the second floor. I'm so blown out on acid that the room is ticking like a clock, and huge purple blooms are puffing out of the ground like mushrooms. I'm used to this by now and I just ignore it. There is a homemade altar against one wall. The altar is made almost entirely of melted candle wax. There are little photos of Indian gurus, assorted beads, shells, feathers, and other glittering tribal relics such as the odd marble, sequin, or pebble gathered from some particularly spiritual beachhead. Rick stands staring at the squirrel who sits on the limb of a fir tree just a few feet from his window. The squirrel looks at Rick, then away, then back at the tree, then at the roof, all in jerky little squirrel movements. "See?" says Rick. "He looked at me."

"Well, yeah," I said. "But he also looked at the tree, the street, and his toes." Rick turned to me with a sad, patient gaze, the gaze of One Who Knows. Then he shook his head and looked at Pam. Pam was a round little thing with a terrific talent and a crush on every guy within forty miles. Most recently it was a smooth-faced seventeen-year-old singer/songwriter who was always hanging around the house playing and singing his newest stuff. His name was Jackson Browne.

Jackson had an air of slight detachment. Like Peter Fonda, he seemed to have a different personal agenda that transcended the trappings of hippiedom. While he hung out with the Gentle Soul, he was more concentrated on his singing and writing, less on the celestial aspects of the cosmos. He would listen to Rick, then look at me, nod, then go back to his guitar. He had a way of tacitly agreeing only in so far as it also didn't mean approval. It just meant "No argument here."

It took people awhile to realize who Rick really was. Other than singing and being St. Francis of Assisi—enough to fill anybody's day—Rick was an astute observer of angels and other celestial beings. Several times a day these cherubim and seraphim made passes over the house.

"Have the angels been over today, Rick?" Pam asks. Rick cocks his head and holds up his hand. Everyone just stands still. In the silence, the air sings. Then there is a whine. I figure it's just more acid shit going on. Rick gazes out the window. "Here they come," he says.

I look out the window. A small private plane, maybe a Piper Cub, flies over the ridge and passes a few hundred feet above the house. Rick glances at me. Have I seen? I look at Rick. Surely, he doesn't mean that this is an angel.

"They don't want you to see them, so they appear as airplanes." Clearly we're in deep here. Stoned as I might be, I still can tell the difference between an airplane and a celestial being. "You have to watch for the ones without numbers under the wings, of course," Rick says. "The ones without numbers are angels. That one has numbers. Of course, angels can do whatever they want. Including having numbers under their wings." So that might be an angel after all, he's just not being obvious about it?

I began to wonder what I was doing there. I began to think that I had been taking entirely too much LSD and smoking too much weed. The answer was plain.

"Rick," I said, "I'm gonna go down the hill and have a beer." Rick was scandalized.

"A beer?" he shrieked. "It'll make your nervous system gross. You won't be able to see the angels anymore."

"Exactly," I said. I hiked down the hill, found a local bar, and drank three beers in a row until I was satisfied that planes were planes and angels were—well, not planes.

It was 1967, the summer of Music and Love. Lou Adler and John Phillips and a man named Alan Pariser had begun organizing a new and conspicuous version of a love-in to be called the Monterey Pop Festival. There had been jazz festivals and classical festivals, and there was always some kind of music at love-ins and be-ins, most recently at Mount Tamalpais. But this was a step in a different direction. This was totally professional. This was big time, not just a bunch of raggedy hippies gathering in a park to get stoned and play flutes, but a bunch of designer-raggedy *rich* hippies gathering in a park to get stoned and listen to the top groups in the world. The other hippies could also come, but it would cost them. In deference to the truly funky, Lou and John had convinced the Monterey city fathers to set aside a part of the fairgrounds for an open camping site for free, but tickets to get into the actual festival were scaled like any other concert. The whole town of Monterey was watching this. We were on our best behavior. The police were very cooperative, very tolerant for the most part. Some of them, swept up in the vibeness of it all, actually wore flowers on their uniforms.

The Beatles didn't come. Ditto the Rolling Stones. But several of the biggest names in music were there: Janis Joplin, Jimi Hendrix, Otis Redding, The Who and The Mamas and the Papas among them. Actually a Rolling Stone did show up: Brian Jones. The whole time I saw Brian there his mouth was permanently caked with a white rime, like a salt lick. He could barely walk. His girlfriend, a six-foot wraith dressed all in black, barely walked with him. They were like two people on their way to view their own gravesite, perhaps even to do a test lie-down. I never heard her say a word. Every now and again Brian burst out in some vague sentence structure before his lips dried up and sealed shut again. I sat next to him during a set by the blues band Canned Heat. Brian loved them. They woke him up. He turned to me between songs. "That would have been us, if we hadn't been so pretty," he whispered. I suddenly had a new appreciation of the Stones. And of Canned Heat. A blues band is a blues band is a blues band. Unless it's the Rolling Stones.

I had a watch from Van, a beautiful handmade silver Mexican watch. Brian wanted it. Entranced by the dope and the hipness of it all, I took it off my wrist and was about to give it to him. I mean this guy was *it*, he was a fucking *Stone*! Then someone came up and got his attention for a moment. In that brief second I came to my senses, quickly slipped the watch back on my wrist and disappeared.

John and Lou had given me the job of being the official honcho of the arts-and-crafts booths at the festival. This involved nothing more than parading up and down the aisle between the booths—which sold everything from stained glass to kachina dolls to three thousand different kinds of glazed mugs—and pretending to have a function.

"Ned, I can't set up my booth. Some guy's in my spot," said one craftsman to me. As far as I could ascertain, he made doorknobs out of gourds.

"Let me talk to Lou about that," I would answer.

"Ned—I'm supposed to get two tickets for Hendrix . . ."

"Let me talk to Lou about that."

"Ned . . ."

"Lou . . ."

"Ned . . ."

"Lou . . ."

Generally, by the time I came around again, the participants had settled the problem among themselves. If they hadn't, I just avoided that section of the fairgrounds from then on.

For this I got a room in a motel and all the marijuana I could smoke. The only rule we had was: No taking LSD. By now, LSD was turning out to be something of a mixed blessing, if not an outright scourge. People were starting to leap from high places while stoned because they knew that the cosmos would not let them fall. Others were ending up in mental hospitals with delusions that would not go away even after the acid wore off. For others, the acid was not wearing off at all and they were starting to live in a permanent state of acid-delusions. Days, months, and years later some were still caught in that dream, unable to work, to learn, to live.

For the first few days of the festival we got lucky. No problems with LSD. Then the Pied Piper showed up, Stanley Augustus Owsley himself, in the flesh, the Johnny Appleseed of LSD who made his own famous brand, Owsley Purple. He literally handed out thousands of free doses to people, one thousand micrograms each, before he could be stopped. Dozens flipped out. They were naked, eating dirt, screaming from the rooftops, rolling in the aisles. We tried to keep them out of sight, and for the most part succeeded. But the counterculture was beginning to show some of its shabby, thread-bare edges. It amazed me, two years later, that there was ever a Woodstock. By 1969 I was so burned out on the counterculture I wouldn't have flown over Woodstock in a 747 at thirty-five thousand feet.

I obeyed the no-acid dictum. Two things had happened recently that helped. One, I had started practicing meditation, which had affected me strongly, and two, I'd given up LSD already anyway. One afternoon I had had a new revelation. I took a dose with a friend and waited for the wong-wong-wonONG to start, the rippling air, the tongue of flame, the Oneness. It never came. I started to feel uncomfortable. Where I usually felt connected to everything, I felt totally foreign. The drug wasn't working. It wasn't bad, it was nothing.

"I'm not taking acid anymore," I said. My friend just stared at me. "Acid's through with me." I couldn't explain it, but inside, in my own mind, I had heard the words: "Don't take me anymore." It was as if acid itself were talking. It seemed like the most natural thing in the world, especially on LSD, to hear an inner voice. At that moment all desire for the drug simply stopped. All I wanted was a double shot of bourbon and about thirty beers.

While booze had fallen into disfavor with the truly hip in the sixties, there were dissenters. John Phillips was an avowed Crown Royal drinker and always kept plenty of liquor on hand at his house along with the bottles of pills and the little mounds of cocaine on top of the piano. Our motto was: It's OK to add something to the pharmacopeia, but let's not get hasty and subtract anything. Alcohol stayed. It remained the one trustworthy drug, the substance that you could measure, use in all company, enjoy for its variety and pleasant, stupefying effect. You could count on alcohol. In fact, I really only liked cocaine because it allowed me to drink more and to drink longer.

I was still loafing along on extra jobs and script reading, enough to pay the rent, buy dope, and play. While all my friends were also playing, they were also working hard.

Terry, Lou, John, were all successful people. The party line in the sixties was that the Establishment was bogus, and that we weren't playing their game. But all the rich hippies I knew played the hell out of the game. They didn't shake the walls, they didn't blaze a new category of economic existence. They all played well within the rules and made considerable fortunes as a result of their efforts.

The only people tearing down the walls of society were the true outsiders, the vagabonds and drifters, the underground politicals. Their rebellious actions were given lip service by the monied freak elite. There was always talk of how "important" these people were to society as an alternative, a dissenting voice, etc. But those vague statements of support, accompanied by the odd check to some free clinic or the occasional Black Panther defense fund was the extent of their participation in the revolution. They hung safely in Bel-Air and Beverly Hills and Malibu, and I hung with them waiting for the process of osmosis to take place. Somehow, if I hung around long enough, something would happen.

In fact, I had started writing songs, trying to emulate people like Jackson Browne, John Phillips, Rick Stanley, and Pam Polland. Scott McKenzie taught me to Travis pick. I bought a guitar. Eventually, I did write a song. Incredibly, John liked it and placed it on a Mamas and Papas album. Lou signed me to his publishing company as a writer. Larry Marks, a friend since high school, used me on a couple of demos at A&M Records as a singer. Then one night, John told me he thought I might be able to sing on my own. He thought I had a decent voice. He had already taken Scott, an old friend of his from early folk singing days in New York, and produced a monster hit, "If You're Going to San Francisco," which began, "If you're going to San Francisco, better wear some flowers in your hair . . ." And some penicillin in your pocket. This credulous lyric made Scott McKenzie a star virtually overnight.

Scott had a beautiful instrument, a pure Irish tenor something like Dennis Doherty's, the lead singer in The Mamas and the Papas, only sweeter and richer. He was a crooner in an era which lacked crooners under the age of fifty. He was a natural for the song. What he wasn't a natural for was the result of having a hit record.

"God, Ned, hide me, willya?" It's Scott. He stands on my porch looking wild-eyed and frightened. He looks as if he's been up all night.

"What's wrong, man," I ask.

"Women. They're all over my place. They're swarming up Laurel Canyon."

"Wait, lemme get a few things, a toothbrush . . ." I said, heading for the bathroom.

"No, you don't understand. I mean armies. Dozens of girls literally breaking into my house to have sex with me." We stood there looking at one another, he pleading for understanding, me for time.

"Toothbrush *and* toothpaste," I said, picking up the pace.

"You don't see it, do you? One month ago these chicks wouldn't give me the time of day, and now they can't wait to fuck me. Why? I mean—it's sick, man. It's perverse. Some of these girls are fourteen, fifteen years old!"

"Toothbrush, toothpaste, and some *gum* . . ."

"Ned, you're not listening. They come at all times of the night and day, they don't care. They have boyfriends, husbands, it doesn't matter. They're like animals. It's not a turn-on at all, it's—terrifying." This was subversive talk and it made me uncomfortable. Since when did a man turn down free pussy? It wasn't in the book.

"Get hold of yourself, Scott. This is what we're here for. You're *supposed* to get all this sex and fame and money. These are the *goods*, for chrissake."

"Then how come it's got me all freaked out?"

"Simple. You're a very sick person, Scott. Now, do you think you could convince some of them, the ones you don't want, that I have a hit coming out, too? Nothing spectacular, I'll just skim off the blow-by." Scott stared at me, turned, and fled.

When John took me to the recording studio, I felt great. I was ready. I could sing. After all, hadn't I sat up night after night singing with John and Michelle and Scott, sometimes Cass and Denny? Didn't John tell me, time and again, that he thought I had a good voice? That I should try and cut a record? It was my turn to get the goods. All I could think of were those girls crawling all over Scott like termites in hot pants.

We got to the studio and another group was still working there. I can't remember who it was, but they asked me if I minded if they stayed while I auditioned for John. Like an idiot I said OK. Fine. I'm on fire. I'm ready. Nothing can derail the success train. Hang around, guys, pick up some valuable pointers.

I stood down on the empty studio floor with John. He put the earphones on me and handed me a joint. I took a few hits and nodded. Look out, folks, the next sixties *wunderkind* is comin' through. John signaled the engineer to start the playback. It was Cass singing a song from one of the M&P's albums. I started to sing with her. I choked. John stopped the playback.

"You OK?" he asked.

"Yeah, fine—just got a frog in my throat," I said. We started the playback again. I blew it again. I couldn't keep myself in Cass's register. I forgot the words. I was slow picking up the melody, even though I'd heard the song a hundred times. What was going on? Another opportunity was passing me by. Panicky, I only got worse and worse. John tried to calm me down. We stopped for a few minutes while he coached me. We had a shot of Crown Royal, a surefire cure. Nothing worked. I was good for a phrase or two, then I crashed. It was obviously not going to happen. I had always been able to do everything brilliantly at John and Michelle's house those long wonderful stoned singing nights. But not here, not in the studio. In the studio, with the whole range of possibilities strung out in front of me, with someone who could actually get a record produced,

I couldn't cut it. The Living-Room Comedian strikes again. Kindly, John patted my back.

"We'll try it again another night," he said. "Maybe," he continued, "maybe you're just not really cut out to be a singer."

I buried my disappointment. I pretended it didn't matter to me. I was by now expert at brushing off failure and disappointment. I was a child of the sixties, I didn't need material things. I sought out my old friend Rick Stanley. While Rick may have been off about the single-engined angels, I never discounted his knowledge entirely, only the most egregious and preposterouse of his flights of ethereal dogma. On a more mundane level, he suggested we go one night to hear the latest spiritual message from a guru, a real guru from India named Maharishi Mahesh Yogi. According to everyone I knew, this guy was really spiritual, or, as it usually came out, *reel spirichul*.

"Can he levitate?" I asked.

"He can do anything. He's at least five hundred years old."

"Yeah. What couldn't you learn in five hundred years, huh? He's probably bored with levitating by now."

"Shit, yes. By now he spends most of his time on the astral plane. He only appears to us because he loves us and wants us to be enlightened, too. He's reel spirichul." Wow.

It turned out that Maharishi was between planes at the moment, so we went to hear one of his disciples, a guy named Jerry Jarvis. Jerry was speaking at UCLA, and when I heard the message it settled into me like a glass of water on a hot day. Cosmic Consciousness in the palm of my hand. Suddenly I saw that I'd been waiting for this forever. Only not just reading it, but experiencing it first-hand through a form of meditation that used a mantra. It was called Transcendental Meditation. Then and there I resolved to get my mantra and start transcending.

CHAPTER

15

As with everything else, I became totally obsessed with meditation. I proselytized everyone I knew, from my parents to Lou Adler to John and Michelle as well as old friends like Richard Lang and Doug Tibbles. No one was safe. People began locking their doors. My father took to hiding in the garage when I came over.

"Keenan, it's Ned . . ." Sharley called as she saw me coming up the driveway.

"Oh, shit!" I saw him scurrying out the back door.

"Hey, Dad! Where ya going?" Here I come, Popsie, your loving son, eyes all dewy and bright with truth and love.

In the garage my father was on a desperate search for something. I stood in the doorway and peered inside, picking him out in the gloom.

"It's in here somewhere . . . this drawer I think. No . . ."

"What are you looking for, Dad?" I asked.

"My ball peen hammer. It's in here somewhere. . . ." My father had never fixed anything in his life. A ball peen hammer might as well have been a half-acre of alfalfa.

"Who are you, all of a sudden, Ozzie Nelson?"

"No," he answered, in a vastly injured tone, "I just need my ball peen hammer, that's all."

"Well, Dad, I wondered if you wanted to go with me to a TM lecture at UCLA tonight. This guy Jerry Jarvis is talking . . ."

"Tonight? Tonight? Oh, Jesus . . . damn . . . tonight . . . hell . . . there's a benefit . . . it's a Stuntmen's Association Ball American Cancer Society Tribute to Ed Wynn kind of Thing For The Occasionally Deaf tonight. I can't get out of it, wish I could, but you know, they're expecting me—where's the goddamn hammer?" He was now fumbling frantically in every drawer and cabinet in the garage, tearing things out and tossing them on the floor. Finally, he reached into one drawer and came out with a half-pint of Smirnoff vodka. "Well, whaddaya know," he said, slapping his skull, "how do you suppose . . ." He uncapped the bottle and raised it to his lips and drained half of it in about five seconds. "*Yaaaaahhhhhhggggaaahhhhdd* DAMN SHIT!" He stood there and bellowed as the vodka hit bottom. Then he turned to me and let out a low, appreciative whistle. "That," he said, "is what I call a ball peen fuckin' HAMMER!"

My father had become a bottle hider. He had half-pints of vodka stuck everywhere. Outside in the hedges, in the branches of the trees, under rocks, in old, defunct incinerators. Inside the house it was harder to do this, because my stepmother was on the lookout, constantly poking through the shelves and sofa cushions.

"Is he drinking again?" she'd ask me. I'd shrug. The question was obviously rhetorical. How could she be missing it? By eleven in the morning he'd be too stoned to stand up. He would go to bed, pass out for a few hours, wake up and start in again. "Why does he think he has to sneak it?" she asked, again perhaps rhetorically. "If he'd do it out in the open it wouldn't be so bad." Again I shrugged. How would that be better? There were no answers, and for once I didn't try to give any.

My disdain for this behavior was compounded by my self-righteous spirituality. I was now an elevated being, a meditator. So I smoked a little weed, drank a little wine. Big deal. At least I never hid half-pints around the house. Of course, I didn't have to. No one was looking for them. In the first six months of practicing TM, although I hadn't stopped drinking or smoking weed, I had stopped taking acid, quit smoking cigarettes, and become a vegetarian. This kind of purity was pretty hard to take.

"What do you mean you can't have a steak?" My mother stands holding a larruping great slab of meat that resembles one of those beefsteaks from the old comic books that people were supposed to put on black eyes back when meat was nine cents a pound. It lolled in her hand like the tongue of a giant dog.

"Well, I uh—it's just too gross."

"Gross!" My mother *lived* at the Safeway meat department.

"I don't mean that way, not ugly, not *particularly* ugly, but just from a less refined level of consciousness. It makes the nervous system gross. Like the opposite of subtle." My mother's mouth worked for a full five seconds before a sound came out.

"Meat is supposed to be subtle? It's excellent beef. It's USDA Choice. It's from Safeway. Meat is judged on color, texture, marbling, freshness. Since when did subtlety become a criterion?" I had to try another tack.

"George Bernard Shaw was a vegetarian. He lived to be ninety-five or something." Her nose twitched. Shaw was a big favorite. Hard to argue with Shaw. She sighed and tossed the meat onto the counter. *Fwaap.*

"Well—what would you rather eat? What's subtle today?"

"Brown rice would be great. Brown rice and some organic broccoli."

"Brown rice? *Brown?*" she spluttered. I shrugged. My mother was a fast adjuster.

"Probably *is* healthier. Those Chinese people live to be a hundred just eating rice and fish," she said, already feeling better.

"Um—no fish, Mom, thanks." She stared off into space, making further adjustments in microseconds.

"Where do I get this brown rice? I mean, we don't have to cultivate a paddy, do we?"

"Ha ha. Very good, Mom. A paddy. Don't worry, I'll get it at a health-food store."

In a way this new phase was more threatening than acid. Acid she had never had to face at all, as I stayed away while stoned. Marijuana required only a can of Glade. But not eating meat was definitely seditious. And the guru struck fear into the hearts of an entire generation.

"Is he here? Is that his car?" A dozen fresh-faced, planet-eyed, beaded, bearded, shock-haired, bell-bottomed hippies stood on the curb peering down the street. We all quivered in anticipation, and the flowers we held in our hands quivered with us. Maharishi loved flowers. Maharishi was in America. He was here in Los Angeles. He was actually coming to this house in midtown L.A. owned by some nice middle-class straights named Olsen, and he was going to speak to us.

The Olsens were typical of the American bourgeois spiritual underground; these were generally very ordinary, well-to-do, respectable people, Catholics in their case, who had this unsuspected streak of mysticism in their veins. There were plain folks like the Olsens all over Los Angeles, people who loved gurus and Eastern mysticism and were long-time supporters of Maharishi from way before this latest wave of spiritual desire had begun to issue from the counterculture. *They* were set. *We* had questions.

When Maharishi arrived, he was sitting in the front seat of a car driven by Jerry Jarvis. The sight of this mystic sitting in a Plymouth was the first of a series of shocks that we were subjected to.

"He's riding in a Plymouth," someone said, scandalized at the banality of the image.

"What do you expect? He would come riding in on a golden chariot pulled by a swan or something?"

"Yeah, but a *Plymouth?*"

"A Plymouth's perfect. The Pilgrims . . . seeking spiritual freedom . . . we're all pilgrims, right? It's perfect. He probably planned it like that." Wow.

My heart was in my throat. The actual no-shit guru was here, the master about whom I had heard for months was about to bring his physical body into my universe and grant me his *darshan*. *Darshan* was like a kind of invisible spray that got on you if you were in the presence of a holy person. It helped you in your quest for cosmic consciousness to get as much of this darshan on you as you could. We weren't positive how it worked, probably something like being in the way of a huge sneeze, but we knew that it made the disciple reel spirichul. By this definition, the Olsens were practically astral travelers by now.

"Maharishi, what about acid?" a guy asked. We were inside the Olsens' house now, sitting on the floor and gazing raptly at the guru. Maharishi looked questioningly at Jerry. I held my breath.

"He's talking about LSD, Maharishi," Jerry said.

"Lysergic acid diethylamide—LSD-25!" the man shouted.

Maharishi nodded and addressed his questioner.

"What it does, this D-twenty-five?" he asked.

"It makes you see God! . . ."

"It makes you see colors. . . ."

"It makes you realize you're all interconnected with the universe and everything. . . ."

"It makes you more peaceful!" Fuckin-A rights.

"It makes you more loving. . . ." Music . . . colors . . . God . . . sex . . . peace . . . cosmic . . . life . . . wong-wong-wongONG. . . .

We weren't worried. Acid's cool. After all, he had long hair, a beard, he was probably astral traveling as we sat there. Rick leaned over to me.

"He can dig it. He's like on acid even when he's just on the natch."

"Yeah. Acid's just chemical meditation anyway, right? We're already so evolved he'll probably tell us we don't need to meditate at all."

"Well," said Rick judiciously, "we may have to meditate for a couple of months. These other people, it'll probably take them a couple of more lifetimes." Wow.

"It's a dream," he answered. Whaaa? . . . Maharishi fluffed his dhoti again and twirled his hair. "This D-25 is a dream." I took a deep breath and down inside I said, no way. Don't tell me acid is a dream.

"A dream!" screamed a local peacemonger, spit flying like darshan. "It's not a dream. I experienced it. It's real!" Now everyone was riled. Even Maharishi was taken aback at the vehemence of this response. But he stuck to his guns.

"It is not real. Only the experience of the inner Self through meditation is real. Drugs are not real." People got up and walked out. The banker-hippie coalition was experiencing meltdown.

"I will allow you your experiences," he continued. "You have had them, they are yours. But nonetheless, this drug experience you have been having with twenty-five? It is a dream. TM is your answer. You may either follow twenty-five or follow me."

It was at this point that the hard core was formed.

Beyond the dope and the sex, I felt no more connection with my contemporaries than I felt with my parents and their generation. I suddenly saw that the whole generation I was attached to was just like me: furious at being asked to consider any alternatives to whatever we had already decided, when we were six, that the world should be like.

Another problem was that I just didn't have any goddamned respect for anything. Not for peace, not for freedom, not for justice, nor equality. I only wanted to feel better. I was against the war in Vietnam because quite simply I didn't want to have to fight in it. I told that to the psychiatrist at both of my induction physicals. Taking a handful of Benzedrine before I went in hadn't hurt either. My blood pressure was sky-high.

"Don't you think the army can handle you, Wynn?" The doctor, complete with identifying goatee and clipboard, sat back in the spare office in the induction center on Spring Street and gazed at me. Outside, hundreds of other young men, shivering and cowed in their underwear, followed a blue line on the floor from one doctor to another getting pinched and poked and squeezed. I had been up all night, terrified. We had actually been told to bring our toothbrushes with us to the physical because we were probably going to be shipped right out to Fort Ord.

"The army can handle me, sir, but I don't know if I can handle the army." I was very nervous. I had picked my fingernails until my hands were bleeding. Oddly enough, I was not intimidated by a black sergeant who had screamed at me in the line for putting my cigarette out on the floor. I had been very cool. I knew my beef wasn't with him. It was going to get down to me and this guy sitting across the desk from me, the psychiatrist.

He had the medical questionnaire we had all filled out earlier sitting in front of him. The questionnaire had been clear on several points: Answer All Questions. Do Not Erase. I had left blanks. I had erased. I had answered NO to the question asking if I were homosexual, making sure that I bore down on the pencil very hard, tracing *No* over and over again until the pencil broke, leaving a streak of graphite on the page. I knew that the shrink would flag that in a minute.

"Are you a homosexual?"

"No, sir. Absolutely not. I love girls. I am completely and totally normal. I'm definitely not homosexual. I don't even like looking at all these men walking around in their underwear. It makes me very uncomfortable. That's how much I like girls. And also, I don't think I can take a shit in front of other men."

"Excuse me?"

"I know you have these toilets in the barracks, right, where there aren't any walls? Just these toilets sitting in a row like Andy Griffith cleaned in *No Time for Sergeants*? I can't do that. I can't shit in front of people like that. Not because I'm a queer or anything like that, you understand, because I definitely am not. Girls, pussy, that's me all over. But this public shitting thing, I just can't do it. Or sleep in a huge room with a bunch of other men snoring and gurgling. Also not because I'm a queer, which is understood, but I just need privacy. That's all." He made some notes and looked up. He nodded. I left. On the way out, I winked at the black sergeant who had already forgotten me and was now screaming at some other poor jerk.

They made me 1-Y and told me to come back next year. When I came back, the same drill took place. I did all the same things, only I didn't even bother with the Bennies this time. Different shrink, same result. They continued to make me 1-Y for the rest of the war.

I still lived inside the emotional skin of a child. The little brown man in the white dhoti and the long hair and the sandals pulled at me because he seemed totally unafraid, even welcoming the storm and laughing at it. This is irresistible to a child. I had attached myself once more to someone rich, powerful, and eventually, after the Beatles discovered him about eight months later, famous as well.

I joined the group of meditators that was the most fanatic. Besides our incessant proselytizing, telling people their lives would be better if they meditated, many of us took on Maharishi's manner of speaking, the lilt in his voice, the way he always started out his sentences with things like: "It is a joy . . ." or "It is the glory of the World Plan . . ." This stilted English became a part of my speech pattern. I began to paint the peaceful attitude on my face, the spacey smile, the deliberate cadences and inflections I assumed to convey a nonmaterial sense of being.

There was also an implicit code of behavior. Everything, every action and thought, "affected the nervous system," and therefore was checked off against a growing list of spiritual no-no's. Life was essentially Bliss. If you weren't living in Bliss, you must be doing something wrong. It could be the food you were eating, or someone you were associating with whose vibe was "low," or a place you were living in. And of course, there was sex. Sex, we now knew, was a function controlled by a very base *chakra* at the bottom of the spine, and it was possibly injurious to the upwardly soaring cosmically evolving meditator. Unless, of course, you meditated before you fucked.

I am sitting on the bed. We are on a meditation retreat high in the Sierra Mountains, in Squaw Valley, California. The whole resort has been taken over by our group, called the Students International Meditation Society. We are evolving our asses off, going to lectures with Maharishi, meditating three and four hours a day, doing our hatha-yoga. It is well known that Maharishi disapproves of short skirts, since he is a celibate, so the women, when in his presence in the lecture hall, place shawls over their legs so as not to attract his all-seeing eye and give him a nonmonkly experience. Other women, longtime followers, wear long skirts, and many of them benefited by this extra cover. But for the most part, the younger women, the new crowd of sixties meditators, are wearing dresses that rarely come much below the bottom of their buttocks.

I have invited one of these girls into my hotel room to meditate with me. I'd seen her around the lecture hall and kind of liked her. Kind of liking someone in the sixties was kind of like being in love. More than kind of liking someone was heavy, man, so we stayed in the kind-of-liking stage for a long time. Luckily, sex was more or less unbridled in the kind-of-liking stage. Still, a certain pro-forma courtship was in order, most of it verbal and all of it splashed liberally with enlightenment-speak.

"It's really a boost to our evolution to meditate together," I said. "We are creating that atmosphere which is more favorable to the flow of positivity, fulfilling the desires of Nature to attaining that state of contact with Being, establishing us in Cosmic Consciousness. Dipping the cloth of Ego in the dye of Pure Awareness, then taking it out and fading it in the sun of the field of action, then dipping, then taking out, then dipping then taking out . . . in and out, in and out . . ."

"Gee . . . you sound just like Maharishi . . . ."

"Er, do I?" Modest, self-deprecating chuckle goes here. "*Sheesh*. It's just that I am so deeply immersed in this program. . . ." Immerse *this*.

I had always used wine and marijuana in these situations, even after starting to meditate. I merely gave the weed some benediction through a quick, memorized spiel about how it was this naturally occurring substance given to us by God, withheld from us by the Forces of Ignorance (formerly the Forces of Oppression, the Pig Right, now merely the Vast Unaware), followed by some aural rajas in the form of the Buffalo Springfield or Bob Dylan. And of course, we all knew that Jesus drank wine.

Now, however, I had my eye on becoming a teacher of TM. Becoming a teacher of TM was a good deal from every angle. You got a big boost on the road to God Consciousness, you could actually tell people you had a job, and, in a not-unwelcome side effect, a lot of meditating women looked on being a teacher as similar to being a sort of minor rock figure. As an aspiring teacher of TM, I had decided to avoid, at least during the retreats, the use of drugs or alcohol. Therefore, I had to resort to other stimulants, like hatha-yoga.

Hatha-yoga is the yoga of physical movement, of bending and stretching, holding poses, practicing breathing, generally preparing the body for not only the dawning but the maintenance of cosmic consciousness. Hatha-yoga is supposed to accomplish this by exciting *kundalini*, known to us vaguely as the Life Force, causing it to begin to rise in the spine through a tiny channel called the *sushumna*. Once this Life Force gets moving, it evidently augers up the spine and through those *chakras* like a cosmic Black & Decker getting hotter and hotter until it reaches the top of the skull where it reams the Thousand-Petaled Lotus of the Mind and poaches the ego like an egg. Our ideas of what that most mystical experience would be like was predictable:

"It makes you see God! . ."

"It makes you see colors. . . ."

"It makes you realize you're all interconnected with the universe and everything. . . ."

"It makes you more peaceful!"

"It makes you more loving. . . ." Music . . . colors . . . God . . . sex . . . peace . . . cosmic . . . life . . . wong-wong-wongONG. . . . Spiritual enlightenment was going to be like this really bitchen acid trip, only you never had to come down. Old ideas die hard.

The more immediate rewards of hatha-yoga were more earthly. For one thing, you could get a woman to disrobe in order to perform it. And there is nothing quite like the sight of a girl in her bikini underwear doing the Plough.

"You know, I think it's a good idea to do some yoga first. I'll meditate while you do your yoga," I say. Then I sit on the bed while the young woman spreads her towel on the rug and starts limbering up. I meditate through half-closed eyes, waiting for that Plough. As she rolls around on the floor, her tiny skirt gets in the way. So she takes it off. Now, in bra and panties, she rocks back on her shoulders and puts her legs in the air. Oh my.

"Don't look," she says. I mumble incoherently, so full am I of the Bliss of contact with Inner Being, so soaked in spirituality that I am incapable of looking, much less maintaining a base physical thought or desire. Holding her waist with her hands, resting on her shoulders and her elbows, she slowly extends her legs back up and over until her toes are resting on the floor behind her head. The Plough. God love those yogis anyway. From this point to consummation is easy.

"Wha . . . Ned! What are you doing? . ." She's breathless and also helpless.

"Just a little tantric-yoga. . . ." I have managed, in my state of Bliss, to roll off the bed and scramble across the floor to where she teeters, upended like a beached canoe. Talk about kundalini rising.

"Is this tantric-yoga anything like fucking?" she asked, still upside down, her ass in the air.

"With cosmic intent," I said.

"Let's get cosmic," she said. Ah, the sixties.

I learned to give lectures on TM. I started speaking at the meditation center on Gayley Avenue in Westwood. I felt for the first time I had a purpose. What I was doing seemed to matter. I believed that I was helping people and at the same time I was being helped. I was drinking less and using drugs less often, sometimes going for months at a time without getting high. I found a group of friends I liked and who liked me. There was a hierarchy here, but I had a chance of being a part of that hierarchy rather than just a fringe performer.

My parents had a noncommittal attitude toward the whole thing. They were just pleased that I was still alive and had all my limbs. My brother had his own problems deciding about how to do his service and avoid Vietnam at the same time, which he managed ultimately by joining the Air National Guard. I assisted his mental and emotional state by drawing a mandala on a piece of paper, sending it to him in boot camp, and instructing him to stare at it for hours at a time until his mind turned to bean dip. It must have worked like crazy, as he came straight out of the service and became an award-winning screenwriter, while I was putting out hotel fires in Spain. But that was later.

I still had to work my way into the inner circle around Maharishi. The trick was to perform some useful function, something that would get me noticed. I had become aware, from that first day when I saw him driven up in the Plymouth, that being around him meant playing a part in his personal ritual. Most striking to me had been the ritual of The Skin.

When the car pulled up, both Jerry Jarvis and Charlie Lutes, the president of the Spiritual Regeneration Movement, had jumped out, waited impatiently for Maharishi to exit, then dove back into the car for something inside. They both, from opposite sides of the car, got a hand on whatever this thing was at exactly the same time and commenced a tug-of-war. After a brief tussle, Jerry emerged victorious, holding in his hand what I took at first to be a leather jacket. It turned out to be an unremarkable bit of tanned deer hide whose significance I did not at first diagnose. I soon learned that this was no ordinary deerskin; this was The Skin upon which Maharishi sat. Always.

Without exception, wherever Maharishi went, he never sat down on anything without this deerskin being placed down first. It performed the function, I supposed, of a spiritual buffer, jamming the negative vibes from any previous set of buttocks. Evidently buttocks played a large role in the spreading around of negative vibes. You never knew if the haunches of the previous sitter belonged to a smoker, for instance, or a meat eater, or a Democrat, any one of which could apparently annihilate the divine radiance emanating from the sacred set of cheeks upon which the Master himself sat. These tamasic gluteal reverberations, echoes of bottoms past, would presumably wreak spiritual havoc with Maharishi's holy keister; therefore, the skin was always placed upon whatever spot he was going to sit, just moments before he actually sat. It was a sort of Strategic Defense Initiative for the rusty-dusty, shooting down and deflecting dangerous low-vibe missiles and sending them crashing back into the cushions. When Maharishi rose again, this skin was swept up and carried to the next spot favored posteriorly by the guru. The nearest I could figure was that the guy who carried The Skin was The Guy. I vowed then and there to get that job.

My quest carried me around the world. In 1969 I went to India to become a teacher of TM. Maharishi's ashram was in Rishikesh, a small village north of Delhi, in the foothills of the Himalayas. There, perched on some cliffs overlooking the Ganges, I lived in a little wood-and-brick hut called a *puri*. The ashram was very rudimentary. There were several brick buildings scattered around, half of them still under construction. There was a glorious little minaretted house right by the river that Maharishi lived in. And there was an open-air dining facility which belonged partly to us and partly to a troop of very aggressive monkeys.

These monkeys were big, about the size and with the personality characteristics of Grumpy the Dwarf. We carried large monkey sticks we had cut from the adjoining forest for protection from these beasts, as they had a habit of confronting us over food. Almost every meal one or two would suddenly drop from the trees right onto the table, generally right in the middle of someone's plate, grab food right out of our hands, and rush back up into the trees above us.

As we were immediately abutted by a forest, wildlife abounded. Indian wildlife. There were spiders the size and color of Best Boy tomatoes, red-legged centipedes six inches long that looked like they came out of a very bad dream, and a troop of silver-gray lobsterlike insects living under my hammock, which stalked the off-worlds on weekends and haunted me the rest of the time. There were scorpions that make the ones in Arizona look like Bambi. Two people on the course were stung. And then there were snakes.

There were not supposed to be any snakes in the ashram because a local saint, Tat Wala Baba, had ostensibly walked the fences that held out the forest, muttering mantras that would discourage snakes from entering. Still, one day I saw an exquisite snake slither through the compound, brilliantly colored and marked.

"Probably a manifestation of Lord Shiva," said Rick.

"Probably a manifestation of a two-step poison factory," said Casey, a friend of mine from Seal Beach. Casey had suddenly decided, halfway through the course, to "go into silence." He wore a sign around his neck that said, THANK YOU FOR NOT TALKING TO ME. He didn't speak for three weeks until I saw the snake. That prompted some fence walking of our own, monkey sticks in hand, to satisfy ourselves that the snake was not a scout for a herd of kraits.

I had a running feud with the Indian workers on the course, one of whom kept stealing my Jockey shorts from the clothesline and wearing them on his head. He talked his pals into this, and soon two or three guys were wearing my underpants on their heads. These were the same guys who kept their donkey thirty feet away from the brick pile and carried the bricks two at a time to the donkey to load it, then led the donkey another thirty feet to the work site.

I never could get the reason for wearing my Jockey shorts, but the fellow would take them, put them over his head, then squat down with his bros and smoke Beedos, a particularly odious Indian cigarette, right under my window while I was trying to meditate and get spirichul. Finally, I went to Maharishi to complain.

"Maharishi, this worker steals my underwear." Maharishi was sitting on his bed, as he did in the afternoons, and receiving disciples and seekers from the surrounding area, many coming from Hardwar, a nearby town known throughout India for its plethora of holy men and women. The immediate forest and riverside beach was dotted with caves and populated by Gypsies and *saddhus*, Hindu mendicants, considered holy and treated with respect in India. Many times I went into Maharishi's house at night and there would be at least four or five of these men sleeping on the floor. They came to him for his darshan, as he was, outside of Tat Wala Baba, considered the top saint in the neighborhood.

"What do they do with your underwear?" Maharishi asked.

"They wear them on their heads," I said. I was incensed. "And they make noise while I meditate." Maharishi appeared to regard my problem with tremendous gravity. He then looked sternly around the room at all the saddhus.

"Have you asked him to stop?"

"Several times," I said.

"And what did he say?"

"That he was sorry and he'd stop. But then he just does it again."

"Beat him with a stick," he said. My jaw dropped open. "Take your stick and beat him."

"Oh, Maharishi, I couldn't do that."

He shrugged. "He is an ignorant man. If you do not, he will continue to wear your underwear on his head."

I quit worrying about my underwear. Eventually the guy got bored and left them alone.

There were about fifty of us on the course. My roommate was Kenny Edwards, the guitarist from Linda Ronstadt's first group, the Stone Poneys. By this time a lot of rock and rollers were TM meditators: the Beatles, several of the Doors, several of the Beach Boys. Kenny and I prided ourselves at having beaten the crowd and got our mantras early. At this time we had both been meditators for about two years.

We spent weeks inside that hut meditating—six, eight, ten hours a day. Sometimes I would go up on the roof of the puri at four A.M. and do *pranayama*, breathing exercises. I was hoping to catch the *nabaswan*, a tiny breeze that came down from the mountains at that hour and was supposed to be the Breath of Brahma. I weighed 149 pounds, ate only rice and dal, and was getting pretty damn spirichul. Except for the sex thing.

The celibacy versus sex issue was very big around the ashram. Maharishi was a *brahmachari*, a monk, and we gathered that was the route to gaining higher levels of consciousness. You screw, you lose. Every drop of sperm is a gross perception, a loss of quintessence. I had a girlfriend on the course, a gorgeous German Valkyrie named Thurid. It was hard to be celibate around Thurid. She was about five foot ten and built like a brick Panzer Division.

"What does Thurid mean?" I asked her. We were lying naked in my hammock after some furious, surreptitious humping. She rolled over and looked at me.

"Thurid means thunder," she growled. Yes ma'am.

The heat increased at the ashram until it reached 120 degrees in mid-April, and Maharishi decided to move the entire course to Srinagar, high in the mountains of Kashmir. Within a week we were all floating in houseboats on Dal Lake in the Vale of Kashmir, one of the most exotic spots on Earth. It was here, a few weeks after having been made a teacher, that I got my shot at The Skin.

I was sitting with Maharishi in a meadow outside his house, rented for him by a wealthy Indian disciple, the wife of the owner of the magnificent Oberoi Palace Hotel, which was just visible down the road. All around us rose the snow-capped Himalayas, and behind us shimmered Dal Lake with its graceful houseboats and *shikaras*. The surrounding hillsides were dotted with cherry trees that were just beginning to blossom. I was having a treasured audience with the guru. We discussed my plans, where I would go, what I would do. All I wanted to do was to be taken care of somehow. I had no ambition beyond being his disciple now. It was much easier than trying to make my own way in the world. I wanted to teach TM full time and make a living thereby, something that was not possible at that time.

"Someday," Maharishi said, "someday I will have teachers making their livings teaching. But for now the money is not there." Abruptly, he stood up. I stood up, too. The interview was over. I realized that we were alone. There was no one here, none of his Indian brahmacharis to grab The Skin. Maharishi turned to me. He smiled. "I'll go in the house now," he said.

"Shall I . . ." I said, "shall I take The Skin?" He didn't answer, but began walking toward the house. I reached down, grabbed The Skin and chased after him. I remember feeling great, with The Skin in my hand, wondering, does everyone see me? Do they know of my close personal relationship with the Master? Am I cool or what?

In all, I spent five years, on and off, with the guru—from 1967 to 1972. In between sessions on the courses like India and Squaw Valley, I would make another foray into the world of reality and try life on life's terms. Each time I met with failure. Whatever I sought, I sought pleasure and reverie over work and accomplishment.

On the way back from India I stopped off in Athens for a week and stayed four months. I lived at the TM center on a mattress on the floor and taught meditation. As I had a beard, many Greeks took me for some kind of priest. In my heart, I wanted to be a priest. A priest who had sex and got stoned. That was my goal. I scored some hash from a hippie just back from Nepal and went to the Island of Paros, where I met three Greek-Americans, Alaric, Stefani, and Michael. We rented a house in the town of Drios and smoked ourselves blind. Thurid visited me for several weeks and we went off to the other Greek Islands and slept on the beaches, drank retsina, and swam naked in the Mediterranean. If I'd had enough money, I never would have left.

I stayed with friends in London for a week before my departure to L.A. It was there I picked up a newspaper and read about some murders that had taken place in Los Angeles on some street the paper referred to as "Heaven Drive." It took me a long time to realize that what they meant was Cielo Drive, the street my mother lived on, and the same street that I had lived on with Terry Melcher and Mark Lindsay. It took a little longer to realize that the murders had taken place in the very same house Terry, Mark, and I had lived in. It took even longer to realize that I had once met the murderers. If there was ever a moment when the sixties seized up and died, it was then. It took me several hours of scanning all the stories in the London tabloids to gather that the Charlie Manson they were talking about was the Charlie that I had met at Dennis Wilson's house one afternoon.

Dennis, drummer for the Beach Boys, and Gregg Jakobson, an old friend, were staying in a rented house, the old Tom Mix log cabin on Sunset Boulevard in the Pacific Palisades. Gregg had called me and begged me to come and meet "Charlie."

"He's a real spiritual guy," Gregg said. "We told him about you and how you knew Maharishi and everything. I think you'd be real interested in this guy." The emphasis was on what a spiritual dude Charlie was.

I tried repeatedly to beg off, but Dennis and Gregg insisted. They wouldn't let up. In testimony to Charlie's prodigious powers it was also mentioned, in passing, that he had all these teenage girls with him and that they would do anything he told them to. Being the spiritual colossus I was, I figured at that point that I really owed it to Dennis to check this guy out.

"Be right over," I said.

Just what I was supposed to do by lending my bush-league imprimatur to this Charlie I didn't know, but when I met him, I was totally nonplussed. He was a small, squirrely little man with pale, pasty skin, close-cropped hair, and an extremely tense, tight way of moving and talking. The young girls who were with him were a disappointment. They were the plainest, dullest women I had ever met. Not one of them had an ounce of individuality or uniqueness. Or sex appeal. They weren't attractive, just young. They were like little mice.

The first thing Charlie did was get out the hash pipe and start babbling about the spiritual effects of smoking dope. This to me, a guy who had spent the past five years of his life in a cannabis stupor. We sat out by the pool, where Charlie went through an embarrassing charade with the girls, making them dive for pennies in the pool. He tried to make them take off their bikini tops, which they were loathe to do. He threatened and cajoled them, they whined and pouted and looked at me. Finally one of them did, exposing her pitiful little tits to the cold air. I squirmed and wished myself somewhere else.

"You know that guy Maharishi?" he asked. I nodded. "Know what Maharishi'd say if he met me?" I shook my head. No idea, Charlie. The hash wall had come down with a thud. I was frozen in my seat. "He'd say, Hey, Charlie, man, where's your beard?"

The hash had made us all hungry and thirsty.

"Feed our guest," Charlie told one of the faceless children. They brought out a bowl of fruit, much of it bruised and broken, the grapes all separate from the stems. Hungry, I started eating the grapes. That's when Dennis started outlining Charlie's philosophy about the wasteful practices of the rich.

The rich, it seemed, including the semiconscious Dennis, were constantly throwing perfectly good stuff in the garbage. I chewed a grape and nodded. In a world full of people who were starving to death, good food, food that could be eaten, was being tossed into the trash. I slowed my chewing way down. In fact, in order to remedy this upper-class atrocity, Charlie sent the girls out every morning to gather food from the rich pricks' garbage cans on Sunset Boulevard. Look at all this bounty, this excellent fruit that they had retrieved from the garbage just this morning. I swallowed. Welcome to Charlie's ecosystem.

The rest of the time I spent at the house that day was spent trying to get away. Dennis and Gregg purposely left me alone with Charlie at one point. I had no reason to fear him. He seemed to me to be just one more fucked-up sixties bullshit artist with his own bizarre agenda. He knew I had written a song for The Mamas and the Papas. He tried to get me to listen to some of his music. I declined. I literally backed out of the place with Charlie right in my face talking a demented blue streak about class warfare, song writing, and how rich fucks screwed little guys like him. When I read about the murders in London, I thanked God and cursed Gregg and Dennis in one breath. Hanging out had lost some of its savor.

CHAPTER

16

When I got back from India, I spent a year in my mother's dining room living on a convertible sofa bed. Nothing was working, including me. I taught TM occasionally, but never with much enthusiasm. The old lethargy and ennui had returned.

A friend introduced me to Jenny Arness, James Arness's daughter. There was a definite attraction, and Jenny and I became involved. We stayed in the dining room with the French doors closed for days at a time. Outside the door we could hear the hiss of Glade as my mother patrolled the hall.

Jenny was a tall, beautiful girl with long flaxen hair, actually flaxen, like in the fairy-tale books. She was shy, quiet, reserved. I continued to preach my endless line of bunk, a monotonous mishmash of marijuana plus meditation plus wine plus sex equals God. I hadn't really changed at all. Spirituality was now just a gig, a routine to practice on myself and anyone else in the vicinity.

For some reason, after a while, hanging with me in my mother's dining room smoking dope, listening to records and talking about God just wasn't enough for Jenny. Within a couple of months she got bored and moved on. In splendid isolation, I went to stay with Scott McKenzie at a house he had rented in a place called Vogel Flat in the Tujunga wash in the East San Fernando Valley. It was an idyllic spot full of horses and yucca trees, canyons and dirt roads. I lived in the cinder-block garage on a mattress on the floor and wrote poetry in the gloom. In three months I wrote one poem.

In Japan
I was thrilled to sleep
on a Japanese bed
on the floor
close to my
footsteps.

I drank wine all day with an actor pal named Timothy Scott, who was also staying there in a tiny guest cabin. We all more or less lived off of our own residuals and Scott's royalties.

I rarely saw my family anymore. When I first got back from India, I had stayed with my father and his family. He was living in an enormous home on North Bristol in the heart of Brentwood Park, one of the most expensive and exclusive neighborhoods on the Westside. It seemed that the worse his drinking got, the bigger his houses had gotten, but this was the apogee. It was exactly the kind of place he used to call a mausoleum when my grandfather had lived in a similar heap of plaster several blocks over on Rockingham. All these homes were either *Godzilla* Mediterranean nightmares or *Friday the Thirteenth* Tudor grotesques, and they ate their owners alive.

From time to time he would lend me his 1967 Dodge pickup. One day, before giving me his keys, he took me to the truck which was parked at the curb and did a quick but thorough search. When he ran his hand beneath the front seat, he came up with the usual half pint of vodka. He grinned as he slipped the little flask into his hip pocket.

"Well, the truck has its gas, and I got mine," he said.

I found it impossible to stick with any job, or to maintain any relationship past some mystical, apparently foreordained six- to eight-week period. I found that no matter how short a relationship was it hurt just the same when it ended. Why did I feel like my guts were in a grinder every day of my life? Everything seemed to be getting to me more and more, and the booze and the dope weren't deadening it sufficiently. I was back where I had been some years earlier before Roger and Juju had given me my first LSD. This time my solution was to try the guru again.

It seemed to me that the TM Movement was the perfect place for an utter flop to wallow undetected by the world at large. I'd about run out of celebrity pals to sponge off of and Maharishi's name was last on the list.

I traveled all over Europe with Maharishi from 1970 to 1972. I drove the car he rode in, I carried The Skin. I stood at the door to his room and played bouncer to the faithful: you, you, not you, not you, you . . . Club Infinity. I had arrived. I had position, I had power; I was The Guy. Or rather I was one of them.

By that time there were several versions of The Guy. Maharishi liked to juggle The Guys, favoring one, then another, keeping everyone on his toes. I had some good friends in this hanger-on staff position including Casey, my silent snake-hunting friend late of Seal Beach and India. Sometimes we did useful things, like teach people TM. More often, we performed useless tasks that had no apparent purpose and were often onerous. But we hung with a vengeance. Where else were we to go?

*   *   *

Maharishi had a real affinity for Mallorca. He liked the weather, and Mallorca was cheap. The Spanish had built dozens of what could only be called tourist bunkers—huge, slipshod resort developments erected primarily for German office workers down from Mainz on an Iberian sun-wine-and-sex holiday. The hotels were flimsy and the amenities few; power outages and water shortages were common. But they had the Four B's: Beds, Balconies, Bars, and Beaches.

The water was suspect, the food horrible, and the locals were a haughty, mulish lot, generally antagonistic to everyone. But when Frantzen and Traudel go on holiday, they bring their own sausages, frolic en masse, and are so utterly besotted with their own bodies, that the leaking pipes, stopped-up toilets, crumbling plaster and indigenous killjoys don't bother them in the least. They tramp right through the Mallorquins, scattering them like sand fleas, a synchronized corps of fully flexed, body-building backpackers from Heinrich's Oberst-Gymnasium. It was in these pilsner-and-paella fleabags that we lived for two years, and it was here that I began the process of plotting my escape.

I am sitting on the balcony of the Karina Hotel in a place called Cala Antena on the island of Mallorca. This is the teacher training course equivalent of Siberia. Things have changed. I am no longer The Guy. There is a new eager beaver from Texas named Billy who is now The Guy. Easy come, easy go.

For the past two and a half years I have had no drugs and almost no alcohol. Without even thinking about it, I have not had a drink in nearly twelve months. Recently, however, I have taken to sneaking down to the hotel bar in the middle of the night and stealing bottles of Guinness stout, the holy black elixir of Ireland, from the refrigerator. Just getting the beer to my room has been an adventure. At three in the morning, in my bathrobe, I have slunk to the grinding, clanking elevator, ridden down three flights to the hotel bar, snuck behind the counter, opened the refrigerator—which is left unlocked because the hotel owners know meditators don't drink nor do they steal—filled my robe pockets and my arms with the little brown bottles, then returned to my room with the glass bottles chinking all the way down the hall. And now I huddle on my balcony staring into the dark Mediterranean night sucking Guinness like a child at a tit. Can he see me? From his hotel room across the plateau half a mile away? Can Maharishi gaze at me with his third eye and see me drinking?

Around me are meditators in their rooms sleeping, dreaming, meditating. Sometimes they come to me in the middle of the night, talking about having seen Maharishi floating over their beds in a cloud, or of seeing angels standing in the corner, or worse, demons sitting outside their windows and grinning in at them. Some of them are young women who are disturbed by their sexual fantasies, which sometimes include the guru.

"This is so embarrassing," the girl says. She sits on the chair in my room. She is still blinking her eyes from sleep. She is wearing only panties and a T-shirt.

"You don't have to tell me. . . ." I say.

"Oh, yes . . . I think I should. He, Maharishi, you know, in his white robes and everything? He stands in my room for a long time just looking at me. It's so weird. Then he approaches the bed and pulls back the covers . . ." Yes? "He puts his hands under my shirt and feels my breasts . . ." Yes? "Then he . . ." Yes . . . yes? "He slides into the bed with me and puts his hand between . . . between my . . ." Yes—don't stop now for chrissake!

"You don't have to talk about this if you don't want to, you know. . . ." Is that me? Shut the fuck *up*!

". . . my legs," she continues. I keep my eyes closed. Sort of. She turns to me.

"Is that bad?" she asks.

"Not at all," I offer.

"But Maharishi!" she says.

"It's just a dream. Don't worry about it. We'll meditate for a few minutes and you'll calm down."

"But I already tried meditating." She gazes wistfully at me. "I'm afraid to go back to my room."

Once again, for a moment, I'm The Guy.

"Well, there is one thing that usually seems to work in these cases," I say.

"What's that?" she asks.

"Do you know how to do the Plough?"

I have my own nightmare: Someone comes in the middle of the night and tells me my father is in the lobby dead drunk. It turns out not to be a nightmare. It's two in the morning, and a girl named Friday is at my door. "Your father's here," she says. The way she looks around the room when she says it, and the way it sounds like an apology, I know he's drunk. When I get downstairs, I see him. Clutching a bottle of vodka in one hand and a fistful of *pesetas* in the other, he stands in the lobby swaying like a palm in a high wind.

"*Hah-haaaah!*" he says, waving the Spanish bills. Then he lets out a long belch. I take the money from him and pay the driver, who flees.

There is a room for my father, and I manage, after considerable effort, to wrestle him into bed. I turn out the light. As I leave, I lift the bottle of vodka from the dresser. "Leave that bottle," he bellows from the darkness. It's uncanny. It's pitch black in the room. I have not made a sound. The bottle did not stick and peel away from the surface of the dresser. Plus, my father has been partially deaf for years, suffering from tinitus. Nonetheless, he has heard the bottle move through the air. I replace it.

It was not a surprise visit. Dad had flown from Germany where he was doing a film, so he could "meet the Maharishi." But somehow the actual sight of him, the first I'd had in two years, was shocking. The reality of my life was put into sharp focus again. In a way, he reminded me of who I was.

In Spain I'd enjoyed something like a special status. I had been to India. I had been a skin carrier, a chauffeur, a reader of the Vedas. I didn't smoke. I didn't do dope. I didn't eat meat. I only stole the occasional few beers from the hotel refrigerator and drank them in secret on my balcony. Someone even hinted that I was in Cosmic Consciousness, which was embarrassing, undeniably pleasing, and utterly ludicrous. Naturally I disavowed this allegation, which is exactly what a person who was really *in* Cosmic Consciousness would do. The more one protested, the more certain it was one was there.

Odd things were happening on the course. People were starting to come unraveled. The official explanation was that they were "un-stressing," a favorite term of Maharishi's, which meant that they were releasing the accumulated stress of years, sometimes in dramatic ways. This was the explanation for the visions and nightmares, and for the erratic behavior of some of the students.

One man developed the symptoms of anorexia nervosa in a misguided attempt at starving himself into CC. Another man jumped from a mezzanine balcony and crashed through a glass-topped table. In the hospital he tried to kill himself by sticking his fingers into an electric light socket. At the same time, I was spending my days with a guy named Bob who simply stared into space with his mouth open and his tongue hanging out. I took him to his meals, sometimes I even fed him. "Tongue in, Bob," was the main drift of our conversation.

The capper for me was Steven, a teacher who, in a fit of jealousy because his girlfriend was having sex with another course member across the hall, cut out the crotches on all her panties and hung them in a necklace on a large poster of Maharishi. I found that inventive. Then he set fire to the hotel. Although the fire wasn't big, and it was put out in a few minutes, it was frightening. I began spending all my free time drinking Guinness on the balcony. When

my father came, as insane as he may have appeared, he was a welcome sight. After all, as W. C. Fields might have observed, he was
only drunk.

My father sobered up long enough to have an audience with
Maharishi. It was a fine performance. He dressed up in a tie and
jacket. He did his best to conceal his shakes and was marginally
successful. It could have been interpreted as anxiety, after all, which
always pleased Maharishi anyway. When people shook he took it as
a form of deference.

Maharishi hadn't a clue as to who my father was, but he had
been informed that Keenan Wynn enjoyed some measure of fame
in his own country. This was enough to put Dad on the B list, the
A list being reserved for CEOs and the Beatles. There was a brief
audience in which Maharishi kept talking about "acting" and pretending to know who my father was, and my father kept pretending
he heard him.

I also introduced Dad to Jane. Jane and I had met in India and
had been friends for several years before things began to change
between us. In Mallorca, we had discovered that we were in love,
and I became very ardent. Whenever we got the chance, we took
long walks through the beautiful countryside or sat on her balcony
and watched the moon on the Mediterranean. Her room was directly
above Maharishi's, and sometimes when we made love we could
hear the high-pitched laughter of the monk coming from below. I
found this oddly erotic, and it seemed to intensify the sexual feelings
between Jane and me.

But more often than not, we were apart, each of us living in
different hotels and having our own jobs to attend to. When my
father came to visit, we had an opportunity to be together. We rented
a car and I drove the three of us around the island. We had to stop
every half hour so Dad could get a drink. Naturally, he got drunk,
became his usual obstreperous self, and we had a huge fight. I was
furious at how he had behaved in front of Jane, and I was relieved
when he finally left. But I was sad, too. Something had changed.

Six months later Maharishi moved the entire course to Italy to
a town called Fiuggi, just outside of Rome. Here, Casey, Rob, Tom,
and I, all former The Guys, were put into a house together and left
to our own devices. We were semiretired, semiforgotten, and we
loved it.

Maharishi lived on new blood; he needed people filled with the
fervor of recent spiritual discovery, people who believed they were
going to get enlightenment at any moment. We knew goddamned
well that wasn't going to happen, so we relaxed. We had no definite

schedule. We meditated for six to eight hours each day. It was idyllic, save for one negative fact: We had no money. We had to eat in the dining room where everything, including the students, seemed to be made of wheat. Imagine our joy the day that Mike Love showed up at our door, beaming, clear-eyed, ready to put out the message to the world. We fell on him like wolves on a bunny.

The program had changed, we said. It used to be about peace and serenity. Now it was all about meat. The Kshatriyas—the warrior caste from which Maharishi sprang—well, these guys ate meat. So now we were on the Kshatriya program. If Mike wanted to evolve, he should get on this Kshatriya program with us. And oh, yeah, wine was on the list of do's as well. We grabbed him and hauled him to a local shop where he bought us two whole roast chickens and four bottles of red wine. Then, back in our house, behind locked doors, we trashed our auras with grease and alcohol.

From then on, I avoided Maharishi, even ducking behind trees whenever I saw the Mercedes coming down the street. Every chance I got I ate meat and drank wine. I showed up at meetings half-blitzed. I had less and less to do with the course or the people. Tom and I went into the hills one day to split a white tablet which someone had given him. We split the tab, swallowed it, and walked for an hour waiting for the stuff to come on. It never did; it was a fake. I was extremely depressed. I wanted to get high.

By this time my father was back in Europe. He had come to Rome to do a spaghetti western and had called me in Fiuggi. I went to Maharishi and told him that I wanted to visit my father in Rome. Maharishi was deeply immersed in a meeting with his latest brain trust. The meeting was about one of the guru's pet projects: How can we get Maharishi the Nobel Prize for Peace? Evidently, my presence rang a bell.

"Ned has been to Oslo," Maharishi suddenly remembered. "Maybe he can organize Scandinavia." Oh, Christ, I thought. I had gone to Oslo the previous summer to find out why one of the teachers there was using TM to further his own personal goals. It had been a tempest in a teapot, really, a small, university town model of narcissism and hero-worship complete with a little cadre of crew-cut students who had pledged undying love and obedience to a sickly, thirty-year-old celibate psychiatrist who lived on spinach and milk and dreamed of taking over the TM movement in Norway. I concluded it was all due to the long days and short nights in the North. Nobody ever slept up there in the summer, so they sat up all night plotting. It was an exhausting, unpleasant experience, and I wanted to remain as far below the arctic circle as possible. Luckily, someone informed Maharishi that one didn't get the Nobel Peace Prize by organizing Norwegian meditators. Maharishi wasn't totally convinced, but in the ensuing lull I took the opportunity to flee while the group changed the subject and began discussing the possibility of taking over the Soviet Union's school system.

My job in Rome became keeping my father sober from the time he got up at six o'clock until he got into the studio car at eight to go to work. The movie company was hoping to get at least one shot in in the morning before he became hopelessly drunk, which he usually was by ten. I was successful about 50 percent of the time. The studio was ecstatic.

It was just like real life. Jane came and stayed with me for a few days. I met some people from Texas at our hotel, and I began to live the high life again. I was drinking, eating meat, making love, and caretaking a drunk. I lived this way for two weeks, then Jane had to return to Fiuggi. Soon, I would have to go as well. Then I had a vision:

I was sitting in a meeting with Maharishi. He was outlining his plan to take over the world. The meeting was in its sixth hour and everyone was on the edge of their seats laughing inordinately at everything the Master said; I was flanked by meditators who had lost their minds. I was, of course, responsible for them. One was crocheting his tongue and the other was cutting out the crotches of his girlfriend's panties, setting them on fire, and tossing the flaming crotches in my face. Suddenly, Maharishi looked at me and said that I was to be sent to West Pakistan to put down a yogi rebellion there. It seemed that the local TM leader had decided that TM works best if you smear your body with fresh cowshit first. I began to yearn for the days when all I had to do was pull my father out of a bar and get him to bed.

Sitting in the Termini in Rome, I tussled with a choice: There was a bus going back to Fiuggi, and a train going to Spoleto and the Music Festival. The bus and the train were fifty yards apart. I actually got on the bus and sat down. Then I got off and got on the train to Spoleto. In effect, I had made my break with Maharishi.

CHAPTER

17

In 1972 I decided to become normal. Since nothing I had ever done, from childhood around the studios and the stars to life with the guru had prepared me for normalcy, all I could do was parody what I thought was a fair representation of the American middle-class ethic. One of the things I knew people did was get married. So Jane and I got married. Another thing I knew was that people got a car. So we got an old VW. People also went to work, so Jane went to work.

Tracy, who had won two screenwriting Emmys almost certainly as a result of staring at the mandala I had given him several years before, encouraged me to try my hand at writing screenplays. I had never written anything longer than a poem or a short story, and I rarely if ever had shown my writing to anyone. But the screenplay form was familiar to me, as I had read literally hundreds of them. Without really thinking much about it, I sat down and wrote one. It wasn't particularly good, but it garnered some interest and helped me to get an agent. The second one got me a job at Paramount doing a rewrite. The third one got me a movie deal.

Lest a wrong impression is made, this process took four years. In the interim Jane and I accumulated a small pile of goods which included credit cards, a condominium, and a used Mercedes. Giving someone like me these small tokens of success was like giving a flamethrower to a pyromaniac. Actually, it was more like giving gasoline, rags, and a candle to an arsonist. I went up in flames, but it took a while for the blaze to get going.

We built a little paradise for ourselves, then we bolted the door. The relationship was astutely political: She was the hostage and I was the Ayatollah. The most dangerous thing in the world is having a thirty-five-year-old baby in charge of your life. Jane was trying to grow up; I was only interested in having bigger Christmases. I became a bourgeois gentleman gardener, a beekeeper, a putterer. I raised cactus. I wrote in the mornings and farmed in the afternoons. Then around five I'd make myself an enormous vodka-tonic, draw my beach chair next to the hive, and watch my bees come humming home from the fields. I was a plantation owner in my own mind.

My father was in the process of scaling down, moving, every year it seemed, to ever smaller houses. My mother was living in an apartment in Beverly Hills, having finally run out of houses entirely.

She was in a constant battle with Van over money. It was a process that seemed endless, and it involved the occasional court date.

We're in Los Angeles Superior Court. The halls are jammed and noisy. The clutches of people, mostly Latino and black, don't recognize the stout, florid-faced man who puffs along in his black suit and homburg toward the courtroom. Twenty-five years earlier they would have besieged him for autographs: now he evokes only the most cursory of glances.

I watch my stepfather, who does not recognize me as he passes by. He is old now, no longer the fresh-faced boy or even the middle-aged man of ten years earlier. He seems almost sexless. "He looks like a rabbi," my mother says. Later, after being closeted with his lawyer and my mother and her lawyer for half an hour, he comes out. "Don't I know you?" he asks me.

"Hi, Van," I say, grinning like a monkey. "It's me, Ned." He stares at me as if he's just seen a bug on the wall.

"Gawd, you look old," he says. Then he turns and chugs off.

Our family's downward mobility was now full-speed-ahead, except for Tracy, who was successfully bucking the trend, and me, who, at least for this brief Chinese-style flowering, was actually holding my own. The fear of living with panty-crotch burners and head-stitchers the rest of my life had me going full tilt at the world of business. I was with an excellent writers' agency, Bobby Littman and Keith Addis, and I was actually in the position of turning down projects. This is the position most valued in the film business. It's also a position that creates danger for people like me who are given to instant arrogance at the slightest hint of prosperity. Instead of realizing how lucky I was, I started thinking it was owed me, that it was my due.

The culmination of my first tiny ripple of success was a movie I wrote and acted in called *California Dreaming*. Originally entitled *State Beach*, the movie was a simple, low-budget youth picture that should have made money. But it was sabotaged by the company that made it, a process that is, by now, routine in the film industry. Question: How many producers does it take to change a light bulb? Answer: Does it have to be a light bulb?

We shot the film in Avila Beach, a small town outside of San Luis Obisbo. It was a time of suspension for me. I was doing a job, getting paid both as a writer and as a performer. In the movie's budget, I was finally "above the line." Jane came up and stayed with me. We rented a condominium in Pismo Beach. I made friends with the cast and crew and was even given a place at the Teamsters' table each week for *Monday Night Football*.

But soon I experienced a wave of the old guilt. I was too lucky, too fortunate. I didn't want to be above the line; what if someone took exception to that? What if one of the extras on the set didn't like me—I used to be an extra, after all. What if the assistant wardrobe girl thought I was snotty? It became vital that I be accepted by everyone all the time. So I would watch *Monday Night Football* with the Teamsters, and then scurry off with the director and the producer for dinner. Does everyone adore me yet?

I also tried to walk a line politically between John Hancock, the director, and Louis Arkoff, the producer, who were at odds during much of the filming. Louis was on the shoot almost every day looking over John's shoulder. He'd see something he didn't like, then he'd get me aside and ask me what I thought.

"Well, I thought it was—pretty good."

"You mean you liked the way Tanya waited until Calvin went into the bathroom with her sister?"

"Oh, that part . . . yeah . . . I wondered about that. . . ." Later, John would take me aside.

"Louis wants to have Tanya confront Calvin immediately, before he goes into the bathroom." I'd shake my head and roll my eyes.

"Christ, the guy doesn't understand how comedy works at all," I said.

Finally, after the film was shot, Louis and John became enmeshed in a tug-of-war over the editing. Louis literally locked John out of postproduction. He would take the film each day and, with the editor, cut it himself. Then, the next morning John would show up at five A.M. with his own key, open up, and recut Louis's cut. Then later Louis would come in and recut John's recut.

It was a disaster. Nothing worked, nothing fit. The story appeared truncated and meaningless. I went to see an early version and felt like someone had hacked out my stomach. It was the same feeling I had in school when I came out at lunch and saw some guy waiting to beat me up. The opening of the film was going to be one more version of recess.

I went to see *California Dreaming* in Westwood after its release. It was 1978. The theater was crammed with little sand warts and skate nazis sitting on their boards in the aisles and loving every second of it. At least here, with the beach rats, kids for whom the movie was really a treat, I felt like I had accomplished something. Without advertising or backing of any kind from the studio, however, the movie died in two weeks. A hundred thousand screaming surfers couldn't save it.

I was offered other writing jobs during the late seventies and early eighties. I wrote various versions of various projects, some of which were made, most of which were not. As long as I was getting paid I didn't worry about it. It was standard in Hollywood to write things and never see them made. Often, I did work that was uncredited. Still, I was a bona fide Hollywood screenwriter, and as such, I felt I had arrived.

My life with Jane had got to a point where everything was peaceful, serene, easy. A familiar feeling of restlessness and boredom set in. Here there were no teachers, no gurus, no one to keep a rein on me. I was free to scratch my itches. I remember standing in the driveway one perfect summer day. The bees were humming, the garden was growing. The air was still and the sky was blue. I thought—this can't last. It's too nice. Subtler was the inclination to get in there and agitate.

I am at a party in the Valley. I have come alone. The party is full of meditators, many of whom I knew in Mallorca. There is beer and wine. Disco is very big, the BeeGees are on the stereo and everyone is trying to dance like John Travolta. I'm so stoned I can barely walk. I see a girl I used to lust after in Italy. I try to hustle her. She knows I'm married, but I explain the new rules. The program has changed, I say, it's all about doing what you want now. Drink, get high, have sex. As long as we meditate, how can we go wrong?

The girl I'm chasing isn't convinced, but she's interested enough to say she'll meet me later. After she leaves, another girl, one who turned me down five years ago on a meditation retreat, walks me outside. We talk a while, then we get in my car. She unzips my pants. I am peaking now. This is it: sitting in a car in North Hollywood getting a blowjob, anticipating a date later with another girl, and my wife safely at home. To top it off, I'm so drunk I can't get off. Does life get any better than this?

For me, the development of the rationale for extramarital involvement was an organic part of my self-centeredness. It was simple: I deserved it. There was no reason, I told myself, why a big-time up-and-coming macho guy like me shouldn't be able to have more than one woman. It was natural. Organic. Necessary, in fact, for the smooth functioning of the creative mind. I also had an ace in the hole: the guru himself.

Maharishi was a prime example of situational sexual ethics. Soon after Jane and I had returned to the States, two female friends of ours had come to visit us. Each of them, at different times and totally independent of each other, had blurted out tales of having had sexual liaisons with Maharishi on a more or less regular basis, one for a period of nearly two years. Though neither of them had thought it particularly enjoyable, they had done it out of, they said, love, respect, curiosity. Do monks have dicks? We added ego to the list. For a while they had both enjoyed an exciting secret life with the guru which had made them feel singled out and special. And of course, there was the old sense of duty.

"Gee," J. said. "I thought it would be good for Cosmic Consciousness. Servicing the guru and all that."

"I think that's *serving* the guru," Jane said.

"Ohhhh. . . ."

I had heard dozens of rumors of Maharishi's sexual escapades, but for a long time I had refused to believe them. After all, these stories had circulated about him for years. Like any true disciple, I could not countenance anything that would put him in a bad, i.e., human, light. So stories of Maharishi chasing his attractive disciples around the ashram had no effect on me. I had rejected them out of hand.

I'm sitting on the grass at John and Michelle Phillips's house with Mia Farrow, whom I have known since I was a teenager. Her sister Prudence is a friend of Schuyler's, and her brother John was friends with my Uncle Sherry. Mia knows I am a meditator, and she is telling me about her trip to India, about the Beatles, and about Maharishi, whom I do not yet know personally.

She tells us that while she was in India, Maharishi made several passes at her which she repeatedly rebuffed. These passes included taking her down to his "meditation cave" in his house at the ashram, putting his arm around her, and trying to get her to lie down with him on a mattress there. She had refused this prodigious honor and finally, in an effort to extricate herself from him and his rather maladroit blandishments, she had simply walked off the reservation.

"He even had me followed," she says. "All the way to Goa." John and Michelle shake their heads, amazed. I blithely discount her story. I'm reasonable and mature about it.

"Mia, he's a *brahmachari*," I say. "He took vows of celibacy with his guru. You must have misinterpreted his intentions." The former Mrs. Frank Sinatra turns to me.

"Ned," she says with great patience, "don't you think I know when a man wants to fuck me?"

I started sniffing at everything I saw until I ran into a stewardess from Texas. She had all the requirements: good legs and a remote address. I began an affair with her that lasted two years. Jane gave me chance after chance to break off and come back, but I was trapped in my own lust and lethargy. I couldn't move. So eventually Jane had to do the moving.

It should have been no shock when she told me she was leaving me. Still, I was devastated. It was as if she had her own feelings,

independent of mine, something I hadn't reckoned on. I tried everything. I got pissed off. I cried. I yelled and threatened. But I wouldn't
give up the girlfriend. It was the only thing Jane asked for, and I
couldn't give it. She became very calm and reasonable. She understood her own role in the marriage, she said, understood that it was
dependent and stifling. It was best if she left.

I was amazed. I didn't think this could happen. I was going to
be a statistic. I was going to be divorced, like Dad. How could I
maintain my moral superiority then? And besides, since when did
Jane have feelings? Where did *those* come from? If I'd known how
she felt earlier, I whined.

"It wouldn't have made any difference, Neddy," she said softly.
Yeah, but what about me? What about the *baby*?

Meanwhile, my father was approaching his own nadir. He no
longer owned a home. He and Sharley had moved to a small cottage
in Brentwood which they rented. When I asked him where his money
went he shook his head and made vague references to having so
much on his shoulders.

"I'm always in the middle, boy. I never get ahead." He was never
clear of just what it was that was keeping him from getting ahead.
But things were about to change.

He had been signed for one of the plum roles of his career, Perry
White in the first *Superman* movie. He was excited. This was a mega-
project, and even though there were better roles, there weren't any
bigger movies. The money and the exposure were there. It was something he'd been hoping for for years, it was The Break.

"Maybe now," he said, "now I can get a little bit ahead."

He flew to London to begin shooting. But in the hotel, before
he ever got on the set, he had a *grand mal* seizure. The English
doctors, after taking a look at his history, ascribed the seizure to
chronic alcoholism. He was hospitalized for a week, put on anti-
seizure medication, and then he came home. Jackie Cooper was
brought in for the role. This scared Dad into quitting booze altogether. For about six months. Then he started again. Within a matter
of a few weeks, he was drinking more than ever.

From 1979 to 1981 I spent a lot of time in Aspen. I stayed either
with Tracy and his family, who lived about a mile up the Roaring
Fork River on East Highway 82—or with Annie Marshall, who had
a house near Red Mountain. Annie worked for Jack Nicholson, and
when she went on location one summer with him, she offered to let
me stay in her house. I had met Jack some years before when Michelle Phillips had introduced me to him. Now, through Annie, I met
a whole new pack of people to hang with that included Anjelica

Huston, Jill St. John, Jimmy Buffet, and Glen Frey—a whole new group of glittering folks who lived and played in Aspen. I was in my third phase of hanging. This time I had it figured out.

I'm staying at Tracy and Kerstin's house. It's 1981. Aspen is hanger's heaven. Hanging in Aspen is effortless: I'm there, I hang. This time I have an air of dubious legitimacy about me because I'm writing a screenplay with Tracy so it's like, well, I'm not just up here to hang, goddamnit, I'm working.

Tracy and I work half the day and then ski the other half. This is how it works when you're in the Big Time. Sometimes, when the weather is particularly nice, we don't work at all. This is Mega Big Time. One of those mornings I find myself standing in the lift line with Jack Nicholson and Bob Rafelson, the director. We're going to ski together and then have lunch on the hill. This moment is *sat-chit-ananda*, the hanger's *samadhi*.

I do some of my best skiing coming off the lift and down the short unloading track. I glide casually, adjusting my goggles, yanking at my gloves, Gold Medal stuff. Jack grins and hunkers over his skis. I make a mental note: Jack doesn't look as good as I do on skis. This thought fills me with a certain gusto. Let the games begin. Bob Rafelson looks over at me. "I'll ski with Ned," he says.

"What's the deal?" I ask. "Aren't we all skiing together?" Jack gazes thoughtfully at his poles.

"Sure," he says. "We'll all ski together." He does two little knee dips. I have often wondered at the size of Jack's legs. His thighs are like beer kegs. I have always thought of them as kind of short. What they are is kind of strong. Jack settles into a semiracing tuck which, it turns out, he can hold for two hours without getting tired. He points himself and takes off down the hill. I ignore Bob's offer and take off directly behind him. It doesn't take long to realize why Rafelson doesn't ski with Jack: Jack never turns. The greatest skiers in the world turn. Jack goes straight.

After about a half a minute of going straight I realize that Jack is not going to turn. Not ever. He's going to ski straight down Aspen Mountain, get on the lift and do it again. Hanging with Jack is rapidly losing its appeal. As it is, I'm now completely out of control. Jack skis near the edge, I ski right over it. Trees are whipping past me like telephone poles in a *Road Runner* cartoon. I'm Wile E. Coyote riding an Acme-Rocket Sled to oblivion as Jack keeps getting smaller and smaller in front of me. In his all-black ski clothes he's a pinprick of darkness, a black hole, a flying, flapping bat out of hell, and me —I'm going so fast tears are running out of my eyes and freezing to my ears.

Then a miracle occurs. I see a way out. To the left there's a kind of escape road like the ones trucks have on steep downgrades. I try and steer for that. On a rise I see Bob Rafelson. How did he get there? He waves at me. It's a curiously reassuring gesture. Later, I find out he's not waving, he's trying to stop me. This is not an escape road.

I perform a feat skiers call catching some air. I catch a good cubic acre of the shit. For a moment I am actually weightless. This feeling doesn't last. I do a full face-plant into a deep snowbank. Through the grace of a higher power, there is no huge boulder just beneath the surface.

I pull myself out of the snow. I've lost a ski. Bob is standing over me. "Lose Jack?" he grins.

"Uh, yeah," I say, spitting snow. Bob nods pleasantly.

"Guy never turns," he says. I spend the rest of the afternoon having lunch. When someone asks me later how it was skiing with Jack, I smile mysteriously. Jack's a private person.

When I returned home, things picked up. Richard Lang suggested me for a *Movie of the Week* that he and Duke Vincent had sold to ABC for Aaron Spelling Productions. The network approved me, Aaron approved me, and I was writing. I had a beautiful new girlfriend, Melinda. I had a large apartment in Brentwood. I bought a new car.

Prosperity was raising its ugly head again.

I'm sitting in my apartment. My father calls me on the phone and asks if I wouldn't mind a visit. I tell him to come on over. He has quietly changed his life in the last couple of years: He has quit drinking. Not gone on the wagon this time, but quit. Entirely. He won't say exactly how long, but it's more than two years.

"That's great, Pop," I tell him. Boy, if anyone needed to quit drinking it was him.

"I woke up one morning," he had told me, "and all I could see was a motorcycle tire. The air valve on a motorcycle tire. I was lying on the ground. My face was right on the pavement. Little rocks were stuck in my cheek. I stared at that tire and tried to understand where I was and how I'd gotten there, but I couldn't. I didn't remember a goddamn thing. I'd been home, I knew that—I had a drink—the next thing, I'm lying on the ground in the parking lot of some fucking bar in Santa Monica. It's fourteen hours later. Where'd those fourteen hours go?"

Now he sat in my apartment and stared at me. He shook his head and looked around the apartment. There were supermarket bags lining one wall. Every single bag had bottles in it. Wine bottles, beer bottles, vodka bottles, tequila bottles. There were more bottles on the kitchen sink. Why the hell hadn't I cleaned this up before he came over?

"We had a party this weekend," I apologized. "Mel and I had a party. We just haven't cleaned it up yet." It was Tuesday afternoon. Dad nodded. He didn't laugh about the bottles like he would have a year or two ago.

"I don't want to tell you how to live, son," he said. He spoke kindly, softly. He hated to give orders or advice. He always backed off. This was painful for him, but all I could think of was, we just didn't clean up the place yet, that's all.

"I don't want to tell you how to live—but this," he looked me straight in the eye, "this—is a hard way to go." I didn't get it. What was a hard way to go? Having a dirty apartment? Having a party? Getting a little drunk on the weekend? What was a hard way to go? "Listen, Ned—believe me, I'm the last guy to tell you anything. You know that. Forget it. Enjoy yourself." He smiled and kissed me. Then he left.

I wrote two movies for Aaron Spelling, one called *Don't Go to Sleep* starring Dennis Weaver, Valerie Harper, and Ruth Gordon, and a pilot called *Velvet*. In between I also wrote a *Movie of the Week* for Mace Neufelt. The two Spelling movies were made and shown on ABC. *Don't Go to Sleep* got decent ratings, which was nice, but I pinned a great deal more hope on the pilot. ABC had a deal with Aaron—they had to buy two pilots a year from him. No one in Hollywood had a deal like this. Working on a pilot for Aaron was money in the bank. I was made. *Velvet* was a lock. Nothing could possibly go wrong. It's like being down on double zero in roulette and seeing that on the table, every number is double zero. There was one problem: For the first time, Aaron had made three pilots in one season.

Richard called me. "They didn't pick us up," he said. "They picked up *Glitter* and *Paper Dolls* and passed on *Velvet*. It's OK. We'll come back with another."

"Right." I knew there would be no other. If you don't hit, you miss, and if you miss, you fail. There would be no other pilot for me in that company. Every game is for the championship.

It's 1985. Portland Mason and her mother Pamela have invited me to their house for a party. I don't get invited to many parties these days. I am increasingly isolated from people I know. Melinda, after three years in a relationship with me which was generally known for its decibel level, got up at five A.M. the day after Christmas, threw her bags in her car, and left.

At the party I meet Dear Abby. She's all in red, a perfectly charming woman. I am my most charming self with her. No one would ever want to fuck up in front of Dear Abby. From seven thirty in the evening until four in the morning I drink. By that time Pamela is running an old James Mason film in her projection room. It's getting a little maudlin. I stare at the screen like a zombie. God, I loved James Mason. Why did James Mason have to die? I'm easily the drunkest person there, but as usual, come time to leave, I am able to stand straight and speak clearly enough to pass muster at the door. I can drive. I'm fine.

As soon as I get behind the wheel, I nearly lose consciousness. I can't focus. Pamela has a long driveway with bright lights lining it. These lights leap out at me, blinding me. I can't really see the pavement, but I judge where I am by looking for foliage and staying out of it as best I can. The driveway is a test, a long test of my abilities. If I can get out of the driveway I'll be fine.

After a long, harrowing trip I make it out on the streets of Beverly Hills and promptly forget which way Sunset Boulevard is. I grew up here, for chrissake. My streets. What's happening to my sense of direction? I wind slowly, carefully, for what seems twenty minutes, until I find Sunset Boulevard which is, in reality, maybe ninety seconds from Pamela's house. It's dry, clear, a perfect night. Forty years of training tells me the direction of home, which is Brentwood. I point the car that way. The roads are empty.

I do pretty well for a while. I keep one eye closed and watch the double line on my left. As I head up Sunset past UCLA, I know that a hundred yards ahead there is a sharp left turn and sudden downgrade with a stoplight immediately at the Bellagio Road entrance to Bel-Air. For some reason I decide that I will not slow down for the turn. My thoughts are crystal clear on this. I like the speed I'm traveling at, about fifty. It's comfortable. I will not lift my very heavy foot from the accelerator. At another time, maybe, but not tonight. My foot is just too heavy to move it. I am going to drive fifty miles an hour and simply give the turn a try. If I make it, great. If not—fuck it.

I don't make it.

First I strike the curb. The car bounces off into the middle of Sunset, spins 180 degrees and starts traveling backward down the street. I can hear the tires screaming, smell the rubber. I am completely relaxed. This is an interesting experience. The car jumps the curb, slews across the grass, and ploughs rear-first into an adobe wall. In my mind the clear thought comes: You're not that drunk; you must just be getting reckless. This thought marks the peculiarity of my condition, both for its stark clarity, and for its total misapprehension of my state of mind and body.

I was able to drive away from that without injury. No police showed up either. I simply started the car and drove it away. When my father saw the damage a couple of weeks later, he looked at me.

"I got hit in a parking lot. Someone was backing up . . ." I started. Dad smiled.

"Must have been backing up at what, fifty, sixty miles an hour?"

"No, really . . ." I said. No. Really.

I was learning the lesson: One drunk can't fool another drunk. All the years I had his number, now he had mine. When I had sat in my car those few seconds after hitting the wall, with the ringing in my ears and the smoke inside the car, I had experienced the miracle of denial, denial so dense that my own mind was armed instantly against knowing the truth. What I *had* known was that whatever I was, whatever caused me to hit that wall, it wasn't because I was drunk. It *couldn't* be because I was drunk. Even after drinking vodka for nine solid hours. I'd been drinking that way since I was fifteen and had never had an accident when I was drunk. A couple of little parked car sideswipes maybe, nothing more. Nope. Alcohol was definitely not a factor here.

The last bastion for the alcoholic is his own logic. In that he seeks his guarantees. If I could continue to prove to myself that these were temporary setbacks, then I could go on forever. But the slide had become precipitous. I realized, however, that something was wrong, so I decided to play it safe. There was an outside chance that drinking and driving were not a good idea right now, given the state of mind I was in. I had a choice. I had to either quit drinking or quit driving. Logic intervened. I quit driving. The car sat in the garage and I walked to the local bars. I couldn't get hurt that way, and I could drink all I wanted. Another logical decision, another guarantee.

It got to the point where I would close the bars at two, walk home, open the front door, get inside, close the door and drop down on all fours. I would then crawl—sometimes this would take five minutes, sometimes an hour—to the bedroom. I would haul myself up on the bed and lie there hoping to pass out. But my mind would be full of thoughts: What's happening to me, what she did to me, what they did to me, what I'm going to do to fix it . . . tomorrow. Sometimes I'd lie on the rug in the hall and stare at the baseboard and think, God, you're drunk.

They say an egotist isn't someone who necessarily thinks highly of himself, just constantly of himself. This described me perfectly. The self-centered prating was incessant. Eventually, I would grab the bottle of Valium that I kept by the bed and take two or three to calm the voices in my head, the committee on world affairs starring me. I'd lose consciousness for two hours and wake in a sweat. I'd take more pills, drink more alcohol, fall asleep again, wake up again.

I had never drunk like this before. The liquor even looked different in the glass, so thick and oily that when I drank I bit the gulps off with my teeth like hunks of meat. I began to dream about worms. In the dream I was usually in a Roman-style arena. All around me people sat watching me eat huge, fat worms, wriggling creatures sweating with juice. I'd pop them like Coney Island wieners in my teeth, then chew and swallow them. Finished, I would grin, worm guts dangling from my lips. The people would cheer. Worm dreams, I knew, and later, feces-eating dreams, were associated with alcoholism. A light bulb went on. I did the only sensible thing, the last refuge for the out-of-control drinker: I went on the wagon.

I'm at another party. This time I have driven my mother to Harry and Marilyn Lewis's Beverly Hills mansion for their annual blowout. I love annual blowouts, especially when rich people give them. Harry and Marilyn own the Hamburger Hamlet chain, and they know how to throw an annual blowout. There is a band, a tent, great food, and most important, three open bars. But I am on the wagon. I am not drinking booze tonight. Instead, I drink nine little bottles of Perrier in an hour and feel superior to everyone with a drink in their hand.

Ricardo and Georgiana Montalban are here. I start talking to them. They're drinking and having a hilarious time, something they seem to do with complete impunity. I have never known two people who enjoy themselves more and never seemed to get in any trouble from it. That starts to eat at me. I'm no different from Ricardo and Georgiana. I haven't had a drink in eleven days. My system has to be adjusted by now. Shit. You can't just stand around at a party talking to friends and drink Perrier, can you?

I find myself asking the bartender for some champagne this time. No Perrier, just a glass of champagne. In self-defense, I say. Someone laughs. In self-defense? Yeah. With all these people around me drinking, I gotta do *something*. The champagne is just what the doctor ordered. One more of those and then something more sensible. Like vodka on the rocks.

Five days later I was still drunk. I'd wake up with a freeway collision taking place in my brain, stagger to the bathroom, rifle the medicine chest until I found some Tylenol with codeine, take a handful of them, and then lie on the floor hoping to die. But it wasn't going to be that easy.

As a teenager, I had heard of the dark night of the soul and thought it romantic and mysterious. The actual descent into the maelstrom, however, was often prosaic, even trite. I ate, I watched television, I puked in the sink. If it weren't for the fact that the pain was so acute, it would have been soap opera. A little raw, maybe, but soap opera nonetheless.

To anyone watching, the solutions were obvious. For me, it was less so. I was paralyzed. I tried to write another script, get another development deal, but my trips to the studios were fewer and my contacts were shrinking. People didn't answer my phone calls, and the fact was I didn't want to speak to them anyway. I knew what they would say, and I knew what they would think.

I prayed for something to happen, for things to change. I made deals with God again, as I had when I was nineteen, telling him if he'd just help me through this latest financial crisis, this latest career crisis, this latest relationship crisis, this latest crisis of pain, I'd give money to the poor, I'd treat women with respect, I'd call my mother, take my father to the movies, whatever the hell God was after.

Each Christmas for the past ten years I had made it a habit to watch *A Christmas Carol*, with Alastair Sim. At the joyous, uplifting ending, eyes brimming, I thought, how great—have these angels come at night, show you your life, grant you a spiritual renewal, and change you into a good and worthwhile human being. Overnight! Bring 'em on! Bring on those angels. I always missed the point of the story: that Scrooge's sad and solitary life was marked by his failure to love others. He was entirely self-centered, and this was the cause of his profound misery.

The irony was that I had drunk from the beginning to forget who I was, and I had ended up more self-obsessed than ever. I was drinking now without the benefit of relief. I no longer got high when I drank. My body got drunk, but my mind was awake and clear. It crackled with noise like water on a white-hot wire. My thoughts were clear, and it was impossible to still them no matter what I drank or swallowed. I drank from nine in the morning until I could manage to pass out. No matter what I did, inevitably I would wake to fear and terror which would stay with me until I could manage to reach unconsciousness again.

The mind is strange. It forgets itself in sleep. And there was always a moment at the very first faint stirrings of wakefulness, before my mind had time to focus, a brief moment in which I'd be absolutely fine. No pain, no regrets, just peace. Then, in less than a single second the self-forgetting would be over, and the realization that I was still here, still me, would roar down like an avalanche. A feeling of utter despair would wash over me. The feeling was bone deep and total. There was not a shred of hope in it.

In the evenings I would take out my revolver, lay it on the table in front of me, stare at it, and drink. Then, too scared to blow my brains out, scared I'd miss, I would return it to the shelf and continue drinking. I began to fear that I was losing my mind. In my mother's era, some of the people we knew had something called a nervous breakdown. They simply lost the ability to cope. My father called it going off the deep end, or, more succinctly, blowing out the back. Rarely was drinking ever mentioned as the cause, unless the person was notorious for it, like he was. I reasoned that perhaps I was having one of those, just a good old-fashioned nervous breakdown. I had been to the doctor. I had told him I was depressed, even drinking a bit more than usual, though I was careful to underestimate the amount by at least half. The doctor had given me Elavil, an antidepressant, and Xanax, a cousin to the esteemed Viscount Valium. He also told me not to drink while taking this medication.

Grateful for the prescriptions, I took them according to my own directions: Swallow with a glass of beer, and, if one doesn't work, take two, if two doesn't get it, take five. I added another tiny lagniappe, a double shooter of tequila back. The result was I found myself, more than once, chewing on the barrel of my loaded .38 at two in the morning. I even went into the bathroom and looked at myself with the gun in my mouth, just to see if I was really doing it. In my sick, sad heart, this insane behavior amused me. I grinned at the macabre image. How dramatic you are, I thought. Why don't you pull the trigger?

Sometimes I'd burst into a squall of sobbing and tears. I would fall on the floor and weep and pray. It would pass, I'd get back on the couch and continue drinking. Then I'd think of something that would bring me to my knees again. Again I'd be on all fours, tears actually splashing off the backs of my hands, screaming and crying to God to either help me or kill me. Then I'd apologize, become meek and obsequious, quiet down, reassure myself I'd be OK. I'd get back on the couch and have another drink. I was finished. I was willing to die. I just didn't have the courage to kill myself.

It had to end, and it did. I think what did it finally was exhaustion. I was physically, mentally, and emotionally whipped. Until I felt this depletion, until I was truly spent, I was still trying to deal and reason with the universe. But finally, I simply had to give up. I had lost, and it no longer mattered what happened to me. I told God that he could do whatever the hell he wanted with me, I had no preferences anymore. I just wanted to stop the insanity and the pain, at whatever cost. I had rediscovered the secret of the old prayer I'd found at nineteen in the driveway on Foothill Road, the secret of acknowledging defeat. Within seconds an idea came to me: This has got to stop. I'm going to have to get some help.

* * *

I pick up the phone. I dial information. I am not like other people. I don't have to go through what they have to go through. I get the number. I dial the number. I have my life under control. I don't need anyone telling me how I should live. Someone answers. Hello? This is not something I really have to do, I am simply going to find out what their program is and see if it interests me. Hello?

The person on the other end tells me his name and asks if he can help me. I tell him I can't stop drinking. I've tried, but I can't. I think I have a problem. I've never told this to anyone before. He tells me I've called the right number, and he gives me an address. I write it down. The next day I don't drink all day long. At seven o'clock, pissed off at the terrible injustice of it all, I go to the address on the piece of paper.

I sit at the edge of the crowd and glower, refusing to meet the eyes of the others there, all obvious losers. I'm not like them and I don't want them thinking I am. Just being here I'm risking the fact that someone might get the idea I'm an alcoholic. In spite of myself, I start to hear things that sound familiar, like pieces of my own life. I begin to listen. The impulse to flee slowly goes away. Afterward, people talk to me. They're friendly, too goddamn friendly. Don't they know who I am?

When I go home that night, somehow I feel different. Inside there is a kind of excitement, a feeling that I may have stumbled onto something here. Then next night I go back. I listen some more. I do this every night. A week later I haven't had a drink. Perhaps this is where the angels will find me.

CHAPTER

18

I stood across the street for what seemed like an hour, watching the little rented house on Westgate Avenue in Brentwood. Forty years earlier, across Sunset Boulevard, two blocks north and four houses west, I had lain in my bed at night listening for Old Bastard in the walls. I had knelt on the cool stone by the pond and searched for fairies in the moss. I had sat in the kitchen and waited for June to give me my chicken foot and seen Cocoa walk away with the strange men. I had walked these streets with my father, played in Ty's pool, and laughed when Gene and Peter and Dad did monkey tricks on the lawn. And one day I had watched my father grow smaller and smaller and disappear as Van drove us away to another life.

I looked at the sky. It was the same sky, bright, and gauzy with clouds, and the air smelled like warm stone, so warm and solid I could almost lay my cheek against it. I suddenly felt small and fragile. But next to the old man in the little house, I was a towering giant full of strength and energy.

My father was dying of cancer. The disease was pernicious, evil, vile, incurable. It was painful beyond imagination, and I quaked in its presence. I had made a mistake about death, I had seen too many movies. There is no attractive, New Age wrapping to put on dying. Death is not interested in mantras, crystals, herbs, prayer cloths, or brown rice. It's not something that unifies families, brings greater understanding of life, and elevates the individual in some holistic way. No celestial music is heard, unless the screams of the dying are someone's idea of a concert in Paradise. People do not make noble statements, or, if they do, the statements sound hollow, flat, and idiotic.

Death is from the ninth century. In its massive, bleak, incalculable power, it is the last true remnant of the Dark Ages come to our time. It rides a pale horse, wears foul rags, carries a scythe, and stands at the window watching from cold, deep-socketed eyes. And every now and then it gives the body on the bed a little tweak, and the body heaves and howls and fluids run from every pore. Sometimes Death plays like this for hours, finding little nooks and crannies where the morphine doesn't reach. I had made a big mistake about death.

* * *

We are all standing in this little bend in the corridor at St. John's Hospital in Santa Monica. My stepmother, two sisters, Wynnie and Hilda, and their husbands, my great aunt, Billie, Ed Wynn's niece, and I. This tiny alcove is supposed to serve as a room where relatives wait for news of loved ones who are in surgery. It's one of the most truly heartless pieces of architecture I've ever been in. There is another family there, filling the space with frightened and anxious people. When the men in their green smocks finally appear, it's evident immediately that there is nothing good about to happen.

The surgeon shrugs. Then he shakes his head. "We found a tumor on his pancreas. It has implants in the liver and the lymph nodes."

"What does that mean? What does that mean?" my stepmother asks, her face red from crying. The surgeon looks at his operating partner.

"It has metastasized, spread to other organs. There is nothing else we can do. We can't remove the tumor from the pancreas because the pancreas's position in the body makes it impossible. Removing the pancreas is not an option."

"How long does he have to live?" I ask. The surgeon shrugs again.

"Eight months," he says. "Six, maybe eight months." Eight months? That's nothing. I've spent eight months worrying about not getting laid. I've stared at the wall for eight months before. I've wasted twenty eight-month clumps in my life and never even noticed it.

"Remember The Trip?" he said.

We were sitting in my father's office in the little house on Westgate. He'd been home from the hospital for several weeks, and he had gotten a little stronger. He had acted very strangely in the hospital. Postoperative encephalopathy, the doctors had said. What he was was off his rocker. He came out of the anesthetic as if he'd been drinking for days. In fact, he'd been sober for nearly seven years by then. But for two weeks he raged and shouted, swore and barked like a madman. I cornered the doctors. They couldn't figure it out. "Did you know he has sleep apnea?" asked one Ph.D.

"You mean, do I know he snores?" I asked.

"Yes," the doctor said gravely. "Well, not just snores. He stops breathing for twenty or thirty seconds at a time. He could die from that." I could only stare at the man in wonder.

"But what about this aberrant behavior?" I asked. "He's acting like someone who's been drinking. We told the anesthetists he was alcoholic. Did the anesthetists make some error in the use of the

oxygen?" No no no. Nothing like that. It's just encephalopathy.
"Doesn't that mean simply that he's not right in the head?" I asked.

"Well, yes," said the doctor.

It took nearly four weeks for my father to regain his sense of
place and time. At one point we doubted whether it was possible
for him to come home at all, but after a while he began to emerge
from the haze. He realized he'd been in the hospital and that he'd
had to have a gall bladder operation. They had actually found the
tumor was blocking the flow of bile from the gall bladder and they
had rerouted the tubes. They told him about that, but they didn't
tell him about the tumor.

"Well, this mental condition—he wouldn't understand," said the
doctor. "We'll wait until he's mentally clear again. We'll wait until
he's lucid."

"Why tell him?" my stepmother asked. "He doesn't need to know.
Why tell him at all?"

"It'll become obvious, Sharley. He'll begin to wonder why he's
not getting better," I said.

"I'll tell him when he's lucid," said the doctor. "I won't volunteer
the information, but if he wants to know, I'll have to tell him."

"OK," Sharley said, reluctantly. "But not unless he asks."

"Remember The Trip?" The way my father spoke about the trip,
he capitalized it. It was always, The Trip. We took two vacations
together in my entire life, one to the Sierras for three days to fish,
and one to San Francisco, which we called The Trip.

I was no more than nine or ten. We drove from Los Angeles
through the blazing hot San Joaquin Valley and I thought it looked
too much like Los Angeles and I hated Bakersfield. We went to
Yosemite and saw the firefall and Half Dome and El Capitán. We
went to Sequoia National Park and visited the redwoods and drove
through a tree with a hole in it. We went to Lake Tahoe and rode
in a speedboat and I won eight silver dollars. In San Francisco we
visited Fisherman's Wharf and ate dinner at the Top of the Mark.

After we came back from dinner, Dad started to leave again.
"Just gonna go to the bar, get a couple of blasts before I go to bed,
Neddo," he said. I started to cry. He got some socks from his suitcase.
"Grandpa used to make one of these for me when he had to leave
me alone to do a show," he said. He fashioned a little doll from the
socks, balling one end up into a head. Then he gave me the doll. I
clung to this little ball of my father's socks and fell asleep.

"Yeah, Pop," I say, "I remember The Trip."

He had twenty-four-hour nursing. For weeks he had to be
wheeled in a wheelchair. Slowly but surely he began to get a little

stronger, until he was able to get out of the wheelchair and walk short distances on his own. He never got much better than a kind of wavering, unsteady gait and needed to be assisted much of the time. Weeks passed. Still he did not ask. The doctor visited him.

"Did you tell him?" I asked the doctor when he came out.

"He didn't ask," the doctor said. Six weeks passed. Then eight. My father was getting better. Not altogether well, but better. And with this he was getting restless. Whenever the doctor came, he put on the face of recovery. Maybe, if he looked good, smiled, joked, and sounded hearty, the doctor would tell him he was fine. Really fine. But he began to wonder why he was not getting any stronger. He still couldn't drive. There was friction in the house between him and my stepmother, between her and the nurses. He wanted to get out, but he couldn't drive or go anywhere on his own.

It's March, two months after he entered St. John's, six weeks after he came home. It's sunny and warm and Dad is feeling pretty good. We are sitting on the lawn in the backyard. The nurse is there. Sharley is there. Aunt Billie and Cici, an old friend of Sharley's, are there. They are frozen in my mind like figures in a glass ball.

"Must have been more than a simple gall bladder operation, huh, son?" he says, ". . . to knock the living shit out of me like this?" I look at the nurse, and then at Sharley. They stare at me. "They must have found something more wrong with me, huh?" The women start chattering. I look at him. Is there a way out of this?

"Well, there was a problem with your liver," I say. What problem with his liver? You mean the implant of cancer in it? Is that what you mean?

"Why can't I get a straight answer around here? Every time I ask about when I'm going to be able to get back to work, get better and start driving again, working again, they just fix my pillow and tell me to be patient."

"I never noticed your being particularly curious, Dad," I say, annoyed and scared. Is there a way I can leave? Can I get out of this? Can we call the doctor? Isn't this his job?

"I'm amazed, Ned. I haven't shown any curiosity? I'm amazed you think that," he says. He stares at me. Sharley sits on the chaise nearby. The women stop chattering.

"Why don't you ask Dr. Keatinge when he comes?" I say.

"When is he coming?" Dad asks. Not for a week, unless we call him. Too late. Too late for that. "I just want to know if I can make any plans. When I can be up and on my own again. I want to know if I'll be acting again, or if this is it."

He looks at Sharley. She hesitates. "What do you mean, Keenan," she says carefully.

"Is this it," he says. "Am I finished?" He looks at me again. I do not want to be here. I do not want to be a part of this conversation. Sharley looks at me.

"Just exactly what is it you want to know, Dad?" I ask. Somewhere nearby I can hear the whine of a leaf-blower. Put it off put it off. Put everything off.

"Am I ever going to work as an actor again?"

"No," I say. "You are a very sick man, Dad, very sick." He stares at me. I hear myself, why do I sound so angry? He purses his lips and puts his hand to his face as if to ward off the next blow. I take off my sunglasses and look him in the eye. "You have cancer," I tell him.

It was like I'd dropped a building on him. All the air went out of him.

"Jesus," he said. Sharley gasped.

I could barely see or hear anything. I was shaking so badly that I nearly dropped my glasses. I hadn't had a drink in nearly a year, but here I was shaking like it was the morning after a bad night. To still my hands, I grabbed his hand which shook all the time, the result of parkinsonism. Together we sat there with our hands locked, quaking like leaves. Dad took off his glasses. Tears coursed down his cheeks. He looked into the sky then back at me.

"Cancer?" he said. I nodded. "Well, that's it then." Sharley got up and went over and hugged him. I started apologizing immediately.

"I'm sorry, Pop . . . I'm so sorry . . ."

"Jesus, Ned," she said, "why did you tell him?"

"He asked" was all I could say. It didn't sound like a good enough reason.

For months he sat in that house. There was no pain, just fear and worry. I went to see him every day. Sometimes I'd stand outside and look at the house for a long time before going inside. I could see him, if he was up, through the window, sitting at the table in the patio in his hat and his coat to protect him against the morning fog. A few friends came, among them Lee Marvin who came up from Arizona. But mostly he didn't want to see anyone. We sat in his office, and later, when he could no longer get out of bed, I'd come and sit next to him and we'd talk a little.

"Emily," he said one day. "I was thinking of Emily." Emily, my youngest sister, had died three years earlier, at twenty, of lupus, a blood disease she had had since she was ten. "She had a bad break, that kid. I lived seventy fucking years, she had twenty." I had put Emily out of my mind—now the sight of her flooded my senses.

* * *

It's fifteen years earlier, and Richard Lang and I are making one of our home movies. This one is from a script I wrote called "Emily," and stars my baby sister. It's about a lonely little girl who lives in a home with drunken parents. One day she starts talking to a little fruit tree in the backyard and the fruit tree talks back to her. Soon she is able to see an apparition in the tree, a lady. She begins to have conversations with the tree-lady. Her parents become alarmed, and one day her father, in a fit of rage, cuts the tree down. As he is cutting the tree, however, it begins to bleed. Emily screams and runs to her room. She looks in the yard at the dead body of the tree. But the lady talks to her and tells her that she is all right and not to worry. She'll come back to her some day. And the next day Emily sees a tiny twig sprouting from the soil.

We never finished the movie with Emily. We shot a few hundred feet and quit. Emily was diagnosed at ten and lived on aspirin and prednisone the rest of her life. She grew up and moved with her boyfriend to Oregon. She lived as normal a life as she could until one Thanksgiving morning she didn't get up. She died in her sleep.

"I can see her sometimes," Dad said. He was not given to fits of spiritualistic reverie. But things had changed.

One morning he was smiling. Now a death's head stared at me from the pillow, eyes sunk back, lips stretched over his face like a thin rubber band, his skin pallid and sweaty. A smile was a matter of interpretation.

"Last night," he said, "last night I couldn't get up, so I peed in the bed. Couldn't help it. The nurse . . . she wrote in her book, 'urine spill.' " He drew out the phrase in a mock Shakespearean voice. "*Urine spill*, for christsake. It's all so fucking grand."

There were periods when he felt well enough to get out of bed and sit in his office. We sat and talked about a lot of things. Especially about drinking and sobriety. He'd been sober seven years.

"All the shit that happened to me, the busted bones, the wives, the houses, even the hearing, it was all booze. I never realized it. But it was all the booze. I don't remember much about the sixties, from 1965 on. And the seventies are mostly a blank." He shook his head. "There's booze in the kitchen. Right there on the counter. Sharley drinks it. I look at it and figure what's the point. It won't help. I could certainly have it if I wanted it, but it won't help. It'll make things worse." He didn't even want the nurse to give him morphine.

"The car," he said to me one day. "Was it a mistake?" The red Jaguar he and my mother had given me for graduation. "It's always bothered me. Was the car too much? Was it a mistake?" Probably.

"No, Dad. It was great. It was a beautiful car." Yes, it was too much. But don't worry about it.

"I dream about my mother all the time," he said. Sometimes he called her name in reverie.

"Do you dream a lot, Dad?" I asked.

"Not enough," he answered.

Not enough.

One day he couldn't get out of bed anymore. He could barely speak. I took his hand.

"How are you feeling today, Pop," I asked. He looked at me. All that moved were his eyes.

"Lousy," he croaked. To me the word *lousy* will always describe the absolute worst a person could ever feel and still live.

When the last days came they were a revelation of pain. He had not suffered overly much for most of the time he had been home. After he learned he had cancer, he took the option of having chemotherapy, even though he knew it could not save him. The oncologist said it should provide a palliative effect, which it did. The regimen was not aggressive, and there were no unpleasant side effects. He thanked me for telling him about his disease.

"At least I feel I'm doing something, not just letting it go. I feel better knowing I'm doing something." But the last three weeks were filled with agony. Nothing seemed to reach where he hurt.

The sound was ominous, a hissing bubbling sound like thousands of beebees rolling in a metal pan. It was his breathing. It seared me like a flame. He lay propped in his bed with this horrendous noise coming from him.

"He's dying," said the nurse. He started to moan and tried to speak. It was difficult at first to understand what he was saying. His mouth wouldn't work properly and he couldn't form the words. I hovered over him.

"What is it, Pop," I said. "What can I do?"

"Helme . . ." he groaned. "Helme . . ."

"Help you, what, Pop, do you want morphine?"

"Helme commi suci . . . helme commi suici! . . ." I was stunned. I looked at the nurse. Was he saying . . .

"I think he's saying 'Help me commit suicide,'" she said.

He cried it over and over again. If I'd had a gun I'd have shot him. Then I realized I was helpless, utterly helpless, to remove him from his pain, and it hurt more than anything I had ever felt. I could do nothing at all except stand there and hold his hand and listen to the rattling and screaming. Then suddenly he stopped breathing, his face contorted horribly, his chest collapsed, his neck accordioned, he looked like he was being turned inside out. A froth boiled from his mouth. The nurse counted his pulse and looked at her watch. He didn't breathe for two whole minutes. Outside the window Death sat on his horse and gazed at us. Oh, God, please take him. Enough is enough. Please have mercy. Let him die. Die, Dad. Don't fight it. Let go of it for chrissake. The nurse turned to me and nodded.

"That's it," she said. Scott, Hilda's husband, called the mortuary to bring the hearse. Then, incredibly, he began to breathe again. He was still alive.

He didn't die that night. Or the night after. He died three days later, October 14, 1986, just after three in the afternoon.

I sat at the foot of the bed and watched him. This time there was no screaming or shouting. He had finally, blessedly, fallen into a coma. The rattling was there as usual. But there was no moaning or crying out. His breathing was very slow. It disappeared for half a minute at a time, then it came back. His body fought for air even though there was virtually nothing left of him to keep alive. The others, my stepmother, great aunt, sisters, and brothers-in-law were all thankfully outside on the patio having drinks. Only the nurse and I were in the room.

I couldn't take my eyes off his face. I touched his hands, his feet, his brow. His skin had taken on an ashen pallor, and felt cold to the touch, even though he was still alive. I watched him as if I could keep him in the room forever with the power in my eyes. He took a breath. He let it out. I waited for his chest to rise again. Thirty seconds later it did. Then he let the breath out. I waited again. I waited a minute. Two minutes. Three minutes. Five minutes later he had not breathed.

"Is he dead?" I asked. The nurse nodded.

"Let's wait this time," she said. Just then the door to the room blew shut. She and I looked at one another. Outside, I could hear the others chatting and laughing, hoping to get through this in their own way. I kissed his toes and his fingers and then lingered to look at him. But my father was no longer there. The body on the bed was utterly inanimate. It looked like an ash in the shape of a human being.

Later, after the men from Forest Lawn had taken his body from the house, Roger and Scott asked me if I wanted a drink.

"No, thanks," I said.

"I'm sure under the circumstances," said Roger kindly, "no one would blame you for taking a drink."

"No, I know no one would blame me," I said. Not even him. Not even the old man.

* * *

I see him on TV in an old movie from time to time. I'm not always certain he's dead, even though I saw him take his last breath and heard the crackle in his throat as he died. Sometimes I think he's just playing out one more of his little melodramas, ever the actor.

"I'm always in the middle, son. Tell your mother I just haven't got the dough this month.

"Do me a favor, willya, kiddo? Write Sharley and tell her I got mugged on the Via Veneto and tell her to have the business manager send me some money to the hotel.

"I'm dying of cancer, kiddo . . . actually, sonofabitch . . . I god-damn well *died* of cancer, didn't I? I just never seem to get ahead."

My life today is different. There's no more puking in the sink, no crawling on the floor; I don't drink or use drugs. A measure of sanity has been restored. I feel the cold wind on me as never before, and I fear death more. But I fear life less.

INDEX